DRAMA
IN THERAPY

Volume II: ADULTS

"*One easily forgets that human education proceeds along highly theatrical lines. In a quite theatrical manner the child is taught how to behave, logical arguments only come later. . . . It is no different with grown-ups. Their education never finishes. Only the dead are beyond being altered by their fellow men.*"

—Bertolt Brecht

Edited by
GERTRUD SCHATTNER
RICHARD COURTNEY

Foreword by Theodore Isaac Rubin, M.D.

DRAMA
IN THERAPY

Volume II: ADULTS

DRAMA BOOK SPECIALISTS (PUBLISHERS)
New York

Printed in the United States of America
by Noble Offset Printers, Inc., New York, New York 10003

Library of Congress Cataloging in Publication Data

Main entry under title:

Drama in therapy.

    Includes bibliographical references and indexes.
    CONTENTS: v. 1. Children.—v. 2. Adults.
    1. Drama—Therapeutic use. 2. Child psychotherapy.
3. Psychotherapy. I. Courtney, Richard.
II. Schattner, Gertrud.

RC489.D72D72   616.89'1523   80-15680

ISBN 0-89676-013-8 (v. 1)
ISBN 0-89676-014-6 (v. 2)

Grateful acknowledgment is made to the following for permission to reprint previously published material:

American Journal of Psychotherapy for "Play, Fantasy, and Symbols: Drama with Emotionally Disturbed Children," Eleanor C. Irwin, and for "Art & Drama: Partners in Therapy," Eleanor C. Irwin, Judith A. Rubin, Marvin I. Shapiro; *New Outlook for the Blind* for "Drama: A Means of Self-Expression for the Visually Impaired Child," Susan Aach; Speech Communication Association for "Developmental Drama for Brain-Damaged Children," Sue Martin; Jason Aronson, New York and *Acta Paedopsychiatrica* for "Dramatized Storytelling in Child Psychotherapy," Richard A. Gardner; *Journal of Rehabilitation* for "Drama: An Outlet for Mental & Physical Handicaps," Marvin L. Blumberg;

and to the following:

Viola Spolin for "Theater Games," copyright © 1980 by Viola Spolin; and Baywood Publishing Company for "The Actress as a Mental Health Teacher" by Hugh James Lurie, copyright © Baywood Publishing Company, Inc., 1973.

10 9 8 7 6 5 4 3 2 1   0 1   2 2 3 3 4 4 5 5 6 6 7 7 8 8 9 9

CONTENTS

THEODORE ISAAC RUBIN, M.D., a practicing psychiatrist in New York City, is president and faculty member of the American Institute for Psychoanalysis, a fellow of the American Academy of Psychoanalysis, and a member of the American Psychiatric Association and the Association for the Advancement of Psychoanalysis. Recipient of the Adolf Meyer Award (Association for the Improvement of Mental Health) and the Social Conscience Award (Karen Horney Clinic), he lives in New York City and is the author of twenty books including *Lisa and David, The Thin Book By A Formerly Fat Psychiatrist, Shrink,* and *Compassion and Self-Hate.*

FOREWORD

ALL THERAPIES have the common goal of returning the self to the self. This means the reestablishment of knowing what we feel, what we want, and having the ability to make free choices and to act accordingly with appropriate and good judgment.

"Acting out," in psychiatric parlance, invariably connotes destructive activity. To "act out" means compulsive, choice-less, impulsive, and often disorganized moves which are counter-productive and maladaptive. Neurosis, psychosis, and sociopathy are each marked by destructive and life-impeding "acting out" phenomena. The afflicted individual is "caught" in an "acting out" matrix or web, fed by unconscious conflicts and forces over which no control is effectively exerted. This matrix, if sufficiently malignant, accounts for the victim's entire life production and exploits all of his or her time and energy. In people who are healthier, who retain some measure of health and choice, "acting out" may be confined to sporadic destructive acts, maneuvers, explosions, and impulse activity.

Drama therapy represents a different kind of "acting out." Indeed, this therapeutic modality may well offer a uniquely effective instrument in both investigating sources of "de-structive acting out" and in remediation of various emotional disorders. I am immediately reminded of conditions in which "acting out" consists of great attacks and damage on constructive action of any kind. From my point of view, severe hopelessness, deadening of feelings, depression, resignation, fear of deeper feelings—especially of anger, all leading to inhibition and even to paralysis are forms of "acting out." Being unable to act in one's own behalf as a result of unconscious forces is then a form of "acting out" experienced through paralysis or no action at all.

We know of course that theatre has a long history as a therapeutic agent for people, indeed much longer than psychoanalysis and other modalities. We are also aware of the process of identification, empathy, catharsis, ventilation, and abreaction—in which we express our feelings as well as words. We are aware of the therapy which ensues and the relief enjoyed after a cathartic reaction takes place and in abreaction activity.

But the art and science of drama therapy offer the above therapeutic modalities and more. This is what this fine, comprehensive work is all about. Its papers are written by artists and scientists, and it has been integrated by editors who are artists, scientists, and therapists. Drama therapy, as conceptualized in this work, provides procedures, examples, and voluminous substance of "integrated or constructive acting out." Through this most serious and unique work we learn how to use the human proclivity for acting in the service of serious psychotherapy. "Integrated acting out" is highly organized and represents planned, cohesive tapping of inner resources designed to promote the cause of free choice and *constructive action*. People do not have to be scientists, therapists, or professional artists to enjoy the therapeutic benefits of involvement in drama. The play's participants enjoy the unique benefits of camaraderie in the cooperative effort necessary to the fruition of the production however modest or ambitious. Playing out a role as an actor can serve as a bridge to mobilizing inner resources in actual life. To involve one's self in creative process taps and activates inner resources.

"Constructive acting out" is then the subject of this important work. Its diverse experts have provided us with a significant contribution to understanding and relieving human misery. Through "constructive acting out" we may understand and dissipate "destructive acting out." Drama therapy gives the patient an opportunity to feel so much more of himself than other treatment modalities. Through acting out he can feel and activate his feelings. He can speak and hear his voice. He can move and feel his body as he moves. He can feel himself in relation to other actors. In short, he can experience the integrating use of his total self as an exercise in constructive acting and living.

These two volumes describe this fine, therapeutic instrument as applied to both children and adults. I am pleased that each group is taken separately because problems and solutions for each, while they have much in common, are also highly specialized. May I also point out that drama therapy as described in these volumes has the capacity to entertain although it is also a methodology for investigation and treatment. This work adds dimension to both fields, psychotherapy and drama, and in so doing rewards readers of all persuasions.

Theodore Isaac Rubin, M.D.
New York City

PREFACE

THIS BOOK IS a collection of papers about drama therapy. It is in two volumes: the first about children, and the second about adults.

It is intended to meet a number of needs. First, there is very little published material on the subject and this book aims to fill the gap. However, even two volumes cannot completely satisfy this need and so, second, it is intended to stimulate further publications that might delve deeper into the different topics introduced here. As a result, third, the book is intended to cover as wide a spectrum as its length permits. Fourth, it aims at an international audience. The need for drama therapy knows no frontiers. Although the majority of chapters are written by Americans, there are equally distinguished contributions from Canada, Britain and elsewhere. Fifth, we hope that the book will interest a wide readership and that the subject matter will gain the significance in society that it deserves. It contains learned papers for the qualified practitioner and there are more popular articles for the layman and the student. Sixth, and finally, this book aims to provide materials for those areas of drama therapy where needs are greatest. To that end, we have included contributions of the highest quality which speak to the most immediate of these.

Both volumes have the same structure. Part 1 looks at Assessment, Part 2 at Special Problems, and Part 3 at Related Techniques. Part 4, however, differs: in Volume 1 it is concerned with Education, but in Volume 2 this part contains material on Theatre. No complete bibliography is given because specific references to each topic are included at the end of each chapter. However, we would encourage the interested reader to refer to the index where cross-references of topics will assist him in his further studies.

G.S., *New York City*
R.C., *Toronto*
1981

ACKNOWLEDGMENTS

GERTRUD SCHATTNER wishes to thank Marcy Syms Merns for her untiring efforts on behalf of this publication, Karin Abarbanel, Ronald Christ, Barbara Eler, and Ramon Gordon for their help and valuable advice. Richard Courtney wishes to thank Ina Dumphie for secretarial assistance. Both authors are thankful to Rosemary Courtney and Edward Schattner, M.D., without whose editorial assistance and personal help the book could not have been written. Their special appreciation goes also to Rosemary Courtney for the preparation of the Index.

The publisher acknowledges permission to reprint articles as follows. In Volume 1: "Play, Fantasy, and Symbols: Drama with Emotionally Disturbed Children," by Eleanor C. Irwin, *American Journal of Psychotherapy*, 31, 3: 426–36; "Art & Drama: Partners in Therapy," by Eleanor C. Irwin, Judith A. Rubin, and Marvin I. Shapiro, *American Journal of Psychotherapy*, 29, 1: 107–16; "Drama: A Means of Expression for the Visually Impaired Child," by Susan Aach, *New Outlook for the Blind*, September 1976: 282–285; "Developmental Drama for Brain-Damaged Children," by Sue Martin, *Communication Education*, Speech Communication Association, 5205 Leesburg Pike, Falls Church, Virginia 22041, September 1977, Volume 26, No. 3: 208–213; "Dramatized Storytelling in Child Psychotherapy," by Richard A. Gardner, from sections of his book, *Psychotherapeutic Approaches to the Resistant*

Child, (Jason Aronson, New York), and sections from "Dramatized Storytelling in Child Psychotherapy," *Acta Paedopsychiatrica,* 41, 1974: fasc. 3, 112–15. In Volume 2: "Creative Dramatics: An Outlet for Mental Handicaps" (reprinted as "Drama: An Outlet for Mental & Physical Handicaps"), by Marvin L. Blumberg, *Journal of Rehabilitation,* 42, 6; "The Actress as a Mental Health Teacher," by Hugh James Lurie, *Psychiatry in Medicine* (Baywood Pub. Co., Inc.), 4, 2, Spring 1973: 183–90.

GERTRUD SCHATTNER is a graduate of the Vienna State Academy for Performing Arts and the Max Reinhardt Seminar for Dramatics. She was a lead actress under Reinhardt and Otto Preminger with Albert Basserman, Elizabeth Bergner, Hedy Lamarr, Peter Lorre, and Louise Reiner. She has also worked extensively as a translator of Pearl Buck, Richard Llewellyn, George Bernard Shaw, Luigi Pirandello, Thomas Wolfe, and others. In the United States she studied drama at Hunter College, Columbia University, and the Henry Street Playhouse, and trained in psychotherapy at the Alfred Adler Institute and the Moreno Institute. She was a staff member at the Adler Clinic and Post Graduate Center for Mental Health; chairman of play production for the Suffolk County Mental Health Association; recreation director and drama therapist for adolescent girls under the auspices of the Catholic Charities, Brooklyn, and at the Riverside Nursing Home and East River Nursing Home; director of her own Theatre for Young People; and instructor at Maria Ley-Piscator Creative Theatre and at the Lincoln Square Neighborhood Center. For thirteen years Gertrud Schattner has been senior drama therapist at Bellevue Psychiatric Hospital where she coordinates the program for volunteers for the entire hospital, supervising them as well as undergraduate and graduate students in drama therapy. She is also a faculty member of the Arts-in-Therapy Program, Turtle Bay Music School, New York City. Founder and first president of the National Association for Drama Therapy, she is a frequent guest lecturer on drama therapy.

INTRODUCTION

I BEGAN TEACHING one of the first courses in drama therapy in the United States ten years ago in the Arts-in-Therapy Program of the Turtle Bay Music School in New York City. Each year, during the opening class, one of the first questions students would invariably ask was "What books should we read?"

Until now, my answer has always been the same: "There are no titles I can suggest, because there are no textbooks or guides to the field of drama therapy."

It was from this need and from my own wish to share my life's work and experience that the idea for an anthology of *Drama in Therapy* was born. Would it not be helpful in creating a recognized profession to find other people who might be doing similar work? The response, as I began searching for contributors, was most gratifying, and I received many articles from therapists working in the United States, Canada, Europe, Israel, all around the world. I was fortunate that I was joined in my work by Richard Courtney. To sift through the mounting wealth of material became a demanding task. As we prepared and organized the selections, we came to the conclusion that the pioneering work of the drama therapists was of such importance that the publication of two volumes, rather than the single volume originally intended, was certainly warranted. With these twin volumes now, after five years of preparation and research, we hope to advance the recognition of drama as an adjunct to psychotherapy as well as a treatment modality in its own right.

The more than forty contributors to *Drama in Therapy* have been drawn to the use of drama as therapy from various fields: education, psychiatry, theatre, speech, movement, and visual arts. Do these specialists have anything in common? Why do they do what they do? There is no single answer applicable to all. For some it is the love of drama itself. Others have observed the power of fantasy and creative expression to reach the mentally ill, the imprisoned adult, the disturbed child.

The reasons why I became a drama therapist and have remained one for twenty-eight years are simple, direct, and have evolved from my life experiences.

My early youth was spent as an actress on the European stage—a career that was interrupted by Hitler's invasion of Austria. During the war that followed, I lived in Switzerland, where my husband was an attending physician in a tuberculosis sanitorium for survivors of Nazi concentration camps. Most of these survivors were young men in their twenties. Physically ill, they were also disturbed and broken in spirit after the horrors of imprisonment. They were quiet and depressed, polite but lifeless as they silently paced the hospital corridors. Many of them died, not because of illness, but because they had lost all interest in living.

I was asked to help them by organizing their leisure time between the medical treatment and the long rests ordered by their doctors. But I wanted more for them than organized leisure time. I wanted to extricate them from their apathy, to make them realize that they were free to communicate, free to build a new life for themselves. Yet what was I to do? I was completely on my own. I had no textbooks. My only tools were my intuition and my experience on the stage. I decided that we would meet in small groups. We would read short stories and poems, and I, drawing on my theatrical experience, would introduce them to role playing.

Following some initial reluctance, certain patients became interested in particular poems that expressed feelings of bitterness and despair. The authors of the poems seemed like friends to the patients. This relationship became even more apparent when we decided to prepare a performance of a play by the great Jewish writer, Sholom Aleichem, about life in a small community in Poland—perhaps very like the villages where most of these men had spent their early years.

It would take still another book to describe how these dispirited young men began to wake up, to enjoy themselves, and to work together. Being involved in the play's production meant becoming part of life again, being needed as members of a group with a joint purpose, working towards a common goal, and being valued for their own accomplishments. During rehearsal they regained their memories, they lost their shyness, they discussed their roles, and they gradually became creative contributors to the art of acting and staging a play. Many of the men had not smiled in years, but drama gave them the gift of laughter again. Drama also gave them the chance to accept responsibility, to rehearse, to redo, to re-create, and, of course, to enjoy the reward of a successful performance.

A few weeks after that performance, one of my actor-patients came to see me. We talked. He told me a little about his childhood and about his recent experience in the concentration camp. He also spoke about what had happened to him through our drama groups and our desire to care for each other, guided by someone who cared. Not only did he wish to cope with the memories of horrors, he also believed that he had gained the strength and confidence to plan a future. Gradually, he had forgotten to hate. Not one of those young men had spoken so intensely or so personally before.

At the time, I did not know that I had taken a very small step into the unexplored territory of drama as therapy. Neither did I realize that my first attempt to use drama as an instrument in the healing process had started me down the road of a long learning process, a road which I am traveling still. Those silent men in Switzerland were my first teachers, and all through the years since, each encounter with a patient has added to my understanding of the wide range of human suffering as well as given me an opportunity to renew myself.

Later, in the United States, I spent ten rewarding years as

drama instructor in a home sponsored by the Catholic Charities. I worked with hundreds of girls. Most of them came from broken homes, and they were troubled by many different psychological and mental problems.

One girl I especially remember is Marie. She spoke only Spanish, was very slow learning English, and her remedial teacher had little hope for her progress. But Marie had a lovely singing voice, and she wanted to play the lead in our production of a well-known musical. "To play this part," I told her, "you must be able to understand and correctly pronounce the words you sing." Within two months, Marie was the best reader in her class. She was taken out of the remedial program, and she became the star of the show. I had helped Marie to learn English, I told myself. What a therapeutic success!

Then there was the Lincoln Square Neighborhood Center in New York, where I worked for eight years with a mixed group of children—the rich, the poor, the healthy, the handicapped. Little Donna walked with crutches because she had had polio. When asked whether she would agree to a rather risky operation that might help her, she said yes and, when the doctor asked her why, she said, "I want to be in our show, *The Wizard of Oz.*" Donna underwent surgery, never used crutches again, and was the happiest munchkin ever to dance down the yellow brick road.

It was during the seven years that my husband was resident psychiatrist at Central Islip State Hospital that my interest in the field of mental health began. I had become chairman of play production for the Suffolk County Mental Health Association, and I numbered among my cast members psychiatrists, social workers, nurses, and theatre enthusiasts from nearby communities. Our greatest success was the production of *My Name Is Legion,* the well-known play based on the life of Clifford Beers, founder of the mental health movement.

One evening, I was asked to help direct a talent show presented by the hospital's patients. It was the first time that I had become involved with the severely mentally ill. I recognized the almost magical outlet that drama gave those patients and realized once again the curative powers of the creative arts in the treatment of the emotionally disturbed. I watched what happened to them when they were allowed to express themselves on stage. I saw the pleasure and gratification they experienced when they knew they were important—when, however briefly, they could be in the limelight, at the center of attention. I learned what happiness some of the patients felt when they believed that they had something to contribute and that they were part of a team. I saw that through drama they felt the freedom and the right to express feelings that had been dormant but could now come to light.

From the moment I first worked with psychotic patients, I knew that I wanted to remain in the field of drama as therapy, to explore it further, and to specialize in as many aspects of it as possible. Although I have worked with clients from the very young to the very old, in many different settings, my most rewarding experience has been the last thirteen years with the patients at Bellevue Psychiatric Hospital.

My road to drama as therapy is just one among many. The chapters in these two volumes present several other approaches to the field, from several different points of departure, by specialists in many different fields—education, sociology, psychiatry, the arts. Assembling these approaches for the anthology, however, I began to realize that merely publishing them in book form would not be sufficient to establish drama therapy as a recognized profession. Something more was needed, and a goal began to develop in my mind: the founding of a national association for drama therapy with the aims of setting the highest standards, promoting public awareness of the field, helping new drama therapists to get the best possible training, making colleges and universities aware of our objectives, and, most important, seeing drama therapy fully accredited as a field of special study.

In June 1979 this goal was partially achieved when the National Association for Drama Therapy was founded with me as its president. Subsequently the American Psychiatric

Association has recognized drama therapy by inviting our association as well as other creative art therapy organizations to be represented at a joint conference with the American Psychiatric Association. With this invitation, drama therapy has moved another significant step closer to acknowledgment as an important discipline uniting therapists whose backgrounds may vary widely but who share a single aim of achieving growth and health using drama as their tool.

Gertrud Schattner
New York City
1981

DRAMA
IN THERAPY

Volume II: ADULTS

RICHARD COURTNEY studied under G. Wilson Knight and Bonamy Dobrée at Leeds University, England, where he was also director of their theatre group. He has been a professional actor, director, and designer (including work with the British Broadcasting Corporation), and an instructor in drama education and therapy since 1948 in England and since 1967 in Canada. His lectures and broadcasts have taken him to various parts of Europe, the United States, Australia, and Asia. Formerly professor of drama at Victoria and Calgary, he is now responsible for graduate work in arts and education at the Ontario Institute for Studies in Education, and is cross-appointed to the Graduate Centre of Drama, University of Toronto. He was president of the Canadian Conference of the Arts from 1973 to 1976, president of the Canadian Child and Youth Drama Association from 1971 to 1973, and a board member of the American Councils of the Arts (USA). Currently chairman of the Task Force on Arts and Education in Canada, Richard Courtney has published over a hundred articles, reports, and books—including *Play, Drama & Thought, Teaching Drama, The Drama Studio,* and (forthcoming) *Peoples in Performance: Perspectives in Drama & Culture,* and *The Dramatic Curriculum.* He is a member of the British Association of Dramatherapists, and a founding member of the National Association for Drama Therapy (U.S.A.).

Chapter 1

THE UNIVERSAL THEATRE: BACKGROUND TO DRAMA THERAPY

Richard Courtney

"Thou seest we are not all alone unhappy:
This wide and universal theatre
Presents more woeful pageants than the scene
Wherein we play in."
— Shakespeare

Spontaneous drama helps people to live. It is a vital and dynamic way of adjusting to existence.

In our century, the use of drama for this purpose has so increased that it is virtually a commonplace. It exists in schools and education, in recreation and leisure, and in the "helping professions." Business simulations are similar to those that train astronauts. Increasingly, the professional theatre works for the personal and social adjustment of both actors and audience. More and more, drama is being used with deprived groups — prisoners and addicts, the retarded and the socially underprivileged, the perceptually and physically handicapped, the aged and the hospitalized. And in clinical psychotherapy, natural play and improvisation are now increasingly used.

Why? What is it about spontaneous dramatic play that seems to appeal to our times?

1

1 THE UNIVERSALITY OF DRAMA

Drama is a universal activity. Children are always at play. Adolescents emulate heroes. Adults rehearse "in their heads" an upcoming interview. Dramatic thought is a key aspect of mind—in both thinking and feeling. We can examine this in three interlinked ways: (1) personal; (2) social; and (3) cultural.

Personal

Our thought is not limited to our brain. Thoughts have relationships to brain and body, the nervous system and heart beat—in fact, the totality known as *mind*. Thoughts, too, are "whole": they include the cognitive, the affective, the aesthetic and the moral. There is no such thing as a "pure" emotion or "pure" intellect: all are woven into total thought.

One quality of mind is *imagination*. It is interlinked with all thought. It is a unifying process which permits "as if" thinking. It allows us to consider possibilities.

Mind receives information from *perception*: our senses provide us with data about the world. By increasing our perceptual awareness, we build concentration and perseverance.

What we perceive is *transformed* by mind. The data we receive are worked upon by cognition, emotion, imagination, the aesthetic and the moral so that they can be dealt with by mind. Sense data are transformed into *images*—mental units with which we can work—which connect into *imagings,* or groups of images along which thought flows. These imagings are of various sorts on a continuum: sets, or the well-worn paths of usual thought; and associations, or the odd, bizarre and "different" connections of thought. The cognitive qualities of mind treat such imagings rationally and logically, while the emotional qualities give them inner meaning and significance. Imagination, on the other hand, allows us to choose between them. At the same time, it re-creates other imagings (possibilities) which allow for even further choices.

Any living organism is dynamic: its energy is provided by the tensions between its parts. The dynamism of mind is provided by *identification* and *impersonation*.[1]

Social

Once an imagining has been externalized in an act it becomes social. "As if" thinking has to be tried out in the world, and the moment that occurs the world has been altered to some degree. Moreover, the world provides "feedback" to the organism.

Dramatic actions become play when we are very young, and the purpose of play is to relate the inner to the outer.[2] This develops with maturation but, at all ages, there are appropriate forms of play; in fact, between birth and death human beings are continually striving to relate mind to the environment. This can best be seen through the generic growth of symbolization: the initial iconography of play is holistic; it develops to the symbols of the arts and religion which, although rich and fecund, are more rational than those of play; finally, the signs of abstraction grow and they need have no referents of any sort ($1 + 1 = 2$ can apply to apples, or to no referent).

Society is created by the dramatic actions of the individuals within it. Our roles create analogies within society and, as Elizabeth Burns says:

> In drama...the immediate "coming to recognize" an unexpected feature of natural or social reality, is doubled. First, drama is a special kind of activity which consists in composing a plausible semblance of human action of an important and consequential kind. Secondly, we use the terminology and conceptual apparatus (the social technology) which makes this special kind of activity possible as a means of understanding human action itself.[3]

Cultural

Historically, all societies have recognized the health-giving qualities of drama and theatre. Yet they have done so in different ways:

(a) *Hunting and gathering societies* created rites through *mimesis* — the simple imitation of action. Hunting rites rehearsed the actions of the hunt which, by "sympathetic magic," gave the whole tribe power over natural forces. The

individual actor-dancer was possessed. He tried to "drive"
his way into the spirit of the animal in order to possess its
power — the bull in ancient Greece, or the wolf amongst the
Nootka on Vancouver Island today. He did so on behalf of all
the people, and this was psychological health.

(b) *Agricultural societies* also gave dramatization a central
place in their psychological life. Out of rites grew the ritual
myths which demonstrated the terror of winter (death), the
sowing of seeds (burial), the hope of spring (life), and the
reaping of the harvest (resurrection). In performance, *mimesis*
gave way to *mime* proper, but the action of the actor-dancer
still unified the individual, the community and nature.

As communities settled and temples were built, the dra-
matic-religious celebrations changed. Liturgy arose, and this
divided the actors (the leaders of the rituals) from the audience
(the participating community). This is the development of
theatre, proper. As time went on, the audience stopped participating and merely witnessed. It was in this context that
Aristotle could speak of *catharsis* — that drama purifies the
emotions of the audience; he says nothing of the actors. The
tragic experience of Aeschylus, Sophocles and Euripides was
acknowledged to be of this order.[4]

(c) *Secular societies* finally made the audience a mere witness.
In medieval Europe, the tenth century trope began the process, and from this grew the Mystery Cycles, the Tudor
drama and Shakespeare.

With the rise of capitalism and communism, secular
theatre was either "entertainment" (providing relief from
societal tensions) or it was didactic — teaching the moral
values of one class to a passive audience. In the nineteenth
century drama of Ibsen, the audience were mere voyeurs
"looking in" at the lives of others. Theatre did not have the
same healthful and organic relation to the ego-strength that
it had in nonsecular societies.

It is in this context that we can view the development of drama
therapy in our century.

2   THE TWENTIETH CENTURY

At the turn of the nineteenth and twentieth centuries, the existential climate had been prepared for a change. Philosophers earlier in the century (Rousseau, Goethe, Spencer) had advocated natural play for both learning and psychological health, and distinguished educators (Basedow, Froebel, Montessori) had experimented with a variety of methods.

Then, suddenly, Einstein's theory of relativity appeared. Old ways of thinking were no longer acceptable: there were no scientific laws, no rules and no absolutes. Everything depended, said Einstein, on the observer's frame of reference. Psychologically, relativity was more important than Freud's postulation of the unconscious; he had merely replaced a fixed system with a more flexible one. But Einstein had opened the door to spontaneity, dynamism, and the validity of the individual's own perspective. Thus drama therapy had a fertile ground in which to grow.

Drama therapy had three origins: (1) theatre, (2) education, and (3) psychotherapy. These occurred simultaneously, yet independently. Originally separate, during the course of time they have grown together into one organic field.

Theatre

Until the end of the nineteenth century, improvisation had not been used in the serious theatre. It had always had pride of place in popular entertainment (the *commedia dell'arte*, the British music hall, the American vaudeville) but, even there, it was as "set pieces" within a *scenario*. [5]

It was Stanislavsky[6] who introduced improvisation to the formal theatre, and he did so for actors. He used improvisation to teach them an inner acting technique: to find the "conscious means to the subconscious." The words of a text were only part of a characterization. There was an unbreakable tie between the psychological and the physical; behind every physical action (and that includes speech) there is something psychological: "The first fact is that the elements of the human soul and the particles of a human body are indivisible." Every word and every gesture reveals inner thoughts and feelings—the subtext. And acting must demonstrate this.

In other words, the crux of acting lies in the value of dramatic action itself—not talking or theorizing about it, or what Viola Spolin calls "playwriting," but the very doing of drama. The dramatic act is of value because it brings knowledge, awareness, understanding—"truth."

The actor achieves this "truth" through improvisation. It leads him to find the physical actions that are right for him and, therefore, the subtext that is right for him. Any actor, as a result, will interpret a character differently from any other performer.

Improvisation in the theatre is now universal—and not merely in an actor's preparation but also in the performance. Viola Spolin, too, emphasizes the relation of body and mind: "Our first concern is to encourage freedom of physical expression, because the physical and sensory relationship with the art forms opens the door for insight."[7] For Spolin, spontaneity is the key: through it "we are re-formed into ourselves" and we "function as an organic whole." Given the objective for a "game" (what Einstein would call "a frame of reference"), spontaneity leads to intuitive creation and learnings. Spolin's evaluation, too, is not about the *why* or *how* but about the *what*. She asks such questions as: Did they solve the problem? Did they show or tell? Did they act or react? Did they let something happen? In other words, Spolin's values center upon the importance of dramatic action itself—like Stanislavsky. Interestingly, although Stanislavsky's improvisation was for the theatre, Spolin first evolved hers for children. Today, many of her improvisational exercises are used by drama therapists.

Education

From the beginning of the twentieth century, British education came to develop the value of dramatic action *per se*. Traditionally, modern dramatic education has the teacher stressing the *what?* and the student creating the *how?*

As a result, the learning of facts is seen as based upon psychological health. Techniques and approaches aim, therefore, to develop the individuality of human beings before (or at the same time as) they assimilate information. Modern drama teachers use spontaneous exercises (for relaxation, creative movement and speech, characterization, and the like) and group improvisation for two objectives: (a) as a subject in its own right; and (b) as a methodology to support other subjects. The techniques of British creative drama are part and parcel of modern drama therapy (see Vol. I, Part 4).

Therapy

Many modern approaches to therapy use drama, both with children and adults. The initial step, however, was taken by Jacob L. Moreno[8] who evolved psychodrama at the beginning of this century. Acknowledging his debt to Peirce and Bergson, he developed a theory of spontaneity as "the readiness to act" — a creative response — resulting in creative products (the cultural *conserve*) which are no longer spontaneous. Moreno's use of drama shifted the emphasis from the conserve (as with Stanislavsky) to the response as such (as with creative drama). In psychodrama, what was therapeutic was the "acting out" of the patient's problem, and this produced *catharsis*. But it was also part of Moreno's theory that all who participate in the psychodrama are helped by the experience: patient, audience, therapist (director) and his assistants. In this sense, Moreno saw psychodrama as a reunification of the total community (actor and audience) and a reeducation — which links with the existentialism of Martin Buber and E. J. Burton. Moreno used improvisation much as creative drama is used in the classroom — just for itself, for its own value. But not quite: while for Slade it provides a "generalized" *catharsis*, for Moreno there was a "specific" *catharsis* because the therapist has directed attention to a specific problem of a patient.

Moreno also evolved sociodrama. In psychodrama, the patient is the center of the drama which tells his story. In sociodrama, the whole group improvise a problem which is confronting that community (a black/white situation where there are racial problems, etc.). Sociodrama relates to both group psychotherapy and sociometry which also originated with Moreno.

In recent years, drama has been incorporated into many "schools" of therapy. For example, both Gestalt therapy as exemplified by

Fritz Perls,[9] and the transactional analysis of Eric Berne,[10] regularly use spontaneous improvisation. In addition, the newer forms of "human growth" therapies (based on Rogers, Maslow, Assagioli and others)[11] use drama. Nor is it unusual to find Freudians, Jungians and others making use of drama techniques.

The ways in which improvisation is used in therapy and education are today growing closer. Moreno had seen this from the beginning: "Learning by doing has been replaced or better said remodelled, with learning by spontaneity training and psychodramatic procedure, in which therapy and doing go hand in hand, one being an intrinsic part of the other."[12]

Today, the links between theatre, education and therapy are forged into a strong bond.

3   DRAMA THERAPY TODAY

Earlier in this century, spontaneous dramatic action evolved separately in theatre, education and therapy. Whereas Stanislavsky used improvisation for the actor alone, creative drama and psychodrama both worked with the audience as participant.

All three, however, stressed the value of dramatic action *per se.* Today, these three approaches have melded into one whole — drama therapy. This term does not sit well with precise definitions which would exclude some activities. Rather, what we can say is: drama therapy is inclusive of all types of dramatic activity which aim to make people "better." Drama therapy includes all types of spontaneous drama which is a "helping" of others, and within two broad types of activity:

(1) *Drama as a therapeutic method in clinical situations.* The spontaneous improvisation is under the supervision of a psychotherapist who is trained in drama techniques. If he is not so trained, someone trained in spontaneous drama can assist in an adjunct capacity.

(2) *Drama as a generalized therapy in non-clinical situations.* These situations are inclusive of schools, recreation and special groups (the deprived, the handicapped, etc.) They do not require leaders with specific clinical training, but they do require trained drama therapists.

These two broad categories of activity are not meant to be mutually exclusive. There are many mixed areas between them. A drama therapist is likely to be eclectic. In clinical situations, he may mix techniques from improvisation, creative drama and psychodrama — but he is also liable to use play therapy, storytelling, and many different kinds of artistic media. In schools, he may emphasize creative drama — but he is also inclined to use all the creative arts, as well as techniques from theatrical improvisation and the therapies.

What matters is the need of the client, patient, student, person. To serve that end, the drama therapist will use whichever technique is most suitable at that moment in time. There is no "one way" in drama therapy. Nor is there any place in the field for drama therapists who regard a particular method as their "own." All that matters, as Gertrud Schattner would say, is "the development of persons." We all use each other's techniques whenever they can be of help to others. It follows that drama therapy is a cohesive field: there is a constant sharing, intermingling and crossfertilization of ideas and techniques. Moreover, the drama therapist must have a myriad of techniques at his or her disposal — each to be used at the right moment and with the right person.

Drama therapy is dynamic and evolving, without precise limits, and is constantly moving toward its potential.

FOOTNOTES

1. Richard Courtney, "Drama and Pedagogy," *The Stage in Canada* 6, no. 5a (1970): 56–57; idem, "A Dramatic Theory of Imagination," *New Literary History* 2, no. 3 (Spring 1971): 445–60; idem, "Education is Play," *Childhood Education* 49, no. 5 (February 1973): 246–50; idem, *Play, Drama & Thought: The Intellectual Backround to Dramatic Education,* 3d ed. (London: Cassell; New York: Drama Book Specialists, 1974); idem, "Imagination & Substitution: The Personal Origins of Art," *Connecticut Review* 9, no. 2 (May 1976): 67–73; idem, "Dramatic Action: A Genetic Ontology of the Dramatic Learning of the Very Young Child," *Journal of the Canadian Association for the Very Young Child* (November 1976), pp. 32–42; idem, "Human Dynamics: Drama & Motivation" (Toronto: Ontario Institute for Studies in Education,

1977); idem, "Making Up One's Mind: Aesthetic Questions about Children & Theatre," in *Theatre for Young Audiences,* ed. Nellie McCaslin (New York: Longman, 1977).
2. D. W. Winnicott, *Playing and Reality* (Harmondsworth: Penguin, 1974).
3. Elizabeth Burns, *Theatricality: A Study of Convention in the Theatre and Social Life* (London: Longman, 1972).
4. Courtney, *Play, Drama & Thought,* chap. 9.
5. Richard Courtney, "Theatre and Spontaneity," *Journal of Aesthetics & Art Criticism* 32, no. 1 (Fall 1973): 79–88.
6. Konstantin Stanislavsky, *Complete Works* (Moscow: n.p., 1945–61).
7. Viola Spolin, *Improvisation for the Theater* (Evanston, Ill.: Northwestern University Press, 1963); idem, *Theater Game File* (St. Louis: CEMREL, 1975).
8. Jacob L. Moreno, *Psychodrama,* 2 vols. (New York: Beacon, 1946, 1959).
9. F. S. Perls, *Gestalt Therapy Verbatim* (Lafayette, Calif.: Real People Press, 1969).
10. E. Berne, *Transactional Analysis in Psychotherapy* (New York: Grove, 1961).
11. A. Maslow *Motivation and Personality* (New York: Harper & Row, 1970); C. Rogers, "Towards a Theory of Creativity," in *Creativity,* ed. P. E. Vernon (Harmondsworth: Penguin, 1970); R. Assagioli, *The Act of Will* (Harmondsworth: Penguin, 1974).
12. Moreno, *Psychodrama,* 1: 152.

Part 1
ASSESSMENT

Assessment is not measurement. It is the ability to judge the needs of the patient and, subsequently, the most appropriate approach for his needs.

In Volume 1, we have examined assessment with children. Many of the styles of assessment listed there — determinist, categorical and analytic, extrinsic, descriptive, dramatic and developmental — can be related to work with adults. For example, of the dramatic styles the *Assessment of Dramatic Involvement* Scale (*ADI*) can be adapted to adult improvisation; and Dorothy Heathcote's six rules of drama apply with equal force to the spontaneous drama of adults.

David Johnson, in the only chapter in this part, puts forward some diagnostic implications in the dramatic style. His general characteristics (spontaneity, concentration and tolerance of delay, transcendence, organization of scenes, patterns in the content of roles, attitude towards enactment) and his characteristic styles (inhibited, overinvolved, compulsive, impulsive) are modes of dramatic assessment for adults. Not merely can they be seen as an extension of related styles for children but, also, they have implications for assessment of children in drama therapy.

DAVID READ JOHNSON, M.S., has been a drama therapist at the Yale Psychiatric Institute and the Soundview Specialized Care Center, and is conducting research on drama therapy at Yale University. Active in community theatre, he is the author of several articles on dance and drama therapy, and vice president of the National Association for Drama Therapy.

Chapter 2

SOME DIAGNOSTIC IMPLICATIONS OF DRAMA THERAPY

David Read Johnson

1 AN OVERVIEW

Drama therapy is the name for the group of therapeutic approaches which utilize in a significant way the nonverbal and symbolic media of creative drama and dramatic role playing. Implicit in our work is the belief that creative expression of feelings and attitudes is a pathway to the achievement of psychological health and insight, and that our bodies and our innate capacity for play can be important vehicles for such expression and learning. Verbal psychotherapy has made an enormous, though limited, contribution to the efforts to help suffering individuals. Drama therapy expands the range of therapeutic possibilities, so that people who have difficulty with verbal media may still grow and learn about themselves through the developmentally more basic media of play and movement. We believe that for the well-functioning individual, too, the re-animation of the spirit which comes from participation in a creative art has an important therapeutic or growth-enhancing potential.

Drama therapists today are fueled by a commitment to our media, and by the positive effects we see time after time in individuals by-passed by other, often more traditional, approaches. In the future, the necessary research and theoretical advances will no doubt contribute to a more exact understanding of the processes underlying creativity, play, and nonverbal behavior and their use in therapy. For now, drama therapists stand, like pioneers, at the edge of a rich, if still uncharted, terrain.

2 DIAGNOSIS AND DRAMA

Diagnosis is the understanding of an individual's personality struc- ture and deficits in terms of some pre-established categories. These may be either the formal psychiatric terms utilized in hospital set- tings, or more experiential, descriptive ones more often used in regard to higher functioning outpatients by the newer therapeutic approaches. Categorization facilitates comparison between pa- tients and between possible treatments, and thus speeds the therapist's initial efforts of setting appropriate goals and utilizing specific techniques.

Limitations of Drama as a Diagnostic Tool

As current psychodiagnostic procedures are relatively reliable and standardized, any diagnostic value of dramatic role playing will, for the near future, largely supplement our knowledge of the patient's symbolic and nonverbal behavior, and suggest avenues of approach and potential areas of difficulty to the creative arts therapist.

Though the literature on the function of play in child develop- ment is very large, and in most cases play is described as critical in the child's cognitive, emotional, and social development,[1] the literature on adult play is nearly nonexistent. According to many theories, child's play in its adaptive function becomes directed in the adult toward work, and in its nonadaptive function becomes internalized as fantasy and daydreaming.[2] Little attention has been given to forms of child's play which continue into adult- hood, of which dramatic role playing is one example. Studies of adult play are extremely restricted in our culture, consisting mostly of expanded versions of latency-age competitive team play (e.g. sports), or games of chance, though more creative forms of play are sometimes evident in hobbies.[3] As a result, many adults are unfamiliar with the medium of dramatic role playing, and associate it with childhood experiences.

Importance of Improvisation

Diagnosis refers to an understanding of the person in comparison with others. Implicit in such an assessment is that the therapist or evaluator has a relatively consistent influence on different people so that idiosyncratic aspects of their interaction do not contaminate the assessment of the person. For this reason, the most reliable diagnostic assessments use carefully standardized procedures and methods of evaluation. The goal of diagnosis must always be to avoid imposing one's own view or characteristics on the person being evaluated. This is not necessarily true of therapy where a critical moment of progress may result from the patient's identification with some strength or characteristic he perceives in the therapist.

In this light, it is clear why improvised role playing has the most applicability to diagnosis — a script imposes a structure and content upon the actor's words and meanings and the personality of the playwright becomes mingled with that of the actor. Especially in improvisational structures, the person is forced to draw upon inner ideas, memories, and images. Even though they may not be original, his choice of them always has a unique meaning for him determined by his history, personality, anxieties, protective devices, and the present situation as he views it. Within an improvisational structure, then, everything which is created has a specific and unique meaning to its creator; and the diagnostician must treat it seriously as having such meaning. Future research and clinical experience will have to establish the specific relationships between the images, roles, and actions on the one hand, and characteristics of the individual's personality structure on the other.

Hopefully, through detailed observation of many different people, relatively consistent patterns will emerge which, when properly labeled, can be the basis of a common language and framework for comparing people's role playing behavior. Important aspects of role playing may suggest impairment or growth in various aspects of the individual's personality, thought processes, or interpersonal relationships. As this knowledge has not been

summarized or tested in any reliable way, I can do no more than
sketch out some of the basic elements of role playing and hint at
their diagnostic value.[4]

3 GENERAL CHARACTERISTICS OF ROLE PLAYING

Spontaneity

Many authors have emphasized the value of spontaneity in the
health of the individual.[5] Spontaneity is the ability to act respon-
sively to situations; it necessitates a degree of self-confidence,
emotional control, and adaptive capability. Therefore the individual's level of spontaneity in role playing can be used as a
general measure of the individual's mental functioning. Spontaneity may be inhibited, however, by a variety of difficulties,
each of which may have very different implications for a diagnostic understanding of the person.

First, spontaneity is inhibited by the person's level of anxiety.
Highly anxious people, by attempting to prevent any increase in
their anxiety, tend to needlessly restrict many other areas of their
functioning (e.g. thoughts, actions, fantasy) which are critical to
spontaneous behavior. Second, spontaneity is constricted by in-
grained patterns of response. These are used by the individual in
many different situations. Spontaneity is characterized by the
person's ability to give a specific response to a specific situation.
Thus, those who tend to act in similar ways in many different circumstances have limited their potential spontaneity. Third, a
person's lack of experience, education, or intelligence may affect
his spontaneity in that alternatives or choices of behavior may not
be known to him. Having a breadth of experience or knowledge
encourages spontaneous behavior.

Thus one's level of spontaneity may have a variety of meanings:
detailed observation of other aspects of the person's behavior is
needed to determine the particular cause of the inhibition in
spontaneity; is he anxious? is he merely using a typical response?
or is he simply not aware of the alternatives in this case?

Concentration and Tolerance for Delay

Another general indicator of psychological functioning is the individual's ability to concentrate on a task, and to tolerate both frustration and delay. The person's concentration, perseverance, and self-discipline in the role playing task are important indicators of his work skills, energy resources, and other adaptive abilities. In evaluating concentration, however, it is useful to take into account the person's apparent motivation to complete the task. Low levels of concentration coupled with little motivation may indicate apathy, depression, or resistance; while low concentration in the presence of high motivation may indicate states of anxiety or else some temporary physiological, or permanent organic, impairment.

A person's tolerance of the frustrations which arise in role playing reflects his ability to control his aggression. Lack of tolerance may severely affect the person's ability to concentrate on the role playing. The ability to delay one's actions necessitates the ability to maintain inside, in one's thoughts, the external situation and one's intentions towards it; disruptions in thinking will clearly interfere with such internal representation. Recent research suggests that greater imaginativeness is associated with a greater tolerance for delay.[6]

Transcendence

Role playing involves a departure from immediate reality: characters other than oneself are portrayed; objects and settings not really present are represented by other objects or mimed actions. This pretend quality is the essence of the symbolic value of role playing, and one which is not readily accepted or understood. I have found that many borderline and paranoid schizophrenics are fearful of this "transcendence" of actual reality in pretend activities.[7] For these individuals, a foam ball for example can only be what it is, and cannot represent a person or even a heavier bowling ball. Similarly, they can only play themselves; to be somebody else is extremely frightening, and they may refuse because it's "silly." I worked with a schizophrenic patient who, whenever I introduced a pretend activity, told me, "I don't want to lie." For him, the very nature of pretending was a mystery. Rosalind Gould, in *Child Studies Through Fantasy*, speaks of the importance of the advance in the child's personifications: from being only himself in his play to taking on the role of the other.[8] It is my impression, too, that an inability to participate in pretend, or transcendent activities is a serious indicator of psychological impoverishment and constriction. Such inhibition can be a defense against confusion: the person fears that if this ball represents a person, then it may literally *become* the person, and then the solidity of the entire real world becomes threatened. The person fears that if he accepts the pretend idea, his fantasies may control the world, turning everyday objects and people into nightmares.

This degree of fear of transcendence is restricted to severely disturbed patients. Nevertheless, close attention to the ability to pretend can reap important information from the role playing of all people. For example, I have an orange "nerf" ball, about nine inches in diameter, which I give to people and ask, "Let's pretend. What could this be?" Answers I have received: (1) "it's a nerf ball;" (2) "it's an orange;" (3) "it's a basketball;" (4) "it's a pillow;" (5) "it's my therapist;" (6) "it's a moosehead;" (7) "it's a bulletin board;" (8) "it's the psychic truth emanating from Zantor to all the peoples of the universe." Responses (1) and (2) may be defined as *concrete* responses, that is, those which depart very little from the actual object, depending a great deal on its actual characteristics (color, shape, size). Responses (3), (4), (5), and (6) are typical of normal pretend responses which involve a greater degree of transcendence, yet are still connected in some way to characteristics of the actual object. Responses (7) and (8) may be termed abstract in that they apparently have no connection to the stimulus of the nerf ball and are probably related only to idiosyncratic associations and fantasies.

People who consistently give concrete responses may be holding onto reality as a way of controlling their thoughts and fantasies; they will have difficulty role playing and will seek out a greater degree of structure in sessions. They will try to avoid unstructured fantasy experiences, especially when associated with their own bodies, and they may prefer movement therapy as long as it does not involve images. Those who consistently give abstract responses are more likely to have difficulty relating to other people in improvisations as they are largely guided by their own internal fantasies. They may even be delusional, being unable to bring their ideas in line with aspects of reality.

Organization of Scenes

Important information about the individual's personality style and thought processes can be gained by observing how he organizes improvisational scenes. How much clarity in the scene can he preserve amidst what degree of complexity? Generally one can assume that a person's mode of organizing a scene reflects his mode of organizing his thoughts. Conflict in the scene can represent internal conflict, and ambiguities or fluidity in his characters, settings, or objects may represent internal confusion in his thoughts or representations of people or situations.

The number of characters the person can represent in any one interaction is indicative of the complexity of his thinking, his ability to view a situation from a number of different viewpoints, and his capacity to keep his thoughts separate from one another. The degree to which a setting is detailed reflects the ability to conceive of a context for his actions and the degree to which he is capable of investing in social reality apart from his investment in himself and his own actions. Shifts in setting or character within the scene indicate a degree of flexibility, and the ability to handle complexity in an adaptive way. Rigidly maintaining one setting or one character seems to reflect some constriction on thought, and may be associated with stereotyped role playing; borderline and obsessive patients typically do not represent such shifts in the action. In some cases, shifts may be frequent and vague, with settings or characters not clearly articulated. They may be attempts to ward off anxieties that develop in a scene and if so, indicate an inability to contain anxiety, as well as the presence of the fluid, confused thinking characteristic of schizophrenia. The ending of a scene is extremely informative and can generally be used as an indicator of how the person will terminate other relationships and commitments (such as therapy, job, school, or hospitalization). To end a scene means to decide to separate oneself from the "pretend" world one has participated in. One may end it oneself by resolving the conflict, running away, or even dying. Or one may not be able to end it, depending instead upon others to do so. For example, one patient ended nearly every scene with an explosion, in which everything in the scene supposedly disappeared. In a striking parallel, he refused to be discharged from the hospital because "there won't be anything left of me." Another patient would end a scene by abruptly cutting off the action, often when he was beginning to interact with another character. After an eight months stay in the hospital he abruptly left against medical advice. His psychotherapist reported that they had just begun to establish a working relationship! The degree to which there is a development of theme or action, instead of a mere presentation of a situation or character, reflects the person's sense of time and attitude toward the future, as well as his ability to conceive of changes in people or situations, and ultimately, himself. True development of the action involves planning and anticipation, important cognitive capabilities.

Character Development

The set of roles one can reasonably portray is called one's *role repertoire,* and the breadth of the role repertoire is one indication of psychological maturity. Developing a character, that is, taking on and articulating the role of another, involves the ability to reconstruct people, events, and feelings. In this process of reconstruction, gaps and deficiencies in the person's system of representing the world internally will usually be reflected in the difficulties met in creating a believable and full characterization.

The reconstruction of a role involves several important abilities. First, knowledge of or experience with a wide range of social roles and situations, and an understanding of basic social processes, are critical for the ability to portray them. Gaps in a person's understanding of social situations often evidence themselves in inappropriate character development. Second, empathy is required: a way of understanding others not through specific knowledge of their feelings but by reference to one's own feeling states. Without the internal reference that empathy provides, the person does not know how to guide his character, and may often confuse his own feelings with those more appropriate to the character.

Third, adequate characterization requires the ability to maintain a constant image of the role, one which will not be easily influenced or changed by variations in the situation or in other characters. Otherwise the role will be fluid and shifting. An example of this is when Don, who was playing a grandmother, ate a piece of German chocolate cake and then a few minutes later in the scene inappropriately assumed a German accent in his speech. Or when Richard, whose character was "watching the Amos and Andy Show," later said that his character's name was Amos. When one's characterization is so susceptible to influence from other unrelated sources, one must suspect that the person has difficulty keeping his thoughts separate and that he has not achieved a constant image of others or himself.

It is important to notice the particular manner in which each individual has difficulty with his characterizations. Impoverished roles (i.e., those without detail or development) may indicate a lack of knowledge and empathy, or may be the result of a defensive effort against becoming confused. Bizarre roles, in which feelings and attributes of the character are unintegrated and inappropriately combined (e.g., the piano tuner who suddenly decides to fly to New York in a jet for a milkshake), may reflect the person's lack of understanding of the social expectations of the role, or even his inability to construct whole people, due to interference from uncontrollable, idiosyncratic fantasies or associations. Stereotyped roles may represent a general blandness or constriction of the personality; or they may be a tremendous achievement for those whose efforts to control their internal world enough to participate in a shared, social reality are only occasionally rewarded. For many psychotic patients, one's initial goal as a therapist may be to have them become capable of representing the stereotype. For most neurotic people, who usually restrict themselves to the stereotype, one aims through an increase in their empathic powers for more detailed, creative character representations. The therapist's attitude to the stereotyped role is different, then, according to the nature of the patient's psychopathology.

Patterns in the Content of Roles

The content of the role playing and the nature of the characters portrayed has traditionally been the major focus for diagnostic and therapeutic efforts.[9] When in Gestalt therapy, for example, a patient enacts a part of his dream (even an inanimate object), it is assumed to represent a part of his personality. Here the focus is on the *what* of the role playing, instead of aspects of the *how* which I have emphasized above. But the question must be asked: what parts of the personality are represented at any given time in the role playing? For example, when does a particular image in the scene represent a specific wish of the person, and when does it represent one of his typical styles of behaving? That is, how are we to make the distinction between the person's current feelings and thoughts, and his more stable personality traits which extend through time and exert a more fundamental, continuous influence on his behavior? In order to make such distinction, one must see the patient over a period of time. Aspects of his personality traits will reveal themselves as consistent patterns across many situations in his role playing: in his selection of roles and the way he portrays them. Once these patterns are perceived, it is possible to see variations in the pattern as reflective of current fluctuations in the person's thoughts or feelings.

I had worked individually with Andrew, who was diagnosed schizophrenic, for a year and a half. At 25, he had been hospitalized off and on for four years. His symptoms included disorganized thoughts, delusions centered around intergalactic travel, inability to hold a job, an extreme hostile-dependent interpersonal stance, and depression.

For several months he had been under a lot of stress in the hospital. His psychotherapist had recently been switched by the hospital administration, and the treatment team was encouraging him to get a job and mobilize himself. A patient he was very close to had recently left. During this time in our role playing sessions, he insisted on playing only two kinds of scenes: (1) either he would be the master and I was to play the slave, whom he would order around, whip, lock up, and generally mistreat; or (2) he would be president of the U.S. (usually Carter, Nixon, or Ford), and I was an underling who would do as he was told.

Over the course of three months this second configuration changed slightly: he now became President Andrew more often, and I was elevated to the role of "presidential advisor." Then, in one significant session in December, this pattern was radically altered: he wanted me to play President Lincoln, who would emancipate the slaves, whom he was to play. The next day he left for home on a weekend pass, and four days later refused to come back to the hospital. He remained A.W.O.L. for over ten days.

Here the ongoing pattern in Andrew's role playing (master-slave; president-servant) was a reflection of important parts of himself: the helpless, passive, and sick part which was being "pushed around by the hospital," and the powerful, aggressive, rageful part (which could in his delusions travel in outer space) that he usually projected onto his therapists and parents. His reversal of these roles in our sessions, so that he played the powerful role, reveals the function of play in overcoming anxiety-producing situations. He could do to me what he felt others did to him, and he could be sure that I would not be completely destroyed, a fate he was in constant fear of for himself. Our work together showed some signs of positively influencing this relationship when, instead of a complete opposition of master to servant, I was gradually seen as having some helpful, if still subservient, role (as his advisor). The sudden and striking alteration of this pattern (combining presidential and slave themes, having me play the powerful role, and adding the theme of "freeing" the slaves) did not indicate a major change in his personality structure; rather, it signaled quite clearly that he was contemplating going A.W.O.L. and perhaps that he wanted my permission to do so. Interestingly, as I learned later, Andrew was not consciously aware of his wish to leave the hospital at the time of the role playing—he said it occurred to him suddenly two days later. Here, then, is an example of how both relatively stable traits and more transient, unconscious thoughts combine to determine the particular content of a person's role playing.

Many other examples can be given of patterns in the role playing which reflect important aspects of personality structure. In some cases, the emergence of the pattern in the role playing precedes its appearance in the conscious thoughts of the patient, as in the case of Andrew. In an exercise in which roles were constantly being reassigned, Ellen would often accept roles, which she portrayed without anxiety. Four months later, she began to talk with her psychotherapist about her fears that she might be a man, or homosexual. She now would become anxious if she was given a male role. Unconscious or latent issues are in this way expressed in role playing, and a perceptive therapist can make use of this information in gently guiding the patient toward greater awareness of these issues.

Attitude Toward Enactment

Another source of information about the person is his attitude toward his own role playing. In general, this is intimately related to his feelings about himself and his accomplishments. The value he places on his role playing, then, is a measure of his self-esteem. The depressed person hates what he did, the paranoid and narcissistic personality thinks the scene was tremendous, the obsessive thinks it could have been a little bit better, and the schizophrenic doesn't care or doesn't know.

In addition to self-esteem, however, one must take into account the person's level of self-awareness, or the "accuracy" of his self-judgments. People who have difficulty distancing themselves from their actions, or who have problems in reality testing, will typically make judgments which are inaccurate. Thus the depressed person who hates what he did when he didn't do very well has better reality testing than the depressed person who hates what he did when he in fact had performed very creatively. Similarly, the schizophrenic patient who shows anxiety about a bizarre aspect of his role playing has attained a higher level than the patient who shows no anxiety at all about some inappropriate action or verbalization. Often what seems to interfere in reality testing is the person's struggle to maintain some consistent self-image and desired level of self-esteem. An important question to ask is: How far will the individual go in denying reality in order to protect a particular view of himself? The potentially psychotic person will go considerably farther than the neurotic who, though conflicted, will eventually succumb to the view which reality demands.

4 CHARACTERISTIC STYLES

I would not like to leave the impression that the diagnostic use of role playing is limited to a straightforward analysis of relatively specific behaviors. Individuals are coherent. Their behavior is not the sum of isolated fragments, but is rather an organization of behaviors: the gestalt, or style, of the person. In role playing, too, there are distinctive styles which characterize people's various means of meeting the demands of the situation. I have found that often they are highly reflective of the individual's personality traits and cognitive style, and thus they have been helpful as general diagnostic indicators. I will now briefly describe some general styles encountered from people who have difficulty with improvisational role playing. While I would not assert that these styles are all-inclusive, they are the most common forms of role playing I have seen.

Inhibited Styles

This group of people find participation in pretend activities extremely difficult and often refuse to join; when they do role play, it is extremely restricted, with minimal involvement. People with this style may be frightened, but they may also show anger and negativism, or in other cases disinterest and apathy.

There seems to be a variety of underlying issues. For most well-functioning people not familiar with role playing, a moderate amount of stage fright at first is entirely normal, but the anxiety should dissipate relatively soon. If stage fright (i.e. freezing on stage, adamant refusals to go on, etc.) continues, it may suggest that the person has yet to solidify his self-image, which role playing threatens by placing him in front of an audience. Adolescents are especially prone to such identity threats on stage, but adults who have had difficulties maturing, or who have especially strong bodily concerns, will also succumb to stage fright.

However, what may underlie other people's inhibitions in role playing is fear of failure and the accompanying ridicule and scorn from the audience. These fears may either have a depressive cast ("They make fun of me because I am no good"), or a paranoid one ("They will laugh at me because they hate me"). Alternatively, inhibitions may not reflect near-normal or even neurotic concerns as above, but ones closer to the schizophrenic's experience. In this case, the issue is that the person simply cannot personify roles, either because he is no longer able to represent other people as having any solidity or reality ("The world has collapsed"), or because by becoming another personality, even in play, he would no longer know who he was; that is, he fears his sense of self would be lost forever.

Thus, inhibitions in role playing should be evaluated carefully, as they are excellent covers for a variety of psychopathological states.

Over-Involved Styles

This set of styles is characterized by high degrees of physical and emotional involvement in the role playing, which in more severe forms may hinder cooperative work with others. The person's mood is typically characterized by enthusiasm, self-enjoyment, and a facile expression of affect.

In its more normal manifestations, the over-involved style is characteristic of the "ham": someone willing to portray in exaggerated form any variety of role, feeling, or situation. The ham, of course, seeks attention through this behavior, but he is at the same time gratified by the intensity of the activity. For some, however, this desire for involvement goes beyond the desire for attention or impulse gratification, and is motivated more by a pervading sense of emptiness and a desire to be filled up by the role, feeling, or action. This is the case of the person who "becomes" his role and holds onto it even after the performances. Here an unshaped identity and an underlying passive orientation can be seen. Another variation in this style is found in the person who overinvests himself in magnificent or grandiose characters as a way of covering his low self-esteem.

Another explanation of the over-involved style has more serious implications. In this case, the person experiences himself as having no well-defined self at all, and in role playing no longer recognizes the separation between his self and the role. Confusion to this degree is probably indicative of nonparanoid schizophrenia.[10] Whereas the neurotic desires to be identified with the role in order to fill himself up, and secretly realizes he is not really his role, the schizophrenic is apt to literally define his identity by aspects of the role and can no longer distinguish between them. Obviously, the degree of self-control is greatest in the ham, who is most consciously aware of the separation between himself and his actions, and least in the schizophrenic, who is prone to confusion and the misreading of others in the role playing.

Compulsive Styles

The compulsive styles are those in which concern for detail and perfection, and efforts to maintain self-control by the repetition of actions are especially evident. In many ways, this style is conducive to good acting to the degree that attention to detail and concern for exact replication of dramatic elements facilitates communication to the audience. However, the compulsive style may be distinguished from this by the degree to which such attention or concern seems to serve efforts at self-control instead of communication.

In its most common manifestation, the development of a compulsive style can be recognized by the individual's overconcern about the characteristics or placement of props, or by a tendency to focus on the details of mimed objects, over and above the development of the relationship to other people. The relationship to props is used not to enhance but to replace the relationship to others, who are obviously less easily controlled. As the compulsive style more seriously interferes with the person's functioning, one

sees a greater attention to order, to making sure scenes begin and
end "properly," and to greater irritation and inhibition when
something goes wrong. Rituals around costuming, entrances, or
posture are also typical.

The extremely compulsive person is unable to function smoothly, and is severely hindered by rigidity in his body, actions, and
role playing. Repetition of actions may reach such a point that no
progression in the scene occurs. For example, a ten year old boy
would run back and forth between the two side walls of the room,
unable to begin a scene because he was unsure if the chair in the
center of the room looked the same from each of the two walls.

The underlying motivation for these behaviors seems to be a
desire to maintain control over one's self and one's actions. The
freedom within the role playing may be experienced as a threat to
those who, if they do not know exactly what they are supposed to
do, may fear themselves giving in to other less appropriate actions
towards others, often of an aggressive or sexual nature. These
people usually are greatly upset by improvisation or other unstructured settings and prefer others whose clear expectations
help to prevent the outbreak of the feared actions. Thus, the fer-
vent request for scripts is usually indicative of the compulsive
style. On a more primitive level, this concern for order and perfection may be motivated by fears that one's own body is incomplete or fragmented. Many compulsive role players can be
recognized by the rigidity in their bodies, which is the counterpart to their need for rigid control of their roles or scenes. Finally,
in its most severe form, the compulsive style is fueled by the fear
of a more general disorganization in thinking, often indicated by
fantasies of the world disintegrating. The compulsive repetition
of actions to the point where the function of communication is
lost is generally indicative of this layer of motivation. The repetition of actions and control of objects are attempts to keep the
self/world from coming apart.

Impulsive Styles

Impulsive styles are characterized by a general lack of control
over actions, unpredictability, and hyperactivity. Generally one
finds this more often in children, but in many adolescents and

even adults this style is readily observable. For example, "pretend" fights or love scenes can become all too real, causing the therapist to intervene lest someone get hurt or mishandled. Behaving in opposition to an external authority is a common indicator of the impulsive style.

In its mild forms, the impulsivity is contained within the role playing: the person plays impulsive characters while others play the controlling, authoritative roles (e.g. police, teacher, parents). Occasionally the person may play these authoritative roles also, but does so in an especially threatening and tyrannical way, usually stimulating rebellious behavior in the others.

In some cases, the person is unable to contain his impulsivity within the role playing and instead turns to the therapist as the external authority who must keep him under control. The therapist will feel it necessary to intervene, with a struggle often ensuing between patient and therapist. Usually this struggle is experienced as relieving by the impulsive person, who is also afraid of his own lack of control and is thankful to have a safe target for his impulses. Unfortunately, once his own sense of safety becomes dependent upon the strength of the authority figure, he must continue behaviors which will stimulate the therapist to be strong and punitive.

In extreme cases neither the therapist nor the role playing are capable of containing the impulsive person, who may feel that if he delayed discharging his aggressive or sexual impulses, he would explode or experience severe internal pain. Only a strong and secure environment (which in some hospitals may involve physical restraint), which sets extremely rigid limits to his behavior, can provide the sense of security and protection he lacks. Role playing then becomes an impossibility.

These four styles represent different attitudes toward the basic issues of identity (inhibited and over-involved) and activity (compulsive and impulsive). The presence of any one style suggests different therapeutic approaches and techniques.

5 CONCLUSION

The ability to play is an important aspect of our personality, one which reflects both cognitive and emotional dimensions of our experience. Inhibitions or difficulties in improvisational role playing may indicate various stages of developmental arrest, thought disorder, levels of anxiety, or learning disabilities. Exactly what these relationships are and how they develop requires a great deal more investigation. I have only been able to suggest areas of correspondence between aspects of role playing and personality structure, based on my clinical experience and research. It is my firm belief, however, that detailed observation of a variety of people in a variety of role playing experiences will provide us with a rich source of information about human development and functioning. All aspects of play expression have a meaning for the adult as well as the child, knowledge of which is largely untapped, though perhaps in part intuitively understood, by clinicians in the field of drama therapy.

FOOTNOTES

1. Jean Piaget, *Play, Dreams, and Imitation in Childhood* (New York: Norton, 1962); Melanie Klein, *The Psychoanalysis of Children* (London: Hogarth, 1932); F. Shaftel and G. Shaftel, *Role-Playing for Social Values* (Englewood Cliffs, N.J.: Prentice-Hall, 1967).
2. R. Waelder, "The Psychoanalytic Theory of Play," *Psychoanalytic Quarterly* 2 (1932): 208–24.
3. L. Peller, "Libidinal Phases, Ego Development, and Play," *Psychoanalytic Study of the Child* 9 (1954): 178–98.
4. Much of the material in this article is also derived from my research at Yale University on individual improvisational role-playing; the Diagnostic Role-Playing Test, a standardized test I have been developing, was used.
5. Jacob L. Moreno, *The Theatre of Spontaneity* (New York: Beacon, 1947).
6. Jerome Singer, *The Child's World of Make-Believe* (New York: Academic Press, 1973).
7. E. Weisskopf, "A Transcendence Index as a Proposed Measure in the TAT," *Journal of Psychology* 29 (1950): 379–90.
8. R. Gould, *Child Studies through Fantasy* (New York: Quadrangle Books, 1972).
9. B. Bricklin, "A Role-Play Rorschach Procedure," *Journal of Personality Assessment* 39 (1975): 453–61.
10. See David Read Johnson, "Drama Therapy and the Schizophrenic Condition," chap. 4 of this book.

Part 2
SPECIAL PROBLEMS AND APPROACHES

This section deals with drama therapy for specific dysfunctions. It also demonstrates different modes of treatment. Each drama therapist approaches his patients in his own unique way.

James M. Sacks examines the problems of acting-out patients, those impulsive individuals whose unreasonable conduct can be helped by enactment (Chapter 3). A distinguished psychodramatist, his approach with these patients is more eclectic than the classic Moreno position. Most interestingly, he says:

> At any stage of development, the potential for dramatic acting remains as a distinct mode of behavior which permits us to mediate between the disparate demands of internal need and the limitations of hard reality.

As we have seen in Volume I, dramatic play is the way in which the child relates his inner world to the environment, and Sacks demonstrates that, with his patients, enactment serves the same purpose. As Winnicott has indicated, dramatic behavior is the key method of mediation between inner and outer for all human beings, from birth to death.

David Johnson demonstrates the use of creative drama and improvisation with schizophrenics (Chapter 4). He provides a most useful structural role model of the relationships within an improvisation, to which he relates the boundary confusions of schizophrenics, and successful methods of dramatic approach. However, apart from its value in dealing with these specific patients, Johnson's model and his treatment of it has implications far beyond work with schizophrenics.

Two chapters then follow about the use of drama therapy with severely disturbed adults: those in a hospital setting, by Robin Reif (Chapter 5); and those in an outpatient clinic, by Stuart Lawrence (Chapter 6). Both are descriptive and couched in terms of journals. Reif describes what happens on a psychiatric ward in Bellevue Psychiatric Hospital, New York. Uniquely in this book, she gives a view from the perspective of an untrained volunteer. Lawrence, on the other hand, provides a journal showing improvisation and creative drama with severely disturbed outpatients. His emphasis is upon socialization.

Marvin L. Blumberg describes group techniques, with similarities to both psychodrama and creative dramatics, used for patients with mental and physical handicaps (Chapter 7). While emphasizing personality development and social behavior, emotional problems also tended to improve. In addition, a twenty minute improvised production increased their personal and social abilities.

The last five chapters, while discussing special problems, also present different types of approach.

Two chapters are concerned with drama in Gestalt therapy. Jon Kogen and Edith Cadenhead (Chapter 8) summarize the use of drama in this approach. Daniel Rosenblatt describes a classic Gestalt method in Gestalt linguistic style (Chapter 9). Virtually a narrative of what happens *now*, his paper specifically describes a one-to-one relationship of drama therapist and patient. As properly befits this mode of therapy, Rosenblatt describes their encounter as "two actors free to create what will happen to the two of them, right now, at this instant."

In contrast, Hannah B. Weiner presents a typical psychodrama approach to the treatment of alcoholism and drug addictions (Chapter 10). She provides a multiplicity of techniques with these patients, together with practical examples of what happens in particular sessions. In an appendix, she supplies nearly fifty additional techniques.

The final two papers are eclectic, though in different ways and in diverse settings. Roy Shuttleworth's treatment of disturbed adolescents commences from the early British concept of the therapeutic community of Maxwell Jones (Chapter 11). He draws on a wide variety of techniques and uses them as required by the needs of the patients. Finally, Claire Michaels draws on many techniques from creative drama, psychodrama and improvisation, as well as a variety of media, in her work with the aged (Chapter 12). In particular, she demonstrates that drama therapy assists the process of recall which has highly productive effects with old people.

JAMES M. SACKS, Ph.D., is a psychologist in private practice and director of the New York Center for Psychodrama Training in New York City. Formerly president of the American Society of Group Psychotherapy and Psychodrama, he is the author of more than thirty articles on the subject of psychodrama.

Chapter 3

DRAMA THERAPY WITH THE ACTING-OUT PATIENT

James M. Sacks

1 DRAMA AND ITS RELATION TO PSYCHOTHERAPY

Drama is a mode of experience which we adults have plagiarized from its inventors. Games of pretending fill the free-play time in nurseries and playgrounds whenever adult supervision is relaxed. It was children who devised the world of enacted make-believe as a protected arena in which ideas and wishes are wedded to fact and action. Their marvelous discovery has helped to free us from our confinement to the separated functions of the entirely mental on the one hand and the entirely physical on the other. At any stage of development, the potential for dramatic acting remains as a distinct mode of behavior which permits us to mediate between the disparate demands of internal need and the limitations of hard reality. Civilization engenders within us such psychological specialization that vital functions, only nascent in childhood, are allowed to atrophy rather than to mature. (While the handwriting of the average adult is clearly distinct from that of a twelve year old, the figure drawings are almost indistinguishable. As children we all draw pictures but as adults we leave art behind as though it were a regression to some early stage of development.) With the decline in pretending goes much of our ability to bring into intimate contact our imagination and our behavior.

Psychotherapy like all education must begin in the areas of the client's relative strengths and, only by degrees, venture into the areas yet to be mastered. This requires a bipolar gradient between the learner's point of origin and his goal. Dramatic acting, being partly in the realm of ideas and partly in the arena of action, is exactly such a bipolar field. In the drama, thought and action may be combined in any proportion ranging from highly cognitive to highly motoric productions. The therapist may thus select scenes which minimize the use of that ego function in which the protagonist suffers a deficit. Once initiated into the drama, the protagonist may be gradually directed towards scenes requiring greater exercise of his disfavored capacity. Thus by reviving the capacity for dramatic play, the therapist restores a natural field on which to treat characterological inadequacies on either pole of the action-thought dichotomy.

The use of drama in psychotherapy has been traditionally valued almost exclusively as a means for helping patients with problems on only one side of this continuum, i.e., those with inhibited action. It is less well appreciated that psychodrama, or the drama therapies generally, are equally applicable to patients with inadequacies in the area of thought and control.

For the former, more reticent patients, the stage is an artificial world where they may test with impunity new activities too risky for the real world. One part of the actor's mind accepts the fictions of the play as being sufficiently real for authentic emotion to be generated. At the same time, another portion of the player's psyche realizes that it is make-believe. The coexistence of these two attitudes makes it possible for the patient to experience what he otherwise could not, either in passive fantasy or in life itself.

2 THE ACTING-OUT PERSONALITY

The second category of patients, those lacking in thought and control, characteristically resort to inappropriate behavioral solutions. They act when they should be thinking, just as the inhibited patients obsessively reconsider when it is time to act. These impulsive individuals exhibit their pathology by continual unreasonable conduct, usually rationalized and not easily influenced by countersuggestions from friends or psychotherapists. While the classical neurotic patient is often paralyzed in his responding to stressful stimuli, the acting-out patient, in a similarly rigid pattern, can not call himself into question, but can only manipulate the environment. While both types of patients misperceive reality, the neurotic resists acting on his distorted views. The acting-out patient sadly encounters the compounding of his problems when his destructive behavior entangles him in its inevitable consequences in the real world.

Acting-out patients may rationalize their behavior very simply or in elaborate ways. Their therapists typically are drawn into an effort to expose the fallacies of these rationalizations. These attempts to make the symptoms ego-alien are usually fruitless, and more frequently result in a compensatory strengthening of the defenses. Should the therapist actually succeed in defeating the rationalizations, the treatment founders on a fresh obstacle. While the patient may no longer make a virtue of his unreasonable conduct, he nevertheless fails to change, despite arduous interpretation. He exasperates his therapist who feels the futility of his interventions regardless of how brilliantly or how tactfully timed and phrased. The patient hears, he understands and he may even sincerely agree with the therapist, but by the next session it is as if nothing had been said. While the interpretations are accepted, their impact is too feeble to influence the powerful negative psychic forces involved.

The dilemma of the patient is that he suffers from a condition which interferes with the very process which is meant to cure him. In order to change his behavior he must allow himself to absorb the full meaning of the therapist's interpretations. This, however, is his problem. Ideas generally, and most especially the threatening ideas which his therapist expresses, are grossly undervalued. For him, impulses have always passed from the unconscious to the musculature while barely passing through awareness. These patients have failed to develop the normal capacity to think be-

fore acting. Deleterious early experience has interfered with their
ability to postpone or inhibit action in deference to conceptualization. Even Fenichel,[1] the orthodox Freudian, confesses
that "treatment for such patients is extremely difficult and may
necessitate modification of the classical psychoanalytic technique." He goes so far as to suggest directly prohibiting the acting-
out behavior.[2] The use of drama fortunately enables us to avoid
such interference with the patient's autonomy and to take advantage of any vestige of observing or controlling ego.

3   GRADUAL INTRODUCTION OF THE IDEATIONAL FACTOR

In psychotherapy via dramatic methods the patient begins with
what he can already do, i.e. act. Next, by gradual degrees, con-
ceptual and interpretive material is inserted into the drama at a
rate which can be integrated.

An intelligent young woman with a demanding, dependent
personality became enamored of the dramatic format. Bored by
conventional therapy, she took at once to the opportunity to
enact her feelings. Although envious when other group members
were receiving attention, she waited all week for the moments
when she could act out her own scenes. These consisted of tearful
diatribes against the various persecuting and thwarting figures in
her current life. She rejected the premature attempts of her
double[3] or alter-ego to insert comments which would ascribe her
inordinate rage to a displacement of the rage against her parents.
Instead she accused the double of devaluing her feelings by rel-
egating them to mere transference. It was necessary for the double
to persist for months in an entirely supportive role, joining in with
her paranoid accusations. This supportive reassurance seemed to
increase her confidence and trust. Later, when the double again
cautiously implied a connection between her past and present
anger, the patient echoed the double's sentiments. She admitted
to the actor in the role of her colleague that he was just like her
father and that she might therefore be especially sensitive to his
slights. The dramatic format enabled this double to titrate the ex-

tent of interpretive conceptualization which this patient could tolerate.

4 JUXTAPOSITION OF THOUGHT AND ACTION

Acting-out patients isolate what they do from what they think. Drama, by its nature, mediates between act and idea and, thereby, forms the bridge. Dramatic acting can facilitate reintegration of these dissociated ego functions. Acting-out persons are impatient and intolerant of tension. They live only in the moment, undervaluing both past and future. In drama, past and future are brought into the present where they can become meaningful for these patients. The acting-out patient tends to use any interval which separates his behavior and his ideas to dissociate his actions from their meaning. By the time the conventional therapist can interpret the conduct which the patient reports, it has already grown cold. To be effective with these patients, the interpretation must be instantaneous — contemporaneous with the action itself. With any delay, the feeble capacity for integrated insight decays. By means of the drama, we can achieve this immediacy and contiguity of act and idea.

It was this opportunity to bring significant material from the past into temporal proximity with the present that helped us to work with Clara. Her acting-out symptoms consisted of repeated submission to mental, financial, and physical abuse from a series of boy friends. When her fellow group members accused her of self-debasement, she claimed that they were unjustly blaming the victim. She received all attempts to connect her present suffering with long past family patterns as curious theoretical formulations that she could not take seriously.

In the course of her drama-oriented therapy she was cast in the role of her father, whom she portrayed as harshly cruel and aggressive toward everyone in the family. By contrast, toward the actress playing the role of Clara, she enacted him as totally cold and disdainful. Returned to her own role, she began complaining to her father that he treated her as if she did not exist. At first she spoke in a wooden way as if repeating prepared thoughts. Soon, however, the anger, longing, and envy of his attention to her sisters became genuine and intense. At the climax of this scene, she unabashedly begged him to stop ignoring her saying, "Please pay some attention to me. I don't care if you hit me!" At this instant I turned her to face an actor taking the role of her current boy friend, saying, "Talk to Phil." She immediately repeated, "Please pay some attention to me. I don't care if you hit me!" sobbing bitterly. In the wake of this scene it became easier for Clara to acknowledge the masochistic element in the pattern of her love life. The idea that she was seeking abuse as the only believable attention she could expect from a man, could not become real for her without the concrete experience of the drama. The license of the dramatist to move back and forth in time, made it possible to bring distant experiences into immediate conjunction with her present life at the very instant of the emotion.

5   DRAMA FOR THE CLEAR DISPLAY OF SYMPTOMS

Since the acting-out patient does not conceptualize his behavior clearly, the version which he describes in a conventional therapeutic situation is notably distorted by rationalizations and evasions. This often makes it difficult for the therapist to know what is actually going on in the patient's life. No such vagaries obscure the behavioral evidence of pathology for these patients. Once in action in the drama, obvious patterns emerge starkly. The true feelings and behaviors, ripe for analysis, become clearly displayed to patient, therapist and group alike.

6   DRAMA THERAPY AND TRANSFERENCE WITH THE ACTING-OUT PATIENT

Even the conventional psychotherapist is not entirely dependent on the dubious reports of his acting-out patients since he also has the material of the transference available. Certain problems exist, however, in the analysis of transference with acting-out patients. Many isolate important aspects of their conflicts to certain relationships, keeping their behavior toward the therapist relatively free of significant symptoms. The blithe assumption that every-thing comes out in the transference is not always justified. One male patient avoided reference to any problems of overdepend-ency in his self-descriptions and, in fact, experienced only casual attachment to his male analyst. He did not miss him on vacations, ask him for advice, or take offense at fancied rejections. Problems of extreme overdependency became apparent only in the scenes re-enacted with his ex-wife, his girl friend and his mother-in-law.

Acting-out patients also have a special difficulty in accepting the interpretations of their transferential behavior. Such patients, barely capable of giving consideration to any psychological inter-pretation about someone not present, can scarcely bear the added tensions when the person in question is directly facing them. They are forced to return to their familiar acting-out, and attack or re-ject the threatening suggestions.

The following example from an individual session illustrates how drama can be adapted as an instrument for interpreting trans-ference with more distance and for obviating direct confrontation.

Frank would commonly exhibit his penchant for hostile with-holding by late payment of his fee. Each month he would offer pseudo-realistic justifications for the delay. My implication that this was a form of hostility was countered with an angry denial that he was angry. When he repeated the request for delay the following month we enacted a role-reversal scene in which I (as Frank) repeated his own statement, "You're going to have to wait for your money this month, I'm afraid." In my role of therapist he obviously chafed at the suggestion but reluctantly agreed to the delay. Next I assumed the role of a hypothetical colleague of Dr. Sacks. "What do you think about Frank?" I asked. To my surprise he said, "He always pulls that. He never went to college but he's as smart as the old Doc here. He collects interest on the money the whole time he holds onto it."

This acknowledgment enabled us to discuss his feelings of educational and intellectual inferiority in relation to his pattern of withholding. Through the role reversal, he could experience himself through the eyes of another person without first having to translate words into concepts and then apply the concepts to

himself. He did not have to lose face by agreeing with my interpretation of the meaning of his late payment as against his own.
He was able to arrive at the interpretation himself. After immers-
ing himself in my role as a therapeutic exercise, a part of this role
remained with him.

7   CONTRIBUTIONS TO EGO STRENGTH

The application of the methods described thus far has been to
facilitate the communication of essential therapeutic concepts to
patients possessing a minimal capacity to accept them, or to incorporate them into their insulated behavioral repertoire. These
methods remain effective despite the anxiety these patients experience at the prospect of any invasion of the therapist's ideas
into their behavior in life. While the drama methods do partially
circumvent the defense system, this is not to say that their highly
defensive stance is uninfluenced by the treatment. On the contrary, the establishment of new insight strengthens the ego,
enabling it to endure greater tension and permitting the relaxation of defensiveness. The fruit of self-comprehending is not only
the acquisition of the concepts involved; the very exercise of the
self-examining function fortifies it. The ego, nourished by its own
courage, grows amenable to more imposing insights.

One therapy group with many acting-out patients rarely
indulged in spontaneous self-exploration. Without external struc-
turing, the group constantly returned to social conversation.
Drama methods were required to ease them into the process of
focusing on their problems. After several months they grew bold
enough to introduce appropriate issues routinely with or without
the drama.

8   DRAMA AS AN AVENUE TO THE
ETIOLOGICAL ROOT OF THE ACTING-OUT
PATTERN

While any act of self-discovery is thus generally beneficial, it does
not necessarily alter the initial cause of the acting out. In
the course of development, children accommodate to frustration
which they normally encounter in progressively increasing doses.

Given time and opportunity to adapt to each new level of difficulty, immediate gratification is slowly relinquished in favor of longer range goals. Impulse gives way to consideration and delay, to more thinking and postponement of action. When circumstance or faulty rearing subject the child to abrupt traumas for which he has not yet acquired tolerance, he is driven back toward blind pleasure seeking. Furthermore, the memory of these painful experiences succumbs to repression. From their lair in the unconscious these mnemonic nexuses of inner disturbance give rise to perpetual tensions. The patient has thus failed to receive the age-appropriate scaled degrees of frustration necessary for the development of patience and tension binding. He is now beset by a constant source of tension from an unknown source. Any step toward unlocking the secret of his problems raises the tension higher. He therefore has no choice but to block out, wall off, or destroy any idea that may threaten the repression.

Ideas and associations diffuse widely so that even apparently innocuous thoughts may conceivably become connected with recognizable derivatives of repressed memories. This mechanism further discourages these individuals from becoming highly invested in ideation.

Eventually this attitude evolves into a semi-autonomous, acting-out lifestyle, no longer functioning simply to evade repressed memories. Conceptualization has become a disfavored experience in itself. For this reason we still have an opportunity of reviving and demystifying the repressed material through a nonconceptual route.

The recapture of traumatic memory by the use of drama methods is clearly illustrated in the case of Larry. He abused alcohol and drugs to the extent that his health was in grave jeopardy. When I tried to discuss the danger of his addictions, Larry would imitate my words with a babyish intonation in an attempt to get me to laugh. Full appreciation of the seriousness of his state was potentially more terrifying than he could face. He fended off all attempts to activate his self-preservation anxiety. The obvious fact that he was in peril was not unknown to him, but this knowledge was devalued so as to protect himself from its full impact. His flow of ideas was severely blunted. He could produce no free associations on his own and, often, did not pay attention when I spoke.

The therapy became more animated with the introduction of drama methods. The regressive playfulness of it appealed to him. At first he stuck to comedy, converting all roles into ludicrous caricatures. Gradually he began to enact the significant people and events of his past in a more serious and affecting manner. Larry's discovery of the emotional opportunities of dramatic expression opened a Pandora's box. He enacted a series of atrocity-like events from different periods of his formative years in which his mother had abused both him and his brother by regular and severe beatings and by subtle psychological torture. His father was depicted as so intimidated by the mother's psychotic rages that his self-protection took priority over the protection of his sons. Larry's mother was finally hospitalized when he was eighteen.

Before enacting his scenes, Larry had no idea what he would deal with. Once begun he found himself re-enacting events which he claimed not to have thought of since the time they had happened. He had no apparent preconception of the relationship of these experiences to his adult personality. During and after each scene, attempts were made to help him establish these connections.

His scenes evolved through several periods. At first he chose to remain mostly in his mother's role, displaying her aggression. Later he preferred his own role in order to purge himself of the counteraggression which he had not felt safe in showing initially. Finally, he exposed the longing and love for better treatment from her. The object of this deeply regressive wish was the only positive mother image he could imagine, namely the depersonalized nipple itself. He fell unabashedly into the baby role, asking to be rocked while he pretended to suck on a bottle. The connection between his dramas and his drinking became firmly established and with the help of other positive reinforcements he eventually came to abstain.

9   SUMMARY

Play acting arises naturally in childhood as an arena on which to work out, by experiment and compromise, solutions to the disparate requirements of impulse and environment. The drama therapist may revive the procedure to assist adults whose solutions have proved inadequate. The dramatic arena is represented as a continuum between two poles: the one of spontaneous impulsive action arising from within, the other as inhibitory mentation arising from concern with environmental repercussions. The overly restrained patient is given a ground on which to move toward the action pole, while the acting-out patient has a field on which he may progress toward rational control. Several drama techniques which facilitate this movement for the acting-out patient are described and illustrated. Threatening ideas are introduced slowly into his more familiar action-oriented context. Interpretive ideas are timed to coincide with the behavior with which they correspond in order to counter the tendencies of the acting-out individuals to isolate action from idea. Drama methods are also used to establish the necessary distance which these patients require to tolerate an understanding of the transference relationship. Finally, drama provides a vivid format for the recapturing and working through of the traumatic memories which originally produced the acting-out disorder.

FOOTNOTES

1. Otto Fenichel, *The Psychoanalytic Theory of Neurosis* (New York: Norton, 1945), p. 507.
2. Fenichel, "Neurotic Acting Out," *Psychoanalytic Review* 32 (1945).
3. Zerka Toeman, "The 'Double Situation' in Psychodrama," *Sociatry* 1 (1948): 436–48.

DAVID READ JOHNSON, M.S., has been a drama therapist at the
Yale Psychiatric Institute and the Soundview Specialized Care
Center, and is conducting research on drama therapy at Yale
University. Active in community theatre, he is the author of several
articles on dance and drama therapy, and vice president of the
National Association for Drama Therapy.

Chapter 4

DRAMA THERAPY AND THE SCHIZOPHRENIC CONDITION

David Read Johnson

1 INTRODUCTION

Drama therapy is the use of creative dramatics toward the amelioration of pathological symptoms in the patient, or the increased potential of the already well-functioning person. In this particular combination of the arts and psychotherapy, drama therapy incorporates aspects of both creative dramatics, in which educational and creative goals are pursued, and psychodrama, in which insight into and catharsis of an individual's specific emotional state occur. The structure of a drama therapy group is more similar to the improvisational theatre group, but its goals are more similar to those of the psychodrama and group therapy tradition. However, drama therapy, strictly speaking, is not psychodrama. The format for psychodrama developed by Moreno may be used, but only as one of several adjunctive approaches.[1]

There is significant divergence in technique as practiced currently by drama therapists. Nevertheless, drama therapy normally utilizes the group experience to facilitate the expression, sharing, and understanding of each individual's problems or concerns. The use of structured, creative tasks usually involving role playing, is often combined with the opportunity for less structured fantasy ex-

47

periences. Ongoing discussion and periods of verbal and nonverbal "sharing" also occur.

Within this general framework, there are a great variety of approaches, with each practitioner independently devising his own approach to fulfill the demands of his situation. There is a need, however, for clarifying the usefulness of particular approaches for different settings and people. All techniques, no matter how exciting or seemingly useful, are not appropriate for all types of people. Specific approaches have not as yet been adequately investigated in this field.[2]

Development of a particular approach to drama therapy has to take into consideration the types of patients, tasks of the group, stage of therapy, aspects of the setting, and the nature of other therapeutic work being done with the patients. It is especially important to have the drama therapy experience integrated into the total therapeutic program being offered to the patient. Further, it is necessary for the therapist to accept certain responsibilities in his own work with the patient. These include: (1) an accurate and detailed understanding of the particular patient's problems and needs; (2) a clear formulation of the therapist's goals with the patient; (3) the existence of a contract with the patient as to the extent of the therapist's responsibility, and to the nature of his interventions with the patient; and (4) the utilization of some method of ongoing evaluation and/or testing of the approach.

The predominantly schizophrenic patients with whom I have been working for the last several years have necessitated a particularly structured and careful approach which has proved useful. I will attempt to delineate some of their major difficulties and explain some of my therapeutic goals, rather than concentrate on the specific techniques and exercises I might use.

2   THE SCHIZOPHRENIC CONDITION

The schizophrenic condition consists in part of a withdrawal from intense, interpersonal relations. The schizophrenic individual lacks a coherent, autonomous identity: his sense of self is insecure, and he experiences both internal and external forces as extremely threatening and at times overwhelming. Unlike the normal or even "neurotic" individual who maintains a relatively unified self-concept, the schizophrenic person experiences any relationship as a potential loss of identity.

> The individual is frightened of the world, afraid that any impinge-ment will be total, will be implosive, penetrative, fragmenting, and engulfing. He is afraid of letting anything of himself 'go', of coming out of himself, of losing himself in any experience... Engulfment is felt as a risk in being understood (thus grasped, comprehended), in being loved, or even simply in being seen.[3]

In order to preserve some sense of identity, to remain in some sort of control over his own experience, the schizophrenic person withdraws from relationships with others and isolates in fantasy his precarious sense of self. This maneuver is paradoxical and can be potentially self-destructive, because he also has a tremendous need for support and protection. His feelings of inadequacy and insecurity in dealing with life situations create the need for someone on whom he can depend. Yet his fear of intimate relationships prevents just such a solution. He therefore retreats from the dif-ficulties of individuation (i.e., developing an autonomous identity while maintaining relatedness with others) because he knows of no middle ground between complete engulfment and a radical isolation of the self.[4]

What allows this threat of engulfment to exist is a fundamental confusion of boundaries between inside and outside, self and not-self, thought and reality.

The establishment of these intrapsychic and interpersonal bound-aries normally occurs gradually throughout infancy. The child's experience of frustration in dealing with reality, which often does not respond to his desires or needs, causes him to slowly alter his primarily undifferentiated, narcissistic conception of the world. He begins to become aware of the differences between that part which is under his control (his body), that which is capable of be-ing influenced (e.g., his mother), and that which is usually not responsive to his needs (strangers, objects, etc.).

Later as his conceptions of self and others develop from this primitive bodily differentiation, the child will begin to distinguish between his thoughts (which are inside), and his actions (which are outside). With the development of language, the child will acquire the tools to make even more exacting distinctions. In this way, normal child development leads to increasing differentiation and awareness of boundaries between a wide range of experiences, coupled with their integration into a solid, but flexible, personality organization.[5]

The schizophrenic, however, has not sufficiently secured this boundary awareness. There is evidence that both constitutional and developmental factors contribute to this fundamental ego-deficit, which seems to be able to explain many of the schizophrenic's cognitive and interpersonal dysfunctions.[6] Disruptions of normal boundaries are obvious when inner thoughts are perceived as reality (in delusions), or when parts of the body are experienced as foreign to the self (in depersonalization). Thus, the schizophrenic's vulnerability to delusions, hallucinations, disruptions in language, fluctuating sense of self, and other psychotic symptoms are understandable. I am reminded of a particularly interesting incident in a drama therapy group some years ago. As the group was holding hands in a circle, a schizophrenic patient turned to me and said in all seriousness, "I have four arms." His experience of his body apparently extended down his arms and up the other person's arm to their shoulder. Given the potential for this kind of experience of the world, it is not surprising that the schizophrenic is so vulnerable to intense anxiety and would resort to a retreat from both interpersonal relations and his own body. The schizophrenic's social withdrawal, verbal incomprehensibility, and lack of bodily integration are all manifestations of this retreat from engulfment and anxiety.[7]

The therapeutic goal, then, is to reverse this process, this vicious circle of primary boundary confusion, anxiety, and retreat from reality. Clearly an environment is needed in which relationships with others will be as nonthreatening as possible, one with distinct boundaries and structure to insure that the insecure personality will not be engulfed. An environment must be created in which something of the inner self can be safely expressed, so that it can be identified and later integrated with the other parts of the self that have been cut off from it. The drama therapy group can be designed to provide such an environment and, indeed, may be especially useful, as it offers the possibility that such a reintegration will occur on a bodily level as well.

In order to clarify the relationship between the therapeutic goals of drama therapy and the schizophrenic's interpersonal difficulties, I must first discuss the nature of role playing and present a special model of the structure of relationships which develop in a role playing situation. Then the specific issues of boundary confusion and isolation will be examined in more detail.

3 ROLE PLAYING

Role playing is a process of identification in which part of the person assumes the identity of another personality. This "other" personality is usually defined by a text, or script, which the actor studies and attempts to understand. The actor will often try to relate certain aspects of his own experience to that of this other personality in order to better impersonate it. Such a role may be called a scripted role.

Another type of role, however, is the improvisational role. Here, a vague situation or general label (such as "salesman" or "customer") is all that has been defined, and the actual personality to be played is spontaneously created by the actor. Thus, the actor must utilize more of his own resources to create and maintain a coherent role identity. He draws upon memories, habits, mimicry, and also more intangible aspects of his own personality, both conscious and unconscious. The result is a characterization that is truly a self-expression; the unstructured nature of the role playing allows many aspects of the self to emerge, some under the control of the individual, some not.

Due to its power-to-reveal, the dramatic situation normally stimulates fears of self-exposure. The possibility that one's innermost secrets, one's most embarrassing faults, might be perceived and paraded around in front of others is, indeed, an anxiety-producing thought. Individuals with excessive guilt feelings, or

those with secret fears of retaliation or punishment, are especially
prone to such anxieties. Curiously enough, the schizophrenic is
usually not affected by these stage fright anxieties. He has structured (i.e. split) his experience in such a way that what occurs in
action is irrelevant to his real, "inner" self. Yet the schizophrenic's
defenses are not adequate to prevent the expression of his own
personality, and often awkward defensive maneuvers are utilized
to hide them after they have already been expressed.

When one does ask a patient like this to "own up" to his
behavior, to admit that such and such a role reflects something
about *him*, one often finds a tremendous resistance to seeing any
connection. The rationalization, "it's only acting," can be utilized
to distance and protect the individual from what is clearly a
representation of his inner self. Yet, to a person threatened with
engulfment, this is an important device to be able to use; the only
other alternative would be further withdrawal. It is axiomatic
that an individual who lacks a coherent identity, who is beset by
confusing internal relationships, also has difficulty portraying
and communicating to others a convincing role identity. For an
individual like this to be confronted prematurely with his confusion, to be made to "own up" to behavior of which he is not in
control, is to court increased confusion, overwhelm him further,
and give him more reason to stay in his crippled, isolated role.
Eventually, though, as he makes gains in self-confidence and
trusts those with whom he is working, the connections between his
actions and his feelings can be made more directly.

In order to understand the schizophrenic's confusion in an improvisation, it is necessary to know what kinds of relationships
exist, what boundaries must be maintained, and what conflicts
normally arise. To clarify these complex aspects of the improvisational situation, and to provide a structure for analyzing the
special problems these patients have, I will present the following
model of improvisational role relationships.

A Structural Role Model

In an improvisation between two people (e.g., Bob and Jane),
each of whom is playing a role (e.g., salesman and customer,

respectively), there are really four kinds of relationships that have to be maintained. I shall define these relationships in the following manner:

A. *Impersonal:* the relationship between the two enacted roles, (e.g., between the salesman and the customer).
B. *Intrapersonal:* the relationship between each person and his own role, (e.g., between Bob and the salesman, and Jane and the customer).
C. *Extrapersonal:* the relationship between each person and the other person's role, (e.g., between Bob and the customer and Jane and the salesman).
D. *Interpersonal:* the relationship between the two individuals, (e.g., between Bob and Jane).

These relationships are summarized in the diagram below:

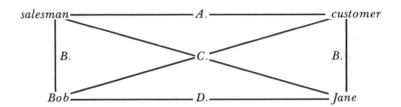

In the improvisation, only the impersonal relationship between the roles themselves is shown; the audience is not usually aware of how the two actors feel about each other, or how they feel about their particular roles. Thus, the intrapersonal, extrapersonal and interpersonal relationships must not be made evident within the enactment. Conflicts between the actors as people often prevent an improvisation from going well, or conflicts between the person and the role he plays may interfere with the enactment (e.g., when a man is asked to play a female role, or a shy person an aggressive bully). Likewise, the role of the other person may be so irritating or engaging that concentration on one's own part is lost. These are frequent occurrences with all types of people. In a drama therapy group an experienced therapist can spot them easily and bring them to the attention of the actors to be worked on in one of two ways. Either the goal will be to increase the level of control within the person, or to explore the underlying conflict with the role or person in question.

4   BOUNDARY CONFUSION

I have been discussing the conflicts which arise between the different structural elements in an improvisation. The actual boundaries between the various elements have remained intact. With schizophrenic individuals, however, there is also the possibility of confusion between the person and his role, the other's role, or even the other person. Bob begins playing the salesman but becomes confused as to whether there is any salesman at all. The improvisation falls apart. Another patient may get so wrapped up in the other's role of Mother that she thinks and reacts to the role identity as her own real mother, which interferes with her intended characterization of the obedient maid.

It should be obvious that these problems are of a different order than those involving conflict within the improvisation. The individual has to maintain and differentiate four kinds of relationships, which I have been calling the impersonal, intrapersonal, extrapersonal, and interpersonal. He is faced with three *other* identities with which he must sustain a relationship while keeping a hold on his own sense of self. One of these (his own role) he must create and regulate himself. For the schizophrenic, this is a difficult task indeed, as any one of these other identities may threaten to engulf him. If he becomes too overwhelmed, he must withdraw and end the improvisation, or else, by showing that he is confused, stimulate others to end it. In this way, the schizophrenic's particular struggle to maintain his identity and diminish the threat of engulfment is revealed to the therapist and to others in the drama therapy group.

The therapist's specific task, therefore, is to help the patient maintain these boundaries, to differentiate between them, and to help him identify the particular source of confusion. It is usually very clear with which area of relationship the patient is having difficulty, and there are a variety of methods through which the therapist can provide assistance. The goal for these patients is not to "open them up," or to "let them explore themselves in new and deeper ways," but to provide them with the necessary structure or support when they begin to flounder, which will hopefully forestall their characteristic retreat from the threatening situation.

Specific Problem Areas

Let us examine these issues in more detail. Four separate boundaries must be maintained. If the interpersonal or impersonal boundaries are not respected, it is evidence of a severe loss in reality testing: e.g., Bob begins to think he *is* Jane (interpersonal boundary confusion), or Bob, the "salesman," begins acting as the "customer," which is Jane's role (impersonal boundary confusion). In either case, the therapist must stop the improvisation and verbally clarify the situation. Confusion of this kind should not be allowed to continue, and may indicate that the patient is currently too disorganized to benefit from the role playing.

Thus, in practice, the two most common difficulties patients experience are in the intrapersonal and extrapersonal areas. In each case, problems arise when the patient: (1) succumbs to his confusion; or (2) in a desperate attempt to ward off confusion, rigidifies his behavior in an exaggerated form.

Confusion in Relation to One's Own Role

PROBLEM AREA 1:   Individual confuses himself with the role he is portraying.

Janet would get upset and confused when she played certain roles, feeling that what she was expressing was very personal. Her enactment would become stilted and a bit bizarre, and her concentration would diminish. The role itself would become very vague. Whenever this happened, she would say that she couldn't go on, that she felt she was exposing herself to ridicule and couldn't figure out the difference between herself and her role.

For Janet, the problem was one of adequately differentiating what is "me" versus what is "not me." The task of the therapist is to help her clarify what attributes are appropriate only to the role identity, with which parts of the role she identifies, and which aspects of the enactment might in fact be reflections of herself. Verbal discussion after an improvisation is often quite useful. All

attempts should be made to point out the differences between the
person and the role; thus, having the patient (or other patients)
repeat the characterization and develop it, often prevents it from
being confused with the person. The temporary use of scripted
roles is also useful in lowering the patient's anxiety.

PROBLEM AREA 2:   Individual finds it difficult to play roles,
and simply plays himself, due to fear of being overwhelmed or confused by the role.

Ellen could not impersonate another person, could not take on
another voice or walk; could only look, speak, and act like Ellen.
She said she would be frightened to do otherwise. Her problem was
in being unable to enact a role, because "becoming" a role personality would be experienced as the possibility of losing her own
identity. Ellen would also not be able to "act" appropriately when
she was on stage: she would talk out of character, ask for a
cigarette, or adjust a sock in the middle of an improvisation. She,
like Janet, could not differentiate between herself and her role.
Unlike Janet, she was so terrified of even taking on a role, of not being Ellen, that she rigidly held onto her own attributes. In this way
she would decrease the possibility that confusion would occur.

The therapist's task is to deal first with the inability to differentiate, then to encourage her to enact different roles. Thus, during
rehearsals for a play, I stressed that when she was on stage, she
was her character, Mrs. Smith, and when she was not on stage she
was Ellen. I insisted therefore that when she wanted to ask me for
anything, she had to come down from the stage. I told her I
would not respond to Mrs. Smith. Thus, a concrete spatial
distinction (between on and off stage) was utilized as a model for
the differentiation between herself and her role. Stepping off
stage in the middle of a scene also pointed out to her how disruptive being out of character was to her fellow actors. By adhering
to this guideline, she was soon able to act appropriately on stage,
and even began to use a different voice for her character. Ellen
has since then been able to take on roles more unlike herself.
However, it was important for her to be given constant reassurance
and support, and for her to be able to become "herself" whenever

she wanted. In this way, she felt she had control over her identities. If it was insisted that she always be Mrs. Smith, and that she could not come down from the stage when she wanted, she would probably have panicked.

Confusion in Relation to the Other's Role

PROBLEM AREA 3: Individual becomes over-involved with and easily affected by the other's role.

Frank was an active role-taker, and could portray many roles with energy and imagination. However, in improvisations he would be so dependent upon the portrayal of the other's role that his role would vary tremendously, and he would often be acting in completely contrary ways within minutes. His shy-and-retiring country doctor would become excited and aggressive, and then German, and then deaf and dumb, depending upon subtle changes in the mood of the improvisation. Traits of the other role would be transferred into his characterization, and Frank would be entirely unaware of it. Also, many times the other person's role would remind him of someone he knew, e.g., his mother or girlfriend, and he would be unable to act since he would be overwhelmed by his feelings about those people.

Frank's problem was one of maintaining his characterization, of not being able to prevent the incorporation of aspects of the "other" into his own role. His identity would be constantly invaded by other identities, leaving his role a shifting, unreal, and empty one. This paralleled his exceptionally compliant, mimicking, and unreal way of relating to others in everyday life.

There are many exercises that can be used to help someone maintain his role, to keep a consistent characterization. However, if the therapist does not realize that the over-sensitivity to the other's role may be a protective defense against a more complete loss of the individual's own identity, then he is merely stripping the patient of his defenses. Rather, the patient must first discover different parts of himself in which he can have confidence, that in some way can feel solid. For Frank, these were reflected in two roles which he often portrayed and which he could maintain relatively constantly: an old lady, and a debonair gentleman.

These represented the part of him that was useless and the target of ridicule (old lady), and the part of him which was charming and engaging (gentleman). Any role which integrated these disparate qualities was especially difficult for Frank to maintain.

Encouragement to maintain his extrapersonal boundaries centered first on the roles of the old lady and debonair gentleman, and then was expanded to include similar roles such as bum and businessman, respectively. Which kinds of roles he could maintain, and which he could not, slowly became clear to him. By identifying these two part-selves, he was able to feel more confident about himself, and was therefore less liable to become confused in an improvisation. Thus, Frank was helped to generalize his ability to maintain extrapersonal boundaries by elaborating on roles which represented two important aspects of himself. He still had difficulty in complicated roles involving subtle characterizations, and in many ways continued impersonating others. However, he increased his self-control in the role playing situation, and was less dependent upon others for his role identity. In this way, the therapist's task involves the differentiation and elaboration of the patient's part-selves.

PROBLEM AREA 4:   Individual becomes insensitive to the other's role, and maintains a rigid, unchanging characterization.

Paul would always pick a very definite role and never alter it, even when his characterization was clearly inappropriate. He would move stiffly, repeat lines, and not seem able to relate to other actors. In one exercise in which people are required to change roles spontaneously, he would consistently drop out. He found it impossible to play "one of the gang" type roles, and instead always picked distinctive leader or victim roles which separated him from the others within the improvisation.

Paul's problem, on the surface, was being unable to vary his role enactments. This would seem to be the opposite of Frank's difficulties. However, both are essentially defensive maneuvers against the same fear of engulfment from an external source (the other's role identity). Paul, who had a distinctly paranoid disposition, was absolutely terrified of being invaded by others' looks, desires, or identities. So he maintained a very rigid, but brittle, barrier in his everyday relationships. Frank, as I have said, employed the defense of being compliant and taking on the qualities of the other person while withdrawing emotionally from the relationship. Both are attempts to prevent more extensive engulfment by the "other" from occurring.

A patient like Paul is very difficult to work with, as any attempt to loosen his rigidly held boundaries is met with intense anxiety. As with Frank, one tries to help him discover parts of himself with which he can feel comfortable. Then, through the elaboration of these and similar roles, the therapist can encourage him to vary his enactments and be more spontaneous.

Boundary confusion in schizophrenic patients, then, is indicated by problems with differentiating, enacting, maintaining, and varying their roles. These are related to either an internal or external focus, and to the degree to which the boundary is defended. This is summarized in the diagram below:

FOCUS OF THE CONFUSION

		Intrapersonal Relationship	Extrapersonal Relationship
BOUNDARY DEFENSE	Undefended	Problem Area 1: *Differentiating* Janet	Problem Area 3: *Maintaining* Frank
	Rigidly Defended	Problem Area 2: *Enacting* Ellen	Problem Area 4: *Varying* Paul

The therapist should be able to understand in what way the patient is confused, and, through methods of differentiation and support, help him to identify and alleviate his confusion.

In a role playing situation involving improvisation, there is an opportunity for patients to see and experience a whole set of complex interrelationships. They can begin to explore and try out on a tentative basis different aspects of their personalities which, with the therapist's help, can be identified and ultimately differentiated. Freed temporarily from the dilemma of deciding who he is as a totality, the patient can take one piece of himself at a time, elaborate on it, "play" with it, and finally learn to control it, instead of being controlled by it. The simplification of the self-presentation process allows the patient to experiment with a limited aspect of the self and correspondingly increase his self-control.

Through the medium of improvisation, important feelings and self-expressions are inevitably released which, if the environment is a safe and protected one, can allow the withdrawn and isolated individual to share something of himself with others. The nature of the drama, with its tolerance for the unreal and the imaginative, entices the inner self of the schizophrenic, which is occupied in fantasy, to reveal some part of itself. The patient finds he can explore with some freedom the various fragments of himself while, at the same time, actualizing them for others. In this way, the inner self makes contact with the world, and the individual's fantasies become part of objective existence. If the therapist has provided enough structure and maintains clear enough boundaries in the sessions, such experiences can serve to lower the individual's anxiety and help to integrate his disorganized personality.

5 SOCIAL ISOLATION

The other major problem in the schizophrenic condition is the radical isolation of the self from meaningful relationships with others. The schizophrenic person retreats from the world because he feels he is not in control of his relationships with others. We have seen how this withdrawal from others is stimulated by the anxieties aroused by his inability to keep inside and outside, self and other, separate and distinct. Thus, the schizophrenic's lack of personal integration is intimately connected to his lack of social integration. The drama therapy group operates toward objectives on both of these levels: (1) to integrate the patient's sense of identity and diminish the boundary confusion; and (2) to integrate him into the group and stimulate mutually satisfying relations with others.

There are several forces operating within a drama therapy group which serve to stimulate relatedness and cause members to become invested in one another. The mere fact that the individual is in a group with other people who have similar problems is important. Each person can see the struggles of others, can learn that many of his own difficulties are shared by others, and can get feedback on his behavior. At times, the group will also provide consensual validation of the individual's experience.

The creative nature of the activity gratifies many deep-seated needs of belonging, and serves to develop a cohesive group feeling. The entertainment aspect of the role playing, in which members perform for each other, provides a giving atmosphere between members, relieving them of their constant feelings of deprivation.

Most importantly, the tasks of the group are interpersonal ones. Each improvisation requires cooperation among the actors, sensitivity to each other's needs, an ability to communicate clearly in words and actions, and a certain level of spontaneity. The positive reinforcement resulting from the appreciation of others, which accompanies the patient's participation in the improvisation, becomes a powerful motivation for him to learn these interpersonal skills. Cooperation and involvement are not sought for their own sake, but for the more tangible rewards that come when one has completed a "successful" improvisation. Warm-up exercises, theatre games, and group discussion also focus on the interaction between members, and serve to encourage even the most withdrawn person to participate in creative group activity.

Apart from these structural aspects of the session, the therapist himself attempts to develop capacities for relatedness within the group. He provides and maintains a safe and supportive atmosphere; he points out difficulties in the role enactments which relate to inadequate interaction; he monitors the group process and attempts to facilitate the sharing of thought and feeling by members; and he continually stresses the possibilities of finding support from others and benefit from a cohesive group experience.

Limits to Group Cohesion

Yet group cohesion can threaten an individual's sense of independence and autonomy, or may lead to a decrease in the structure of the session. Resistance to group cohesion may develop as a response to these threats. Often individual members will try to undermine developing "group" values by engaging the therapist in a one-to-one dialogue. The implicit message (or perhaps hope) is that members can not really benefit from each other, only from the powerful therapist. Other maneuvers, often extremely subtle, will be employed by members to diminish and derail growing group cohesion. Unfortunately, fears of engulfment are often stimulated by positive group experiences. At times, increased group interaction and good feeling lead to increased fears of engulfment which, in turn, cause a massive retreat back into isolation. The moment the group begins to work *too* well, and relationships get too close, it becomes a desert of "false selves" merely going through the motions of involvement. Personal investment and spontaneity dry up, and the therapist wonders what went wrong. Thus, by the very nature of the power which the drama therapist has due to his technique, he can unknowingly re-create the threatening interpersonal conditions which caused the schizophrenic's withdrawal in the first place.

Therefore, a careful, moderated approach to the creation of a positive group experience is required for the drama therapist working with schizophrenic patients. The group must be supportive, not engulfing; permissive, but not unstructured. The slow, tentative investments that the patient makes in the group have to be encouraged, not insisted upon. Every effort to decrease the patient's sense of isolation must be connected with simultaneous efforts to support his sense of personal autonomy and self-control. A long time is needed—many advances and retreats have to occur before real progress is made. There are many potential pitfalls along the way.

The following group story illustrates the ambivalent feelings of members toward their integration into the group. This example was collectively written by a drama therapy group at the end of a session, by having one member at a time spontaneously make a sentence to which the next person would add another. The entire story was created in less than a minute.

A man walked to the top of a high mountain and saw a vicious mountain goat who charged him. The man grabbed it and sang a pretty song into its ear; the goat began to dance wildly. But then the goat began running after him, and the man turned to his friends down below and shouted "Help!" and his friends ran after the goat until everyone collided. They held on to its legs and hair and tail and the goat angrily stomped on them and they turned all red and bloody. Then they stuffed the goat's hair into their mouths and carried it up the mountain where they all danced wildly, just as the mountain goat had done in the beginning.[8]

Here the frightening struggle to become integrated with others, without being engulfed or eaten up, is clearly portrayed. The lone man "on top of a mountain" first attempts to fend off the beast by himself, then requires the help of his friends "down below." The violence and mangledness of the collision between man, goat, and group represent the fears that an intimate group experience can generate. It is when the group incorporates the beast (stuffing the goat's hair into their mouths), and *shares* him, that they partly overcome the fear. They become like him, dancing wildly, but are together, where only one man stood before.

FOOTNOTES

1. Jacob L. Moreno, *Psychodrama*, 1 (New York: Beacon, 1946).
2. Susan Sandel and David Johnson, "Indications and Contraindications for Dance Therapy in a Long-Term Psychiatric Hospital," *American Dance Therapy Association Monograph* 3 (1974): 47–65.
3. R. D. Laing, *The Divided Self* (London: Tavistock, 1960), p. 83.
4. For a discussion of this issue with the schizoid-neurotic, see Harry Guntrip, "The Schizoid Compromise and the Psychotherapeutic Stalemate," *British Journal of Medical Psychology* 35 (1962): 273.
5. See H. Werner, *Comparative Psychology of Mental Development* (New York: International Universities Press, 1948).
6. See S. Blatt and C. Wild, *Schizophrenia: A Developmental Analysis* (New York: Academic Press, 1976).
7. For more details see A. Shimkunas, "Demand for Intimate Self-disclosure and Pathological Verbalizations in Schizophrenia," *Journal of*

Abnormal Psychology 80, no. 2 (1972): 197–205; Martha Davis, "Movement Characteristics of Hospitalized Psychiatric Patients," *Proceedings of the Fifth Annual Conference of the American Dance Therapy Association* (1970).

8. David Johnson, Case Material: *Drama Therapy Groups, 1974–75* (Unpublished paper, 1975).

ROBIN REIF was a member of the Hartman Theatre Conservatory in Stamford, Connecticut, where she studied, performed, and taught drama workshops for children. A writer of articles, poetry, and fiction, she currently lives in New York City.

Chapter 5

DRAMA THERAPY WITH SHORT-TERM PSYCHIATRIC PATIENTS IN A HOSPITAL SETTING:
Observations of
a Student

Robin Reif

1 INTRODUCTION
For several years, Bellevue Psychiatric Hospital Activities Therapy Department has sponsored an ongoing program of drama therapy. While working as a Bellevue volunteer during 1976, I participated in the weekly drama therapy groups organized for an acute in-patient service ward for men and women short-term patients.

The Groups
Drama therapy on the ward was always conducted in groups. The staff, comprised of Gertrud Schattner, drama therapist, Nancy and Sarah, both activities therapists, and myself, was consistently the same. The patients varied from week to week. There were usually between ten and fifteen patients present, all of whom attended on a voluntary basis.

The Sessions

The sessions had a flexible structure that could be adapted to the needs and abilities of the patients. The repertoire of activities included creative drama, movement improvisations, pantomimes, and a variety of theatre games. Sessions lasted approximately one hour.

The Value of Drama Therapy on a Short-Term Basis

Short-term drama therapy at Bellevue was considered primarily recreation. We rarely saw a patient more than once; therefore, long-term therapeutic goals could not be formulated.

What, then, was the value of a single recreational drama therapy session to a short-term patient? Although, as a student, my understanding of psychodynamics was limited, I immediately sensed the value of these sessions to patients. I saw exhausted, isolated people being drawn into the joy and surprise of participation in group activity.

How was this achieved? First, drama therapy offers unusual tools for self-expression. Many patients who seemed unable to express themselves verbally were nevertheless able to use creative movement and drama improvisations as a means to communicate their thoughts and feelings. Secondly, the individual drama therapy activities are designed to foster social interaction. Most of them are exercises requiring close cooperation with partners to achieve a mutual objective, or coordination of group efforts to achieve a collective goal.

Another key element in the value of these sessions to patients was the warm and supportive atmosphere created by Gertrud and her staff. That made it easier for patients to move from withdrawal to active involvement. Gertrud's encouragement was especially important to those who worried about failing to do an exercise "right." There was no "right" or "wrong" way in the drama therapy sessions. The willingness to participate was success in itself.

The Patients

Patients on the ward were between the ages of 16 and 90. Each was hospitalized because he was considered by the admitting psychiatrist to be unable to care for himself or to be a potential danger to himself or to others. Some patients were old, some chronically psychotic with histories of several past hospitalizations. They seemed almost hopeless — barely able or willing to engage in human interaction. Others were young, alert, intelligent and experiencing their first bout with mental illness. Many appeared somewhere between these extremes.

The majority could not manage challenging activities, either physically or mentally. This was partially due to the effects of medication. Others, however, were extremely restless and eager to discharge their excess energies. Some spent sessions periodically attempting to pray, and some were continually trying to seduce other patients (and sometimes staff); some were overly verbal and some entirely mute; some spoke only English, and some spoke no English at all. Gertrud's great skill is that she is able, each and every week, to cull from these disparate elements in very difficult circumstances, something of a unified group experience.

The Log

I wish to share my experience in these sessions with the reader. Therefore, this chapter is based on events recorded in a weekly log which I kept throughout the year. For the purpose of organization, episodes from many sessions are condensed into one narrative.

2 GATHERING

Gathering patients for the drama therapy session is a unique experience in itself. We arrive on the ward, and a psychiatric aide locks the door behind us. Gertrud, in her inimitable voice, calls out "Draaa-ma." Nurse St. Denis, a formidable Jamaican woman, chimes in in her own authoritative style: "Dra-ma, people! All de people for de dra-ma!"

In the day room I find Margaret "Hughes," a patient who claims she is the widow of the late millionaire Howard Hughes. She is sitting silently, staring into space.

"Margaret, we're having a drama session. Would you like to join us?"

It takes her a moment to focus on me. She breaks into a slow,

almost toothless smile. "Oh yes," she answers demurely, and begins
to shuffle down the hall toward the recreation room.

I see Gertrud standing over a bed. Whoever is in it has the sheets
pulled over his head. Gertrud speaks softly, "John, why don't you
come to the drama session? It will be better than sleeping all afternoon." Slowly John emerges from under the sheets, and I am surprised. He is an unusually handsome man of about 35 with glassy
blue eyes which at the moment seem groggy and dazed. "Okay,
Gert," he manages to say thickly. As he gets out of bed, I notice his
arms are heavily tattooed. His open pajama top exposes a stomach
torn with scars. I am struck by the incongruity of his appearance
and his behavior. He looks like a real "tough guy," yet he follows
Gert down the hall like a devoted child.

Finding patients in bed at two in the afternoon, seeing them
wander aimlessly through the halls, or sitting idly in the day room,
I realize that the actual *event* of the drama therapy session is
therapeutic. It provides some structure in the day's activities, and
the opportunity to meet and thereby relieve some of the loneliness
and boredom the patients feel living on the ward.

3   BEGINNING

The patients gather in the recreation room at the end of the hall.
Most are heavily medicated with "anti-psychotic" drugs, and move
as though in slow motion.

When everyone is finally seated in a large circle, Gertrud introduces herself and the staff. She explains that we are going to
play some theatre games, that everyone is welcome to participate.
An elderly man with a swelled, red-veined nose grumbles about
thinking he was going to see a play. He seems to feel cheated, and
walks out.

Gertrud begins the session with the "Name Game." The rules are
that one person in the circle says his name; the person to his right
repeats that name, and then says his own. The next person repeats
the first two names and adds his own name. This is a good introductory exercise for both the patients and the staff. Because of
the rapid turnover on this ward, some patients are introduced to
each other for the first time in the drama groups.

The game gives me a chance to look around the room at

everyone. The patients are all very different. John, whom Gertrud had earlier found in bed, has undergone a real change of mood. He is now alert and enthusiastic. Tammy, a teenager, is very thin and pretty. She seems shy and seductive at the same time. Presently, she is holding Gretta's hand and flashing charming smiles at both men and women in the group. Gretta and Tammy have crayoned their faces with lipstick and eyeshadow. They both look like tattered, painted dolls.

Beatrice participated in the drama group last week. She seems intelligent, but deliberate and sad. She tells Gertrud that last week's session was the highlight of her week, yet she is totally devoid of enthusiasm as she speaks.

Across the circle is Jim, a huge middle-aged man. His pajama shirt is opened, exposing his enormous belly. He is staring at the wall just above my head, with a half-smile on his face. He reminds me of a Buddha statue.

Adela is a 90-year-old Caribbean woman. She maintains a continuous babble that intermittently becomes louder and more agitated. Sarah, the activity therapist, is doing her best to calm Adela, saying "Shh, Mama....shh, Mama." For minutes at a time, this silences the frail looking old woman.

Other members of the group introduce themselves as Henry, Margaret, Ellen, and Maria.

The patients have difficulty playing the "Name Game." Several cannot remember the names of all the others who preceded them in the circle. Mama (Adela) continues to mumble in Spanish and makes it difficult for everyone to concentrate.

4   MIRRORS

Next, Gertrud leads the group in the "Mirror Exercise." She asks us to pair up and to face our partners. The rules are that one person in each pair is to move any part of his body very slowly so that his partner is able to copy all movements as a mirror would. The challenge is for the leader and the follower to move as synchronously as possible. This requires real cooperation between the two. The exercise encourages awareness of oneself, one's own movement, and the movement of one's partner. It gives each person the chance to experience the different roles of leader and follower. I have noticed that when patients are able to concentrate, this game generally has a calming effect.

Tammy, my first partner, immediately begins to lead. Her movements are nervous and bird-like. Intermittently, she breaks into high-pitched laughter, freezes in one position, then suddenly begins her disjointed dance once more. When it is my turn to lead, she does not follow my slow, sustained movement, but continues in her own staccato style. She seems not to understand the rules of the game, even when I re-explain them to her.

When there are patients like Tammy in the group who seem unable to understand and perform the exercises, Gertrud nevertheless welcomes their participation. There is no pressure to do and exercise "right," and no judgment involved.

My next partner is Ellen, a young, attractive woman with large brown eyes. She is dressed in men's overalls and a sweatshirt from a summer theatre. She wears her hair in a crew cut. Last week the group composed a collaborative holiday poem. Ellen's contribution was: "And let us seek to re-experience the original spirit of Thanksgiving." I was puzzled by this verbal, reflective woman. She seemed to have a greater sense of reality than many of the other patients, and acted in a maternal way toward some of them. Elise, a very disturbed middle-aged woman, sat through last week's session drooling and occasionally screaming out at something she seemed to see in the air. This upset most of the other patients, but Ellen held Elise's hand and tried to soothe her.

I begin moving first, and Ellen mirrors me very well. When it is her turn to initiate, she is graceful and moves slowly enough for me to follow closely. At one point, Ellen brings her hands over her eyes as in a game of peek-a-boo. It is a playful gesture that makes us both laugh. I begin to relax, and forget some of my own fear as I feel real contact and exchange taking place between Ellen and myself. I cannot say for certain, but I believe she is experiencing similar feelings.

5 SHOW HOW YOU FEEL

Gertrud introduces another movement activity called "Show How You Feel." Each participant is asked to give expression to his present feelings through movement. Many of the patients have great difficulty verbalizing their thoughts and feelings, even when relatively healthy. During periods of acute psychological distress, verbal communication may be that much more cut off. Structured movement exercises offer a means of self expression and of communication with others at a time when it is greatly needed.

Maria volunteers to begin. She slowly puts her head in her hands, and holds it there, staring at the floor. She doesn't look up, but says, "I want to go to sleep and never wake up." "Why, Maria?" Gertrud asks gently. Maria says that she doesn't wish to speak about it now.

Next it is Nancy's turn. She does a happy little dance, snapping her fingers and wiggling her hips, accompanying herself with "La-de-dah-de-dah." Everyone enjoys her antics—especially Jim who swears that, "After seeing that," he knows he's "gonna make it through the day." The remark is said good-naturedly, and everyone, even Maria, laughs. It is the first time Jim has spoken since the group began.

Instead of resuming his Buddha pose, Jim now joins the group activity. He walks to the center of the circle, and extends his arms to his sides. With eyes closed and a peaceful smile on his face, he slowly turns around in a circle.

"Are you feeling as happy as you look, Jim?" asks Gertrud. Jim's answer seems indirect. "I'm walking through fire, but things are going to be better in the future." His grin gets wider, and he sits down looking very satisfied with himself.

Throughout the session, John has been chattering. His behavior is distracting to everyone. Gertrud attempts to channel his attention into the group activity by asking if he would like a turn. "Sure, Gert!" he cheerfully replies.

Suddenly there is a change. He stops talking, and for a moment seems confused. His eyes are as clouded and sad as when I first saw him today. Finally, he stands up, and lifting his right hand, he waves tentatively at everyone in the circle.

"John, in what way does this show us how you are feeling?" asks Gertrud.

"I'm waving good-bye because I feel like I want to get out of this hospital and go home."

At this, Maria begins to cry. "That's why I'm so depressed. I want to go home and see my children." John looks puzzled. Maria is more moved by his expression of how he feels than he is himself. By identifying with what John just said and did, Maria is able to verbalize and release the feelings she couldn't speak about before.

The example of the patient who communicates his feelings is sometimes contagious. Others become freer and more willing to express and invest their real emotions in the day's activities.

6   IMPROVISATION
Going Home

Margaret "Hughes," who has been totally silent throughout the session, now says quietly, almost to herself, "Yes, I want to go home, too."

Gertrud asks Margaret whether she would like to enact a scene about going home. To my surprise, Margaret whispers a dispirited "Okay."

"Margaret, who is the first person you are likely to see when you arrive home?" asks Gertrud.

"The desk clerk."

My heart sinks as I recall the single room occupancy hotel where she lives along with several other ex-mental patients. (We conducted an outpatient drama therapy session there several weeks ago.)

John, not uncharacteristically, volunteers to be the desk clerk, and the play begins.

Margaret shuffles up to John who is standing behind his imaginary desk, and asks if she has received any letters while she has been gone.

"I'm sorry, Margaret, old girl, there's no letter for you."

Margaret's face begins to tremble almost imperceptibly.

"I'm supposed to receive a letter."

Nancy jumps up and enters the circle, handing Margaret an imaginary envelope.

"Special Delivery letter for Mrs. Margaret Hughes."

Margaret takes the imaginary envelope and "looks" at it.

"I didn't want a letter. I wanted my check."

In my ignorance, I run in with a "special delivery check" for Margaret from the New York State Lottery.

"Oh no, I can't take this. My check is from Welfare, not from the lottery."

I feel terrible. I don't know what to do. Finally John breaks the silence. He begins slowly. "Well, Margaret, you really want that welfare check, don't you?"

"Yes."

"Well, I'd like to make you an offer. Y'see, I've been hiding your welfare check the whole time as a joke. But out of the goodness of my heart, I'd be willing to trade it for the lottery check. What do you say?"

They exchange imaginary envelopes, and Margaret returns to her seat with a quiet "Thank you" to John, and as much of a smile as she can manage.

I don't know whether receiving her welfare check during the improvisation has relieved any of Margaret's anxieties about going home, but I think it was simply valuable to enact a scene about something that is important to her. Also, Margaret had previously been very withdrawn. It was good for her to participate and to receive some attention from the group. John, a patient, came up with the solution that brought about a happy ending for Margaret. In the drama therapy sessions, patients have the valuable opportunity to help each other.

In a Taxi

Next, Gertrud manages to engage Henry, a very withdrawn patient, in an improvisation.

Henry is a middle-aged man from Eastern Europe. He mentioned earlier in the session that he used to work as a cab driver. Gertrud uses this information to construct an improvisation set in a taxi. Henry agrees to play the driver. John, the most talkative and friendly member of the group, seems the best candidate for the role of passenger. Happily, and predictably, he volunteers for the part.

John gets in the "cab," which consists of two chairs, one behind the other, and asks Henry to take him to the Empire State Building. Both men fall silent. Ten seconds later, Henry announces that they have arrived. John gets up without paying and goes back to his seat. Henry doesn't even ask for the fare.

I begin to think that this improvisation will not take off at all when Maria, who has cheered up considerably, volunteers to become the next passenger.

She asks Henry to take her to her cousin's apartment on the Upper West Side. Henry takes off.

"You're going up the wrong street, Henry."

"Listen, Miss, I've been driving here for years and I know the way."

He has spoken! A whole sentence! I know that Henry has talked to almost no one on the ward since he arrived last week. He has given one and two word answers to any questions directed at him, and has been reluctant to do even this. What is it that draws a man out after so prolonged a silence?

"No, you don't."

"Yes, I do."

"Well, if you *do* know the way, then it must be that you're purposely driving up the wrong street just to get more money."

Henry, who appeared to be getting angry, seems to make a fresh decision.

"Well, you're right. I *am* driving up the wrong street, but it's only to avoid traffic." There is a glint of humor in his eye.

"Oh yeah? Then why are you driving around the same block again and again?" (*Touché!*)

"Well, lady, traffic is *especially* bad today!"

The group enjoys Henry's punch line. Something important has just taken place. Henry has moved from silence to a willingness to speak with others and participate in the group. This is a minor victory for Henry who has finally joined us in spirit, and also for Maria who has helped to bring it about.

Song

Suddenly Gretta calls out that she wants to sing a song for everyone. Is there something contagious that is beginning to infect the more reticent patients? Last week Gretta sat smoking in slow motion with a vacant expression on her face throughout the entire session. She would not participate in any of the activities, and thus far, she has not participated this week either.

Gertrud immediately says, "Certainly, Gretta, go ahead."

Very hesitatingly, Gretta gets up from her chair. She walks as if on a tight rope, and it actually takes her about a full minute to go from her chair to the center of the circle.

Standing there, she begins shifting weight from foot to foot, looking like a nervous schoolgirl giving her first recitation in front of a class. Her eyes dart out over our heads. They do not focus on any particular point, but keep skittering from place to place.

"Now is everyone listening? Everyone look at me! Everyone be quiet!"

Everyone has been very quiet for the last few minutes, watching Gretta in pained silence.

She seems about to begin, but suddenly becomes acutely self-conscious. She turns around and around, looking at us. It seems to dawn on her that no matter which way she faces, part of the audience will be behind her.

"I can't sing if there are people in back of me."

Gertrud speaks gently. "Gretta, do you know about theatre-in-the-round? The audience sits in a circle, and the actors are in the middle like you are now. It is perfectly all right for you to be in the middle. We are all watching you." Gretta's fears seem calmed, and finally she begins her song.

"Because of you, there's a song in my heart…"

Suddenly, she stops. Then, tentatively, "Because of *ME*? Me? You? Me?…Who am I?…I don't know who I am." Somehow, her confusion seems to pass, and she prepares to begin again, repeating the overture of weight shifting, hesitation, apologies, and demands for undivided attention.

She finally manages to get out most of the song's first verse, and then abruptly runs back and clings to her seat. Gertrud seems happy with Gretta's performance, and tells her that her song was beautiful. Gretta responds with a tiny, uncertain smile.

I feel that Gretta has taken a real step forward today. For the first time in a drama therapy session, she has made the bold and active choice to express herself before the group. This was very difficult for her, and yet she persevered and came close to completing the task she had set out to accomplish.

A Group!

Suddenly, Maria bursts out, "Y'know, I studied opera for five years at the Conservatory in Italy. I could have been a famous opera singer." She hits a high trembling note, and breaks into an expansive aria. The volume is assaulting, but her voice still has some sweetness and resonance.

Gertrud moves quickly. She goes directly to Maria who has been singing with increasing agitation, looks her straight in the eyes, then says quietly, "Maria, you *do* have a lovely voice." Maria immediately stops singing and looks at Gertrud as though awakening from a dream.

"I know. I could have been a famous opera singer."

Gertrud stands there for a moment before she speaks. "Would you like to play the role of a famous opera singer in an improvisation?" Maria hesitates for a moment, then says, "Yes, I would."

Gertrud suggests a group improvisation in which several famous people gather at Sardi's Restaurant for dinner.

Everyone seems enthusiastic about the idea. Gertrud says she will play a famous actress while Jim decides he will play Enrico Caruso, and will accompany the actress and the opera singer (played by Maria) to dinner. John and I play waiter and waitress, and as soon as our "guests" are seated, we begin running around filling imaginary water glasses, taking orders from Gertrud for roast pheasant on rye, and from "Mr. Caruso" for stuffed rooster.

Nancy enters the scene as a kid from the Bronx wanting to break into show business. She barges in on the party of famous people with an unsolicited chorus of "East Side/West Side." Henry and Margaret, playing two autograph hunters, timidly approach the table of celebrities.

The situation is getting very lively as Nancy competes with the autograph hunters for the attention of the famous people. To enliven the scene still further, I decided to enter in a huff, saying, "We have no cabaret license, so will the kid from the Bronx please leave the restaurant, and would the autograph hounds please leave our guests alone." No one is listening to me, not even John the waiter, who is supposed to be my helper, but who has just told "Mr. Caruso" that he is a singing waiter and has now joined Nancy in a duet.

This improvisation may seem somewhat frenetic. The players are certainly very shabby and no one will ever put it on a stage. The plot and the acting are far from brilliant, and yet appearances are deceptive. What has just taken place in this room is something I feel like celebrating. The high level of collaboration and group feeling generated by this activity is remarkable.

The improvisation was catalyzed by Maria's outburst, and has alleviated some of her distress. She derived real pleasure from playing out a fantasy role. She enjoyed being catered to by the "restaurant personnel," and laughed during Nancy and John's duet.

What makes a group improvisation successful? Everyone must consistently act within the imaginary circumstances and maintain his imaginary role. Although it is common for patients, in a group improvisation, to become confused, today all were able to maintain clarity about the fiction of being at Sardi's.

Group improvisations require spirited and involved interaction among the participants. Although some of the patients in today's group have been very withdrawn and others have never spoken to each other before, there was a high level of interaction taking place among all the players throughout the scene. Also, group improvisations require a collective, synchronous use of imagination to invent roles that can be simultaneously played as part of the same scene. Today everyone invented his own role, and exercised an unusual level of imagination and playfulness in carrying it out. Moreover, only an hour ago, many of these patients could not even successfully play the simplest of games: the "Name Game." Now, most of them are functioning with a higher level of awareness and concentration than they were earlier in the session. There is a playful, energized spirit within the group which represents a considerable journey from the somber, unfocused atmosphere of the beginning.

7   WISHES AND GIFTS

Gertrud concludes the session with the "Wishing Circle." She asks us all to stand and form a circle, placing our arms around each other's waists. She then says, "Close your eyes for a moment and think of one wish you have for yourself, or one gift you would like to give to the group if you could. Let your imaginations go; the wishes and gifts can be anything you want them to be. When you are ready, open your eyes. Everyone will have the chance to act out his wish or gift as a pantomime."

Nancy is the first volunteer. She gets up, and begins to carve slow, graceful circles with her arms. As the arm circles get faster, she simultaneously begins a comical prance around the room.

"Nancy, I cannot guess," says Gert. "What is your wish?"

"It's not a wish! It's a gift, Gert! Can't you guess?" Nancy says this as if her pantomime should be easily decipherable to anyone watching.

"A bird of paradise?" asks Ellen shyly.

"No."

Jim looks annoyed with everyone. "It's very clear to me what it is. It's a washing machine for the ward. Your arms are the blades that swish the clothes around."

Nancy laughs out loud. "Oh, no!" She's almost breathless, but she doesn't stop. "Come on, someone, guess already!"

"I don't know, Nancy...I really don't...uh, is it a jump rope?" John is eager to give Nancy the satisfaction of guessing before she collapses.

"I give up. You guys won't get it. It's the sun! I give you all the sun!"

A moment of silence passes as some of us cast sideways glances at each other, wondering how to respond. Then everyone bursts into a mixed chorus of laughter and exclamations of "Oh, now I get it!" and a few very sincere "Thank you's" to Nancy. I notice that this whole exchange makes no visible impact on either Tammy or Gretta. I didn't see it happen, but at some point during the session, each has fallen back into her own private universe and is no longer fully with us.

John is the next volunteer. He seems uncomfortable. "I hope

you don't think this is crazy...I want a doll...to remind me of my little girl who was taken away from me." John's words are so strong, and yet he communicates no emotion as he speaks. It is almost as if he were speaking about someone else. Again, others seem more moved by John's contribution than he is himself. One of them is Gertrud. "No, John, I don't think it is crazy at all. That is a beautiful wish."

Margaret wishes aloud for "strawberry shortcake like they used to have at Bellevue when I stayed here last year."

Jim agrees that this addition to the menu would greatly improve conditions on the ward, and he himself wishes that "they would put Kool-Aid instead of ice water in the pitchers set out in the day room."

Beatrice, who has been almost totally inactive throughout the session, raises her head slowly. "I wish everyone hope, so that you all will look at the donut in life instead of the hole." Her expression is lifeless, and her eyes seem opaque. And yet there is something about her mouth, a slight sense of embarrassment and something of a smile breaking through that gives me a feeling of her utter sincerity in saying this.

Maria gets up to take her turn. She looks different to me. The tough, sarcastic lady of the taxi improvisation, the agitated soprano of the scene at Sardi's, the emotionally paralyzed woman who wanted to "go to sleep and never wake up" are all but gone. Despite her heavily penciled eyebrows and the deep lines of stress carved on her face, she looks very young right now.

She pantomimes taking someone's hand. It seems to be a child's hand because she bends down to take it. She walks around the inside of the circle with her imaginary companion three times, then bends and kisses the "person" who has accompanied her on her journey around the circle. "This is my girlfriend, and we are going home."

8 LOOKING BACK

At the time I was at Bellevue, I was a pre-medical student with an interest in psychiatry. I wanted to get a sense of what it is like to work with psychiatric patients in a hospital setting. At first, I found myself standing back, emotionally sickened by the level of disintegration and helplessness. The patients seemed to have lost or abandoned the ability to respond to anything or anyone in their environment.

Many barriers to communication had to be broken down. In our drama sessions, trust was gradually established through the group experience. We all participated in creative movement, role playing, improvisations, composing poems, and singing. The group feeling that was generated was very special, and a warm sense of togetherness and human connection emerged.

When the drama sessions ended, I remained on the ward for a few hours to visit informally with patients. Those who had participated in the session often seemed willing to talk with me. There was generally an intensity and an openness in our conversations, triggered by the implicit demand for truthfulness I sensed from many of the patients. This forced me to cut through my habitual, mechanical responses, and moved me to a keener awareness of my own real feelings.

STUART LAWRENCE, a lecturer on creative arts therapy, conducts drama therapy workshops in schools and mental health clinics throughout the United States.

Chapter 6

JOURNAL: *DRAMA THERAPY WITH SEVERELY DISTURBED ADULTS IN AN OUTPATIENT CLINIC*

Stuart Lawrence

1 INTRODUCTION

One of the main reasons for recording this journal is to stimulate other members of the helping professions. I work at a day hospital for severely disturbed adults, in a treatment center called Helping House. Referrals are encouraged by all concerned agencies and citizens; for example, local psychiatrists, psychologists or social workers, hospitals, religious organizations, and social services agencies; individuals may also seek admission on their own. I established the Drama Club primarily as a process in socialization dynamics. It forces its members out of isolation — a condition often suffered by such clients and one that can perpetuate itself. Being with other people for a purpose is a first step in relating and relearning socialization skills, as well as building a self in relation to others. Commitment, consideration, compromise, loyalty, and promptness are all part of the resocialization achieved in drama activities. One can begin to learn about oneself by seeing oneself spontaneously act out. Patterns of behavior become obvious, self-exploration ensues and opens the path to self-understanding.

Drama therapy allows the individual to release emotions in controlled situations. This is socially productive: it rechannels energy into useful acting out, tests reality relationships and can deliver the client from a sometimes threatening bondage. Art therapy uses art, painting and sculpture to help the client better understand his perceptions. Dance therapy uses movement. Music therapy uses music. Drama therapy uses all these elements if it desires: dance, music, art, dialogue and, of course, dramatic activity. All the creative arts therapies can be done on an individual basis — except for drama therapy. One can paint alone, make music alone or even dance alone, but one cannot do drama alone. The nature of drama implies group relationship and social activity.

2   THE BEGINNINGS

Helping House, being a therapeutic community, has a very open atmosphere. Experiments, new ideas, groups and methods of working are encouraged. Leather craft shops, cooking class and a photography group are some of the activities that had developed while I was there.

The executive director of the hospital readily agreed to the idea of a drama group. I mentioned my plans for a drama group at the next community meeting of the hospital. This is a weekly gathering of all members and staff to discuss issues and plans that may have arisen over the previous week. The response of the group was enthusiastic.

That afternoon I called a special meeting for all interested clients. About twenty members appeared. I explained that anyone who wanted to join was welcome; that no one would have to act any part or do any improvisation that he did not want to do; and that the major aim of the group was to foster an enjoyable atmosphere. I spoke of interaction with people, self-expression and consideration towards the people with whom one works. As we concluded, one member of that introductory meeting yelled, "I can't wait."

3 PARTICIPANTS

These made up the core of the group:

Marilyn. Marilyn is a 29-year-old female. She has been hospitalized for eight months. She shows signs of psychomotor retardation and has been diagnosed catatonic schizophrenic.

David. David is a 28-year-old male. He has had intermittent hospitalizations totaling about three years. He is severely depressed and has been diagnosed paranoid schizophrenic.

Mark. Mark is a 28-year-old male. Chronically depressed and insecure, he has been diagnosed paranoid schizophrenic.

Ken. Ken is a 36-year-old male. He has been hospitalized for seventeen years. He is a victim of congenital brain syndrome. He has been diagnosed congenital psychotic.

Stan. Stan is a 21-year-old male. He constantly feels isolated and left out, is withdrawn and suspicious. He has been diagnosed as schizophrenic—undifferentiated type.

Sylvia. Sylvia is a 23-year-old female. Hospitalized for four years, she seems to be extremely fearful of people and responsibility, and has been diagnosed as paranoid schizophrenic.

Chris. Chris is a 30-year-old male. He has a long history of intermittent depressive episodes, culminating at times in suicidal attempts. He has been thought to be fearful of people and any responsibility. He has been diagnosed as schizophrenic—undifferentiated type.

Lucille. Lucille is a 23-year-old female. She has been hospitalized for two years and has been classified as paranoid schizophrenic.

Vinnie. Vinnie is a 31-year-old male. He has been in and out of hospitals for five years and has been classified as paranoid schizophrenic.

Nancy. Nancy is a 26-year-old female, and has been diagnosed paranoid schizophrenic. She has been hospitalized for two years.

4   JOURNAL

Session 1

ACTIONS

Today's session was basically an introductory orientation to the group. I described the concept of improvisation: "Improvisation is the key to what we do here, friends," I said. "It draws upon the unconscious and has the advantage of being shared, explored, and is a great aid in understanding the self. Through the improvisations we will better get to know ourselves."

"Let's get started," yelled David. He was right — drama is acting, not talking. I taught the members today some warm-up exercises so that their minds and bodies would be ready for work. The first was the mirror exercise. This asks participants to break into couples and imitate the movements (as close in time as possible — as if "mirrors") of the other partner. This went extremely well. Marilyn and David were really in tune with each other's movements. Ken and Sylvia did extreme movements with their fingers, demonstrating an amazing precision. Stan seemed somewhat frustrated in his movements with Chris but struggled with this and did not give up, a healthy sign.

We then did physical exercises such as toe touching, arm stretching and hip twisting to limber ourselves up. They seemed to enjoy this.

"O.K.," I said, "who is going to break the ice for everyone and act something, anything?" I really just wanted to get the drama moving, to set some sort of example for the group, and to start the freeing, releasing process.

David said that he had always wanted to be a right-wing politician: "A strict conservative," he said smiling, "and now I have the chance." David asked me to introduce him, and I did. He entered the room and headed for the podium from which to address a crowd at an imagined factory. David was forceful, energetic and believable in his new role. He was quite tough, saying that "if elected the people can't do this and can't do that — they can't ask for a four day week, they must remain home on weekends, no pay increases, no increases in social security," and so on. The crowd roared.

Time was getting short and we had already been in session for one and a half hours. I asked David how he felt and he said, "great," for a reason he couldn't explain. "It's something I've always wanted to do and now I did it, it just feels good," he said.

SUMMARY

I was satisfied with this first session. Everybody seemed to enjoy it, and to follow the limits prescribed for them. I was especially cognizant of Stan's endurance with the mirror exercise, as he is normally withdrawn and isolated, often gives up easily, thereby reinforcing and perpetuating his "out-of-step role." Could this be a path to a new road inspired by a little motivation?

David's improvisation amazed me. This might well be a clear-cut case of projection and release of tension and hostility. David often feels oppressed. He feels demanded of and, therefore, hostile, angry and tense. By playing the oppressor he let others know of his emotions, while releasing them in a safe way. This is what drama therapy is all about.

Session 2

ACTIONS

Today, when the group met, they started warming up quickly. They did their physical and mirror exercises. It was interesting to note that partners stuck with those they had last week. Although unable at this point to reach out for new partners, the group was beginning to attain a feeling of cohesiveness and responsibility. Without being told, they themselves got up to do the appropriate exercises.

Then I asked for improvisations. Nobody moved. I then asked if anyone would like to act out how they got up in the morning and what they did to get ready for the day.

Everybody responded and we decided to go one at a time. Mark started and did excellently, except that he forgot to brush his teeth. He said that "It's funny, but I often forget to brush my teeth." Stan, Marilyn, and Sylvia forgot to wash. We stopped here and spoke of the importance of washing one's face and hands, and other grooming techniques; and of how they enable one to feel better in the morning and start the day off on a better foot. It struck me as quite revealing that three people all forgot to wash.

Chris set quite a good example, outlining very clearly all the procedures necessary to start the day off appropriately by taking good care of oneself. He smiled and said that, although he knows what to do, he doesn't always do it. This may help him to reinforce what he should do.

Lucille, a new member today (and one who has drifted in and out of the group), did an excellent job. It is interesting to note that she is a young lady who tries desperately to always appear proper and well taken care of.

SUMMARY

Today, a big element was the socialization process, both in process and in content. The group was beginning to take care of itself. They demonstrated this by commencing the opening exercises themselves. They acted out socialization–personal skills, bounded by the scene of getting up in the morning. Through the acting out, members obtained some awareness of themselves, such as forgetting to wash in the morning. The group began to explore the reasons for this together, as well as realizing the importance of grooming skills for personal and mental health. By reinforcing and setting socializing skills examples, clients are made aware of what could be done to feel better. There is no question that in this session Marilyn and Stan have learned that they often perpetuate the process of their feeling worthless or abused, by abusing themselves the first thing in the morning.

Session 3

ACTIONS

Today the group, without any instructions, started the session by warming up with the mirror exercise. However, a few members reached out and ventured new partners. Marilyn matched up with Sylvia, and Mark paired with Stan. It was Sylvia who initiated the change, something she ordinarily does not do.

Chris began by pantomiming eating dinner. I always let the

group go where it wants to go so, as Chris finished, any new types of improvisations were welcomed. The group decided to continue with eating patterns.

Mark followed Chris' improvisation, showing how he eats breakfast, and Ken followed with an improvisation of eating lunch. "I never really feel comfortable eating," Ken told the group, and we began to explore this with him. "I always feel somebody is watching me, and I'm doing something wrong," Ken continued. The group spoke to Ken reassuring him that he seemed to display proper eating actions and had nothing to worry about. The group continued to discuss the issue of eating habits and differences in them when eating lunch, breakfast or dinner. For self-assurance Ken re-enacted another improvisation of eating.

The group then took a turn. Marilyn and Ken decided to improvise a couple dining together. Both interactional improvisations were very detailed, appropriate and well done. The applause from the remainder of the group reinforced that.

SUMMARY

Today was a special day for the group. In the mirror exercise, certain members felt confident and strong enough to test themselves against a new partner, quite an accomplishment for them. Sylvia, by initiating a change, demonstrated the intimate, comfortable atmosphere the group has developed, which fosters self-acceptance. Normally she is afraid to join activities of any sort, let alone initiate changes.

Again they focused on socializing skills, and this was especially helpful to Ken who revealed a fear of eating in public due to a feeling of inappropriate expertise. Through discussions and visual models, Ken was given a sense both of confidence and of the irrationality of his fear. He was also given the chance to enact his fear "in public;" he really confronted it and worked through it. He showed remarkable strength.

The third major accomplishment of today's session was the interaction component. These clients, usually isolated and withdrawn, made their first attempts at interacting on a social level and were quite successful. It seems that the group provides a safe, comfortable atmosphere in which the members can begin to test reality skills, that some of them have lost touch with.

Chris ended today's session by screaming out, "I love this group!"

Session 4

ACTIONS

Today the group started off by telling me that they were warmed up and felt they had so much energy that they wanted to get right to improvisations.

Stan said something had been bothering him: he was afraid to ask a girl on a date and could he act it out? "Of course," I said. He asked Sylvia to join him in the scene. He set the premise of the situation, saying it was a girl he met at a musical concert, and he would be calling her over the telephone. We got the props—a telephone from an old toy closet. Sylvia was told to act as she felt and was not given any instructions. As it turned out, Sylvia said she was busy for the particular night but would be happy to go out with Stan on another night.

Stan was devastated and took Sylvia's response as a rejection. He said he would never ask her out again. At this point, the group stopped and discussed the issue with him. We talked about rejection as well as mislabeling something as rejection when it was not. Stan talked of rejections in his life, as others talked of theirs.

Mark enacted a rejecting situation he had recently had with a girl friend. Chris did the same. Marilyn then suggested that Stan act a situation that he felt accepted in. I thought this an excellent idea. Using Sylvia again, Stan "acted" acceptance.

Ken then acted "rejected" and "accepted," two scenes back to back. Stan asked to act out another "rejecting" scene with an old girl friend. During this scene he yelled and even cried a little. He sat down, said that he felt much better and had a sense of relief that freed him.

Marilyn said she always had trouble in dealing with rejection, and would like to act out a serious, angry scene with a teacher. She did so, and said that if she had to do the scene in "real life" again she would now defend more of her own rights and dignity—even if it took more yelling.

David and Mark finished the day improvising a scene in which David was rejected for a job.

Lastly we spoke about rejection and acceptance and how we feel about it. We pointed out ways of reacting—by indicating the scenes that were acted for us, and describing some of the ways we, in the group, overreacted and mislabeled rejection.

SUMMARY

During the session I asked Chris why he seemed not to participate much today and he simply said: "I did so much last week, I felt it only fair to give the others a chance!" This showed a keen sense of loyalty to the group, and a growing sense of group cohesiveness.

Today was a true turning point in the group. The members revealed themselves on a very personal level. Rejection is a hard fact of life for anybody, yet the group members confronted it with a healthy attitude. Stan and Marilyn emotionally and cathartically released anger and hostility that may have been building up inside themselves for years. The group shared, trusted and worked through together a very tough, frightening issue. As well, we gave helpful hints to each other in coping with rejection.

The group showed psychological health in not leaving the session speaking only of the dark side. The other side of the coin, "acceptance," also emerged, was worked on and shared.

Session 5

ACTIONS

After the opening exercises Chris and Stan started with an improvisation of two alcoholics meeting on the Bowery in New York City. The skit was amusing and sincere, but did show a touch of awkwardness as both actors had trouble establishing a rapport.

Mark and Marilyn then acted an improvisation in which boy met girl at work. Mark said he always had trouble meeting people and felt that an improvisation such as this would help him understand better what goes into meeting someone.

These two improvisations led to a group discussion about meeting someone, especially of the opposite sex. We spoke about how to act naturally, what makes one uncomfortable, and so on. This discussion tied in with the previous one on rejection.

Mark then acted out an uncomfortable situation making him tense; then an accepting situation allowing him to be natural and comfortable.

David, Chris, and Stan acted out a scene in which three old buddies got together again, talking about the good old times.

The group discussed the new improvisations, citing what makes us comfortable, the differences in feeling tense and natural, and how other people pick up these differences.

SUMMARY

Today the group felt the need to do more than the usual warm-up exercises. This was a sign of the individual members reinforcing their responsibility towards the group goals. To work well in the group requires standards the members have to meet: awareness of obligations, consideration and responsibility.

Also they learned the social skills of meeting and relating to other persons. It was especially rewarding for Mark, who revealed his fear of meeting new people. He worked through both an uncomfortable situation and a comfortable one, and began to feel and understand the differences. By acting out he also saw himself as successful, setting a model of achievement for himself.

Session 6

ACTIONS

Today's session was somewhat of a free-for-all, with improvisations coming from all directions. Chris and Stan did a job interview scene, as did Marilyn and Nancy. Chris, Mark, Stan, David, and myself improvised a scene in which we all played professional athletes who sat on the sidelines all day and every day. Marilyn, Nancy, and Sylvia did a rock and roll singing scene.

The group discussed the best types of interview techniques, and how to relate to interviewers as interviewees. The job interview scenes were well done and related to our previous discussions of how to meet people, how to introduce ourselves, how to deal with rejection and acceptance, and how to feel natural and comfortable.

There was a sense of enthusiasm that brought joy throughout the session.

SUMMARY

An interesting element was the awareness of behavior patterns. Marilyn pointed out to Stan that he always seems quiet and shy in his scenes. As well, Chris said that Mark always seemed so quiet and soft-spoken that sometimes it was hard to be sure if he was serious.

Mark thanked Chris upon hearing this, and the members asked Stan and Mark to be aware of how quiet they were in their everyday dealings. It was pointed out that sometimes they might feel another person is not listening to them and might interpret this as rejection, when actually the person just can not hear.

I thought this to be a true sign of trust in the group; a trust that helps the group confront, help and share with each other on a very personal level.

Session 7

ACTIONS

Today the group wanted to do scenes involving everybody. The first scene was in a bar-discotheque. Mark was the bartender along with Ken. Stan was at the bar trying to meet Marilyn, a waitress. Then Chris and David came in as friends, hoping to meet Sylvia at the dance. It was quite an impressive scene in which Chris and David let off steam at each other after a hard day's work. Stan introduced himself and began relating to Marilyn; Mark and Ken demonstrated skills in working and organizing together; and Chris moved over to meet Sylvia. All our previous discussions culminated in the acting out of this scene, demonstrating skills of interaction, introduction and rejection.

I also noticed that Chris and David let off steam, getting angry at each other in a controlled and acceptable way. Expressing anger is a problem for many members of this group. We discussed it and acted it many times. In our past vignettes the members had attempted to express anger yet often could not fully release it. Today David and Chris truly expressed anger. (I spoke to David and Chris separately after the scene — asking if, in fact, they were really angry with each other since it seemed so real. They told me that they

were not angry at each other, but Chris said that in the morning he
had been very angry at his father and he had re-directed that anger
in the improvisation.)

SUMMARY

Today's session was important for three reasons. First, it seemed
to summarize many of the concepts we had been working on. Interaction, interpersonal relationships, and conducting oneself with
people in real situations were demonstrated. Second, members of
the group showed that they could express emotion that, up to now,
they had kept bottled up inside themselves. They were learning to
cope with real feelings, to be aware of them and of the necessity to
express them. Third, and very important from a group viewpoint,
was the cohesiveness that the group had developed. The group
decided to do a scene involving everyone working together towards
one project. This certainly represented a significant sense of obligation and responsibility on the part of each member towards the
group, which had progressed from individual pantomimes to a
group scene.

Session 8

ACTIONS

Today, the group started right away with improvisations. Marilyn, Stan, Chris and Mark improvised a scene in which they were all
members of a communal family out west. During this scene, Marilyn
expressed real anger and hostility at each of the men: Chris for coming late to dinner; Mark for not doing his share of work; and Stan
for not fixing what he was supposed to fix. A great deal of emotional
tension was released for Marilyn during this improvisation. Also,
during the scene, domestic chores and tasks, and interaction between those with close personal ties, were well exemplified. Marilyn
said: "Boy, that feels good to let go."

Sylvia, normally a very shy girl, astonished me by going over to
Ken and initiating a scene. They improvised meeting on a bus.

The big event of the day was another group scene in which all
members joined in a "country-sing hullabaloo." Everyone had to
share something with the group: a song, an imitation, a pan-

tomime, or an improvisation. Marilyn sang a song, as did Ken, David, and Sylvia; Mark and Chris shared an improvisation; and Stan, Vinnie (another drifter in-and-out of the group) and Lucille (previously mentioned drifter) did imitations of famous personalities. While a member was on stage, the rest of the group served as audience and thoroughly enjoyed the show. It was a real letting go, a sharing; and it was rewarding.

Before breaking for the day I went back to Marilyn to ask how she felt. She said she felt good and had become aware of her anger and hostility. Today she had something else to think about. She said, "It seemed that my anger and hostility was directed at men. I purposely chose this scene and these guys, and did not choose any women for the scene." This is where drama therapy is valuable — in expressing, releasing, and understanding oneself — in being made aware.

SUMMARY

Today's session demonstrated the trust of the group. Marilyn was able to release pent-up aggressions; Marilyn and Sylvia could elicit, without fear, responses from other group members. The members felt the obligation, responsibility and consideration necessary to partake with others in someone else's struggle. They felt for each other, were concerned about each other, and were learning how to handle such responsibility. Throughout this process of dealing successfully in a group, each group member was learning to "own up" to himself.

The big "hullabaloo" event demonstrated the sharing capacity and cohesiveness of the group. Members were able to share and make themselves vulnerable without fear of ridicule or rejection. They stuck together, were considerate of each other, and learned to help each other express themselves in an open, nonhurting way.

5   CONCLUSION

To me the group has had two overriding functions: (1) self-expression; (2) sharing, which incorporates giving, accepting and receiving. I felt that the group accomplished these goals. The sharing did not stop within the boundaries of the group experience. I noticed that Stan and Mark became good friends, and they now visit each other frequently. There was also more interaction between Marilyn, Chris and Sylvia. A sense of comradeship is experienced now by many members of the drama group in Helping House: a natural progression from a sharing experience.

This experiment seemed to work well. Severely disturbed clients, usually put aside and considered as beyond repair like junk automobiles, proved that they, too, are capable of an experience that is heightening, beneficial, rewarding, therapeutic, and enlightening. These patients are able to take the responsibility that goes with sharing, accepting and receiving, and with expressing oneself and supporting others. The Drama Club has come a long way. It has made members feel better about themselves, with the help of other members. It has made people feel comfortable and human. And it was accomplished by people who, many say, are not capable of much at all. Maybe more of us need to learn how to receive?

MARVIN L. BLUMBERG, M.D., is chairman of the Department of Pediatrics at Jamaica Hospital, Queens, and associate professor of clinical pediatrics at the School of Medicine of the Health Sciences Center at the State University of New York at Stony Brook. He is vice president and medical consultant for United Cerebral Palsy of Queens.

Chapter 7

DRAMA: AN OUTLET FOR MENTAL AND PHYSICAL HANDICAPS

Marvin L. Blumberg

1 INTRODUCTION

A physically and/or mentally handicapped person has sensitivities and emotions as poignant as any nonhandicapped individual. Parental and societal attitudes of overprotection, patronizing pity or rejection often aggravate the handicapped person's inability or reticence to express his feelings, thereby creating more frustration, a further sense of inferiority and often despairing withdrawal. Self-confidence develops from the realization of being needed or wanted and in fulfilling the expectations of others. Also, peer relations can lead to social interaction in the proper milieu.

A training workshop can teach skills and, thus, give confidence to many handicapped persons including the mentally retarded. A general recreation program of social dancing and sports is pleasurable. There are, however, the shy ones, the withdrawn, the insecure who feel inferior to the people of the outside world. These individuals need help to develop broader vistas, an opening of the imagination and courage for new dreams to strengthen their egos and to transform them into social beings. To this end creative dramatics can play a very beneficial role.

In pretending to be that which he is not, a person may better understand that which he is. The inhibitions that suppress the ego are often shed during the concentration required to perform and the enjoyment in play acting. Creative participation in a group experience with his peers can help him to develop self-confidence and increased independent functioning. The relaxation of acting make-believe situations with others enables the shy, insecure or withdrawn one to attain satisfactory personal relationships.

2   MATERIAL

The United Cerebral Palsy of Queens Center is a multidisciplinary, multifaceted institution that affords, on a diurnal basis, treatment, schooling and training to individuals from infancy through childhood into adulthood. The client population includes mainly neuromuscular disorders in the younger ages and a mixture of physical handicaps and mental retardation in the adult group.

For the dramatics workshop, the training program counselors were requested to refer young adults of their selection and at their discretion. They were accepted without discrimination.

The first session of the workshop consisted of six men and women whose intelligence ranged from markedly retarded to dull normal, and whose ages extended from 23 to 40 years. Their brief profiles were as follows:

BA: 29-year-old woman with athetoid cerebral palsy since birth and dysarthric speech. IQ 87.

DH: 23-year-old woman with chronic brain syndrome, mild neuromuscular deficits and mild speech disorder. IQ 54.

PL: 33-year-old woman with congenital defects of vision, hearing, coordination and gait, emotional instability and past history of surgery for congenital cardiac defect. Average intelligence, no IQ available.

BR: 34-year-old woman with questionable simple schizophrenia. IQ 80.

RS: 35-year-old man with simple schizophrenia, depressive features and emotional instability. IQ 82.

EZ: 40-year-old man of borderline intelligence. IQ 74.

Five other clients joined the group at subsequent times:

HH: 42-year-old man with mental retardation. IQ 61.

GP: 23-year-old woman of borderline intelligence, possibly from neonatal brain damage. IQ 71.

DB: 22-year-old woman. IQ 87.

DB: 21-year-old man with brain damage, and markedly immature and inappropriate behavior. IQ 76.

BB: 22-year-old man with Downs syndrome, marked mental retardation and congenital heart disease. IQ 51.

Every member of the group had been a client in one of the Center's training workshops for at least several months since his or her initial evaluation and placement. Some were referred to the dramatics group at their own request, and others because their counselors recognized their need for help in social adjustment or in overcoming their insecurity. Sessions were held weekly, except for holidays and the months of July and August, from the group's inception. The attendance was remarkably regular for all participants although four left the group. One quit the Center program. Two lived at a considerable distance, and their parents were concerned about their late homecoming. One left because of medical reasons.

3 METHOD

For this project, a preconceived, carefully delineated prospectus was drawn up. However, this was set aside at the outset when the aspect of the group was observed, in favor of a dynamic innovative continuum in which the director (author) took cues and clues from the members and proceeded accordingly. There were some similarities to psychodrama and some differences. The emphasis was not on correcting emotional problems as such, although this was often a serendipitous benefit. The main objectives were personality development and social improvement toward better job potential in the outside employment situation.

The author's observations agreed with those of Blackhurst[1] that frequently the proficiently trained retarded individual may have to leave his employment placement because of his inability to interact successfully with his employer and with other employees. There is need for social adjustment on and off the job, in addition to the mechanics of employment. Creative dramatics provides an avenue for acting out solutions to problems of social interaction rather than only discussing them. It further evolves an understanding of the feelings of others.

Group technique was always employed. The sessions were held after training workshop hours in a pleasant room and lasted only one to one and a half hours to avoid too much demand on anyone's attention span. As in Moreno's technique,[2] all performances were ad hoc rather than in a theatrical *mise en scène*. There were exceptions on special occasions for performance before an audience.

At the start, each individual sat without affect, emotion or anticipation. There was neither spontaneity nor group interaction. For the first two or three sessions the director read aloud and then had each able member read aloud various short poems of imagery that were then discussed. Two of the poems used were Carl Sandburg's "Fog"

> *"The fog comes*
> *on little cat feet.*
> *It sits looking*
> *over harbor and city*
> *on silent haunches*
> *and then moves on."*

and Rachel Lyman Field's "Skyscrapers"

> *"Do skyscrapers ever grow tired*
> *Of holding themselves up high?*
> *Do they ever shiver on frosty nights*
> *With their tops against the sky?*
>
> *Do they feel lonely sometimes*
> *Because they have grown so tall?*
> *Do they ever wish they could lie right down*
> *And never get up at all?"*

These poems and others like them proved to be good stimuli. The group began to respond. Several members brought in other short poems that they found in books at home. One young woman enlisted her mother's help in selecting a book of poems in the public library. One young man wrote his own unmetered, unrhymed "poems" that, nevertheless, conjured up images or presented somewhat philosophical thoughts. Initiative started budding in several persons but interaction had not yet developed.

In the next phase the director recounted selected short stories from fiction, history and mythology that were not too complicated in plot or significance. He involved each member in questions, answers and opinions, inviting their comments about each other's remarks. Criticism, however, was neither encouraged nor discouraged. Some spontaneity now appeared which was to increase as time went on.

It was apparent that none of the group had the concentration powers or the ability to memorize by rote. Assignment of short poems to recite from memory at the following session had met consistently with failure. Therefore, for the next step of creative dramatics, it was decided to employ the technique of improvisation. The director would narrate a story in summary such as "The Courtship of Miles Standish," "The Emperor's Cloak" or "William Tell." He would then assign roles, including all of the members of the group according to their intelligence, shyness and other characteristics. The group would act out the playlet with minimal guidance and direction. Their dialogue and spontaneous sound effects such as laughter, groans, horse's clip-clop and background conversation were audiotaped. At the end of the act, the tape was played back. This helped to improve their self-esteem and their egos. They enjoyed hearing themselves in the recordings and then realized what they could do. A sense of humor appeared in all of them and some began to teach each other good-naturedly. The young women especially reacted pleasurably to teasing by the men.

It was interesting to observe that there was never anger, impatience or intolerance on anyone's part. Criticism was usually gentle or even humorous. Everyone listened with remarkable aplomb whenever the severely athetoid woman spoke with a noticeably hesitant speech impediment. In like manner, no one resented or

expressed antipathy toward the young man who frequently exhibited hyperkinetic inappropriate behavior.

Towards the end of the first season, the group was ready for
something big. The Annual Awards Night of United Cerebral
Palsy of Queens was to be held in June. It was decided to write
and to produce an original play for the expected large audience.
With a measure of initiative and some originality on the part of
the more intelligent and outgoing members, with the eager
cooperation of the others and with the evocative leadership of the
director, a play was outlined entitled "New Frontiers in Research."
No specific dialogue was written because the play was to be
rehearsed and presented in improvisation. It was a twenty minute
production concerning a scientific research trio working on a cure
for cerebral palsy. They chose the athetoid young woman as their
research subject and she, with a game sense of humor, accepted
the role eagerly. Props and costumes were collected and one
member created the format of the printed program. The production was a smash hit.

By this time reports from the Center's workshop counselors and
from the client members' parents were uniform in their praise of
the great improvement in every one of the group. Their sociabili-
ty and cooperation on and off the job had increased markedly.
Their enjoyment of their participation in the dramatics workshop
had made them happier persons. The following Christmas the
group, now deciding to call themselves the UCPQ Players, presented another original one act play before the Center audience,
again to "rave reviews."

The group was exposed to music in order to observe their reactions. After three sessions during which recordings were played of
impressionistic, colorful works such as Ferde Grofe's "Grand Canyon
Suite" and Rimsky Korsakov's "Scheherazade," it was apparent that
no one had any appreciation or imagined any thoughts from the
music. Attempts at provoking discussion raised no interest. Thus,
this project was dropped.

Then the group was introduced to some awareness of news
items. This was something that they had never bothered to consider before, but they became motivated to discuss current topics
in the media.

4 COMMENT

The use of psychodrama with mentally ill institutionalized patients has been recorded sporadically in the literature. This modality has been employed as a psychotherapeutic group technique to help patients to abreact their subconscious personal problems and to attempt to cope with them. Less often can references be found to creative dramatics being used with the retarded, and these are most often applied to the institutionalized ones with emotional problems. Most extracurricular activities for workshop day clients have been described as recreational with no reference to dramatics.[3]

Moreno developed psychodrama as a treatment procedure for the mentally ill. He wrote, "Acting gives the frustrated individual the chance of at least playing on the stage the part he has always longed to play, but never succeeded in playing, in real life. As a result, he often discovers new tasks which he can discharge satisfactorily in real life. Many a human life has been enriched by this means, many a choice of job made easier." Pankratz and Buchan[4] used psychodrama with institutionalized emotionally involved retardates who participated both as actors and as spectators, providing the source of the material and the production. The subjects in both groups benefitted by the catharsis.

Twadros[5] found role playing and spontaneity training possible with retarded adolescents with IQ's as low as 50. Guldager,[6] working with retarded adolescents in an institutional setting, noted that role playing by the subjects offered profitable information to the professional worker who is attempting to bring about behavior changes in the patients. It was apparent that acting attains its greatest value in a group setting where insights can be shared with other participants.

Orff-Schulwerk, a creative process involving elements of music, movement and language, was combined with creative dramatics by Morgan[7] in the treatment of retarded children under 12 years of age in an institutional setting. His objectives included increased freedom of self-expression, body awareness and ease in functioning as a member of a group by voluntary participation.

The method and approach employed in the dramatics workshop

at the United Cerebral Palsy of Queens Center reflect some of the techniques of the authors quoted. To a large extent, however, the development was innovative and it was guided to some degree by the feedback behavior of the members. The results in personality improvement and social adjustment were obvious to a greater or lesser degree in each member of the group. For the more severely retarded this means self-satisfaction for them and their families. For the less severely retarded, it will hopefully result in greater productivity and outside placement in gainful occupation.

5 SUMMARY

Handicapped and retarded persons, although trained in skills in a sheltered workshop, and exposed to more or less passive recreational programs, may still feel at a disadvantage in society. Their overprotection or rejection by others and their own reactions to their handicaps may prevent them from making an adequate social adjustment and hinder their potential for employability. Creative dramatics can greatly enhance the physically or intellectually disadvantaged young person's self-esteem and his or her ability to relate to others. This results in happier persons who can then fulfill their residual potentials to their own satisfaction and to society's benefit.

FOOTNOTES

1. A. E. Blackhurst, "Sociodrama for the Adolescent Mentally Retarded," *Training School Bulletin* 63 (November 1966): 136–42.
2. Jacob L. Moreno, "Reflections on My Method of Group Psychotherapy and Psychodrama," *Ciba Symposia* 11 (1963): 148–57.
3. W. Lynch, "Recreation, Role in a Rehabilitation Center," *Rehabilitation Record* 13 (May–June 1972): 18–19.
4. L. D. Pankratz and L. G. Buchan, "Techniques of 'Warm-Up' in Psychodrama with the Retarded," *Mental Retardation* 4 (October 1966): 12–15.
5. S. M. Twadros, "Spontaneity Training at the Dora Institute, Alexandria, Egypt," *Group Psychotherapy* 9 (1956): 164–67.
6. L. Guldager, "Role Playing with Borderline and Mildly Retarded Adolescents in an Institutional Setting," *Exceptional Children* 36 (November 1969): 206–8.
7. D. Morgan, "Combining Orff-Schulwerk with Creative Dramatics for the Retarded," *Therapeutic Recreation Journal* 9 (1975): 54–56.

JON KOGEN, Ph.D., is a licensed clinical psychologist in private practice. He is director of the New Institute for Gestalt Therapy; former chief psychologist at Mt. Sinai Hospital; and training consultant and supervisor at St. Vincent's Hospital, Long Island Consultation Center, St. Joseph's Children's Services, and the Jewish Family Service, New York City.

EDITH CADENHEAD, M.A., is a Gestalt therapist in private practice. A graduate of the Yale School of Drama, she has been a stage and television actress and is administrative director of the New York Institute for Gestalt Therapy, New York City.

Chapter 8

DRAMATIZATION IN THE GESTALT THERAPY PROCESS

Jon Kogen
Edith Cadenhead

Gestalt therapy has become an increasingly popular approach to psychotherapy over the past twenty years. The method was given its name in the book *Gestalt Therapy* written by Frederick Perls, Ralph Hefferline and Paul Goodman in 1951. Until his death in 1970, Frederick (Fritz, as he liked to be called) Perls was the leading popularizer and developer of this approach.

Fritz was a well-trained European psychoanalyst whose thinking began to diverge from Freudian theory and eventually resulted in a form of treatment which differed greatly from the psychoanalytic model. Gestalt therapy has its roots not only in psychoanalysis, but also in existentialism, psychodrama, phenomenology, and the Gestalt theory of perception.

Gestalt therapy uses experimentation to heighten experience so that awareness may be increased. The goal and the method are trusting, accepting, and taking responsibility for what *is*. The primary intent of the Gestalt therapist is to focus the patient's awareness on the "here and now." The emphasis is on bringing to the patient an active, experiential exploration of *how* he is causing himself pain, *how* he is stopping his energy, and *what* he is doing to avoid taking responsibility for what is happening to him, both existentially and internally. A goal that Gestalt therapy does

111

not emphasize is *why*, in an historical sense, you are the way you are. In Gestalt therapy the *how* and the *why* become synonymous.

A viewpoint promulgated in psychoanalytic theory is that the patient is "driven" by forces not accessible to consciousness (repressed) and is thus subject to their "pushes" and "pulls." Current Gestalt personality theory sees the individual not as the passive victim of his or her neurosis, but as active participant, not only as author of the script, but director and enactor as well, and therefore personally responsible for any feelings (or lack of them) that emerge.

The natural state of the human organism is seen as one of movement and growth, of active process rather than passive state. Such growth and change do not have to be produced, but simply allowed. This is a fundamental precept of Gestalt therapy and pervades the attitude of the therapist at all levels.

For example, passive words or descriptions often used by patients to avoid direct experiencing are not accepted in the therapy session. Thus, "I am anxious" translates "I am scaring myself." "My stomach is tight" becomes "I am tightening my stomach." "I am bored" becomes "I am controlling my excitement" or "I am deadening myself."

This represents first level awareness. Often the patient will balk and merely mouth these lines, still unwilling to acknowledge responsibility for what he believes is being done to him. (One is reminded of Oedipus' angry refusal to hear the wisdom of the seer Tiresius when he reveals, "Creon is not your enemy. You are your own enemy.")

Once a patient accepts that his current body state represents something he is doing to himself, the therapist will then suggest that he explore: *how* is he scaring himself; *how* is he tightening his stomach or deadening himself. At this point an excellent way of increasing the patient's awareness of his or her process is to have him identify with the offending symptom or feeling. Here the use of psychodramatic techniques often produces remarkable results. For example, when a patient identifies with his "tightening" stomach he may begin to realize that he has the capacity to tighten, to squeeze or to pressure. Fearing the hostility of these capacities, he has failed to recognize that they also represent the capacity for healthy assertion and aggression. By acting out these "mean" feelings the patient learns, firstly, that there is an aspect of his personality that is meaner than he was aware of heretofore. As he squeezes a pillow, he may actually experience a diminution of the tightness in his stomach. Countless headaches have been relieved in therapy sessions by asking the patient to identify with the headache. When speaking for himself, the headache "victim" usually says things like "I feel pain, pressure, a band around my head, etc." When he is asked to identify with and personify the headache, and give it a voice (a common Gestalt technique), the person may immediately feel (if he is able to do this) more powerful, less victimized, and "meaner" than he did before. He may even feel a glimmer of pleasure in being the victimizer instead of the victim. Psychoanalysis has a lot to say about the dynamics involved and their genesis. The Gestalt therapist merely points out that although the patient may not approve of his "meanness," owning it enables him to feel better. That is an experience, and it is very difficult (although not impossible) to deny one's own experience, especially when the therapist is consistently making it difficult for the patient to avoid this awareness.

Often the starting point in therapy is an exploration of the patient's script, usually some melodrama written long ago in childhood and recreated over the course of the individual's adult life. He has unknowingly committed himself to the preservation and reenactment of this ancient melodrama, condemning himself to repeat the past until he becomes aware how he turns the wheel on which he turns.

Dramatic techniques enable him to try out new behavior within the relatively safe matrix of the therapy session. Here the dragon may be confronted and its various dangers explored so that the patient may have a somewhat deeper knowledge of himself before exploring the real life conditions. In the session the patient is introduced to an impactful situation, either some dimension of his own dreams or fantasies, or some related circumstances suggested by the therapist. He is then instructed to continue the drama, in a sense "creating" it as he goes along. This, of course, is merely a conceit, since this spontaneous creation of the psyche can never really be divorced from the self that creates it. There is by definition a relationship. The "active imagination," as Jung labels it, simply rediscovers what has always been. The patient begins to sense how he projects those feelings that he fears and judges and therefore disowns. He comes to realize how he does not *want* to be responsible for these feelings.

This ability to confront and thereby eventually to own and assimilate rejected parts of the self is, if not a prerequisite, at least strongly correlated with the ability to empathize with, and respond to, others. As the individual begins to develop more skill in identifying with disowned parts of himself he will become more sympathetic to, and empathic with, similar characterological manifestations in the other. The process of enactment, the taking the part of the other in oneself, is critical to psychological growth. It seems indeed paradoxical, but until these unowned selves are acknowledged, inordinate amounts of our energies are consumed in rejecting and projecting them. In other words, we become obsessed with what we are trying hardest to deny in ourselves. This denial requires rigid control mechanisms which have a disastrous effect on our ability to be spontaneous, i.e., to respond, and this applies to both internal and external stimuli. To the individual obsessed with the need for control, an unselfconscious "felt" response to the world around him is difficult, if not impossible. Lacking this responsiveness, the individual's operational stance remains constricted, de-energized and passive.

A method which is frequently used to advantage in the therapy session is improvisation. The patient is asked to verbalize aspects of his experience of which he has not been aware up till now. This technique is termed identification and can be applied to many different aspects of the patient's experience. The therapist will suggest that the patient "become" one particular aspect of his experience that he disowns, i.e., that he experiences as "not me" or "not like me." This disowning can take place in the most subtle ways. "Symptoms," for example, are experienced as "not me," allowing the patient to feel victimized by them. Often he enters therapy only in order to have "them" removed. Similarly in dreams wherein other people, monsters and/or objects threaten the dreamer, these are experienced as "not like me" or "not me" and conveniently projected.

The world of fantasy is an extremely powerful adjunct to the Gestalt method. Often it becomes necessary to dislodge old introjects, personality parts "borrowed" from influential persons in our lives (most frequently a parental figure) and carried inside as though they were us. The use of dramatic techniques helps to bridge this gap between fantasy and reality. For example, let's explore this brief excerpt from a therapy session:

THERAPIST: O.K. Now, that pillow represents your mother, and you're going to tell her to stop ordering you around. You want to let her know that she has got to stop making decisions for you if you're ever going to grow up. How are you going to tell her this in a way she is going to understand? How can you express yourself so clearly that she will be absolutely certain you mean what you say? See if you can figure out how to do that.

PATIENT: (Grinning) I feel like telling her to stop sticking her finger up my ass.

THERAPIST: Then say that to her now.

PATIENT: Tell her? You want me to do that now? (Now the grin disappears and the patient is beginning to squirm a little.)

THERAPIST: Yes, now.

PATIENT: I don't think I can do that. I couldn't say that to my mother.

Patients often have a great deal of difficulty in seeing such situations as fantasy and may, at this point, require assistance from the therapist of a somewhat paradoxical nature. Observe:

THERAPIST: What mother? Where do you see your mother? That's a pillow.

The therapist has pointed out to the client that his fear of expressing his true feelings is correlated with the omnipresence of his own "mother-part," which judges and condemns him. Thus the patient is enabled to proceed with the very scary work of con-

fronting his mother introject. Obviously there need to be many
script changes before this show is ready to open and the client is
prepared to confront his real mother, but the process has begun.

Another way that fantasy and reality are brought together
psychodramatically is via dreamwork. The therapist first asks the
patient to tell the dream in the present tense, as if it were happening in the here and now. Then the therapist may work with
emerging feelings, or he may ask the patient to identify with some
person or object in the dream. For example, the patient might be
asked to identify with a monster in a nightmare. This monster
may be described by the patient as scary, mean, vicious, etc. and
certainly "bad." At this point the therapist might ask what the
patient actually *feels* as the monster, pointing out that the words
"mean" and "hostile" are concepts, representing judgments or interpretations, but not experiences. For instance, a patient brought
in this dream:

> PATIENT: A giant spider is locked up in a room and is trying to
>   escape. I have a big pole and I'm trying to kill this spider.
> THERAPIST: Be the spider in your dream.
> PATIENT: I'm big and black and soft and mushy. I feel a little
>   disgusted with myself.
> THERAPIST: What's your disgust about?
> PATIENT: It's my softness. I'm too soft. I'm disgustingly soft.
>   Like a woman.

Here the patient begins to be aware of the fact that he sees his
"softness" as something disgusting and "bad."

A psychoanalyst might limit his exploration of the dream to its
sexual symbolism and the toxic introject. However, when asked to
experience his identification with the spider more deeply, the patient found that as the spider, what he most earnestly desired was
help to get out of the room. At this juncture he started to
recognize that he himself avoided asking for help because it was
too "soft" and that he also saw his need for help as an "ugly"
aspect of his personality.

Similarly, this technique can be used to help the patient to identify with a "symptom," i.e., to act out the symptom or dramatize it

in order to find out what aspect of his personality he was disowning and how it was being expressed in the symptom.

For example, if a patient is beginning to feel his throat becoming tighter, the therapist might ask him to become the "tightener." The therapist might ask him to do it with words, e.g., "I am tightening you, choking you, choking off your words, etc.," or he might ask him to do the tightening with his hands, to a pillow. Very often, in the act of expressing the symptom, the symptom disappears. Fritz termed this phenomenon the "paradoxical theory of change." Change occurs spontaneously when the individual stops trying to change and accepts who he is. By identifying with the choker in himself, this patient may learn how he chokes off his expression. He may become more aware when he does this and learn how his symptom helps him avoid the anxiety entailed in expressing himself. After a while, he might also learn that instead of shutting himself up, he might do well, at times, to shut someone else up.

The technique of identification is also used as a way to open up contact with different parts of the body. It is a way of focussing attention and associating words with movements that have been suppressed.

For example, a patient's phrase, "I feel like a pushover," led him to enact a conversation between the upper and lower half of his body. This dialogue revealed to the patient how he cut off energy to the lower half, thereby allowing himself no sense of contact with the ground. Without this contact, this essential grounding, the patient was indeed a pushover, and the slightest impact was enough to throw him off balance.

Much of what has been called "repressed" by psychoanalytic theory can be demonstrated to be either aspects of feelings that are not paid attention to, or where the movement component of the emotion has been blocked. Many theories of therapy fail to take into account the fact that each emotion has an action or movement component, and that a contraction or muscular spasm must occur for a feeling to be blocked or suppressed. Talking is movement. Many patients have contractions around the musculature of the jaw either chronically or when a particular content area is approached. When the words are spoken, the holding back in the jaw is released to a certain extent. The result is very different from when the patient speaks *about* the anxiety provoking thought or feeling.

The externalization of internal events such as conflicts, dreams, sensations, melodramas, fantasies, etc., can serve to clarify as well as enhance awareness of the person's process. Thus change is facilitated in a more efficient manner than is achieved by merely talking about or explaining such feelings, thoughts or behaviors.

DANIEL ROSENBLATT, Ph.D., is a practicing Gestalt therapist in New York City. He is a fellow of the New York Institute of Gestalt Therapy, has taught in a number of medical schools and universities, and is the author of *Opening Doors, Your Life is a Mess,* and *The Primer of Gestalt Therapy.*

Chapter 9

THE DRAMA OF GESTALT THERAPY

Daniel Rosenblatt

I sit in my rehearsal room in the Lincoln Center area, awaiting my partner. What will we improvise today? Our script will depend on how the two of us make contact with one another. Our production today will be created from a mutual exploration of what inheres between us.

My partner shuffles across the room to take a seat. I am impressed with his gait, his posture, his musculature. Is he aware of them? I do not want an immediate answer. We have begun to rehearse — that is, to explore.

I ask him to enter the room again, being as aware as he can, of how he moves, of how he feels, of what he is expressing as he shuffles across the room. So today we begin with body work.

Where will my lead take us? I cannot know because I have left a large part open to my collaborator, but I have a rough script from which I am ready to depart. Yet I have certain assumptions: if I succeed in leading my partner to contact his gait, his posture, his musculature as he shuffles across the room, he will very likely lead me into his blocked past, situations, emotions, memories which are dramatically unfinished and which interfere with his growth, his openness, even his creativity, to become himself more fully.

So I have taken charge. I have called out the first notes to our duet. How compliant will my collaborator be? Will he play Trilby to my Svengali, Liza to my 'iggins, Horatio to my Hamlet? Or will he play deceitful Iago, perfidious Caliban, mischievous Rumpelstiltskin? I welcome any of these or whichever part he himself chooses. Happily he brings his own mixture.

He grins as if he were Jackie Cooper, looks with appealing little boy eyes as helpless as Jackie Coogan, gestures inarticulately as if he were James Dean, requests help as if he were Andy Hardy. I recognize quickly that he has chosen to play the Little Boy, appealing, helpless, compliant. I am sympathetic and willing to be seduced: I prepare to answer as Judge Hardy, as Lincolnesque Raymond Massey, as sympathetic Wallace Beery. Yet there is more to both of us than these limited roles.

Clearly he wants support. At the same time he wants to limit my lead by playing more helpless than he is. Which message will I respond to? Can I respond to both? Gently I laugh with him at his helplessness, and gently I remind him that he is an intelligent graduate student with a wide range of resources. I urge him to try again and to produce more.

So together we have widened the drama, we now have two separate, but interrelated subplots: can my collaborator connect with himself, his body and all the memories that are locked within; and how much will he cooperate with me as I attempt to bring him to these hidden realizations? Which subplot will take precedence? Again I lead, but he is free to challenge, to rearrange my script according to his own. I focus away from Judge Hardy and lead him back to his body. Try taking just one step. Can you feel the different parts of the body that are involved? What are they? Do it again? What do they feel like? He stays with me, and then begins to produce his own material. I gambled and won. For the moment he has left the Little Boy behind, and now we are for the moment, Henry and William James sharing secrets of human behavior and motivation. The Little Boy is put aside, though we may choose to return to him later.

How long has all this taken — one, two, or at most three minutes? A flow of words erupts. My collaborator's earlier embarrassment and awkwardness are replaced with his excitement as he shares with me his feelings, memories, awareness. He can feel his slightly hunched shoulders, his retracted pelvis, his gliding steps. I ask him to do it again, walk more deliberately so that he can be especially aware of what he has previously been doing without letting himself know it. He recognizes that he is signalling to everyone, the rest of us: "See, I am not a threat, I am not dangerous, I am not sexy. I minimize my genitals, I am not aggressive, I will not hurt you. Now please be kind to me too."

The Little Boy has returned unexpectedly to our script. Now he claims center stage. Here I am free to be inventive once again. Shall I work with the Little Boy at this moment, and if so, in what way? Shall I ask him to speak directly, or shall I return to the adult and more body work? My psychological dramaturgy tells me that since the Little Boy is so much here today I had better attend to him. I choose to leave body work for the moment and, instead, I deliberately invoke the Little Boy. I direct my partner to create a memory, a fantasy, I don't care which. At this moment I am not a lawyer or a judge, so I am not concerned with the literal truth of what emerges. This is an improvisation, useful for what is produced now, a throwaway to be used without judgment or guilt. I urge my collaborator to return to his childhood. Now he is four years old. I ask him to speak in a four-year-old voice, to move in a four-year-old way; to talk about his four-year-old perceptions with his eyes closed, taking his time to remember — to create — to improvise what he was like then.

The Little Boy rewards me with a monologue of his life then, his fears, his pleasures, his discoveries. His personal narrative is compelling and, as he elaborates the events which lead him to stress his lack of aggression and his lack of sexuality, he begins to weep, then wail. I remain a silent witness, a sympathetic audience, and then a chorus. I repeat key phrases from his narrative, and this time he is silent as I reflect back to him what he has produced. Then we both sit silent. For my part, at this moment, I am aware of sitting with the graduate student, the Little Boy, the monologuist and my partner. Each has a right to be there, each is at peace with the other. I hope that he is aware at this moment that I am friend, partner, audience, director, therapist. We pause.

How shall we proceed with the second act? I ask, "Would you like to go on with body work?" He agrees, but he has a dream he would like to work on. I reply that I feel sure we will have time for both.

Refreshed, I return to body work. I ask my collaborator to in-

vent a whole series of new gaits for himself, to create new
postures, to experiment with new ways of holding his musculature.
Gaily he takes my direction. He will be John Wayne, tight-assed,
stiff, hulking; he will be Dustin Hoffman, tense, intense, eager; he
will be Burt Reynolds, cocky, sexy, slick; he will be Jimmy Stewart,
boyish, charming, sweet. And now from all of these, he will find
himself. He will rehearse different walks, struts, slouches. If he is
courageous enough, I ask him to dare to be Marilyn Monroe, Elvis
Presley, Bette Davis, Dirk Bogarde. I let him explore different
identities and find how he can construct his own: what he wants to
do with his hips, his wrists, the balls of his feet, his ass, his
shoulders. As we work together, he is free to be Adam, Dr.
Frankenstein, the Golem, Galatea, the Tin-Man, or the Wizard
himself. He is free to switch between creator and created, active
and passive, sexy and sexless, assertive and fearful. And once again
we rest. He is not finished. Yet he has a sense of his possibilities, his
potentialities. By himself he can continue to explore his walk, his
identity, himself.

Now he leads. I want to work on a dream. We have begun Act
III. First I led him to his gait, and he led me to the Little Boy.
Then I led him to explore adult men and women. Now he leads me
into his dream. Will Act III be related to what has taken place
earlier? It need not, and yet, who knows? I try to hold myself free
enough to go in any direction—a well-made play, a Spook-sonata,
even a minstrel show, if it seems appropriate. And that is what is
critical: If it seems appropriate. I can be led up a tree or round the
mulberry bush, but at some point, I reserve the right to become
Prospero, the magician, and ask: "What is the point of all this,
how is it that we have come to Erewhon and to what end?" We can
play as much as we like, and then we can also be serious.

He is not sure what he has in mind. He trusts himself and me.
He risks what he doesn't know. I feel he is sincere and I listen with
my eyes, my ears and my breath.

He tells me his dream. He enters a men's room, a comfort sta-
tion. There is a man standing at one of the stalls, urinating. He
looks at the man in the mirror. The man is himself.

Now we have a script to explore. He is the playwright and I am
the director. I direct him to play himself in the dream: I want to

find myself as a man. I need comfort. I feel split off from myself, unsure, anxious. I direct him to play the man at the stall: I feel my genitals, full-sized, mature. I am an adult man, with no confusions on that score. I direct him to be the stall in the men's room: "I will give you time, I will help you stall. I will hide and protect you until you are ready." The man in the stall: "I am grateful but I can come out now. I don't need to stall any longer."

I direct him to be the mirror: I can look at what is happening, I can reflect events as they are. I do not need to distort or hide what is.

Then I ask my playwright to see himself as all these different parts—the man, his double, the stall and the mirror.

And now we look back at what has transpired in our rehearsal today. Yes, it all fits together. The themes of the dream are the same as those of the body work and our work with the Little Boy—we have been exploring different elements of how to be a man, a worthy task for a graduate student.

We are not finished. We will continue with our exploration of our relationship at another time, just as we will look at how he pursues his manhood sexually, as a friend, as a man about to make a career. We may need to bring back his parents to find out more about the Little Boy and how he is still holding on, holding back from growing up. But these dramas are for another day. We are both content to let the curtain fall for now.

This sample of a private session in Gestalt therapy is reasonably typical, not in terms of what happened, but how it happened. The two actors are free to create what will happen between the two of them, right now, at this instant. Any means are appropriate, so long as the contact between the two partners is enhanced, so long as awareness is maximized. Therapist and patient are both as active or passive as they choose. Each is the collaborator of the other, even if this means that at particular moments they become opponents. If this all suggests that Gestalt therapy offers a wide departure from traditional psychoanalytic roles for analyst and analysand, so be it, although the thoughtful Gestalt therapist reserves the right to play psychoanalyst, too, if that makes sense.

In a creative manner, the sensitive Gestalt therapist reserves the right to play with the principles of Gestalt formation: he will reverse figure and ground, offer support or withdraw it, confront or avoid confrontation, support resistance or challenge it, work nonverbally or with dreams and fantasies, play dumb or make interpretations. Throughout he will be guided by the desire to make this moment vivid, alive, filled with excitement and freshness. You ask, is this not a tall order for a therapist? The answer is yes, but the stakes are high, and the drama is unique: two souls in search of healing, of growth, of development. Each has something to learn from the encounter and the innate drama cannot be overlooked. It must be remembered that the major innovators of Gestalt therapy were all very much concerned with theatre and the performing arts. Fritz Perls loved opera and knew at first hand the work of Max Reinhardt, the director. Paul Goodman wrote plays and libretti, and Laura Perls is a talented musician and writer. To them drama and theatre are not something foreign which happens on a stage or a cultural center. It is the stuff of life.

I can learn from them as forebears, but I need to be aware that I do not become a little Fritz, an ersatz Paul, an imitation Laura. I am free to take from each what I need, but then I am faced with the necessity of making it mine, of developing my own style, of integrating what I have taken and assimilating it. That is, I must destroy what I take and recreate it in a new mode as my own invention, suited to my own needs. And this act becomes a part of my own drama as I grow as a Gestalt therapist.

One final note. I have not dealt with group therapy as it is practiced by Gestalt therapists. Here, everything I have pointed out about the two collaborators is vastly enriched. With the addition of twelve new cast members, fuller dramas can be enacted, the chorus can offer a wider comment, the dialogue can be more elaborate, the audience can be more potent. At its best the group can represent a circus, a solemn mass, a comic farce, a tragic opera, a mythic dumb show. To be an integral part of these unique dramas is one of the richest joys I know.

HANNAH B. WEINER, M.A., is founder and director of the East Coast Center for Psychodrama, New York City; co-founder of the Theatre of Today; former associate of Dr. J. L. Moreno and past president of the American Society of Group Psychotherapy and Psychodrama; a member of the board of the World Academy of Psychodrama; and a former director of the Moreno Institute, New York City, and Beacon, New York. A certified psychotherapist, she both teaches psychodrama and trains psychodramatists, and is the author of numerous articles on psychodrama and role playing.

Chapter 10

RETURN FROM "SPLENDID ISOLATION"

The Uses of Psychodrama, Sociodrama, and Drama in the Process of Recovering from Substance Addiction

Hannah B. Weiner

1 INTRODUCTION

I am a psychodramatist, a Morenoan, who enjoys working in the community in a form of public living-life theatre. I find especially rewarding my work as a trainer, consultant and counselor in the field of alcoholism and other drug addictions.

When I became part of the psychodramatic family, we were a tiny band of believers in a method that was immediately loving and involving, as well as therapeutic, experiential and exciting. Later, it became controversial, then accepted and international. As a philosophy it is cosmic; as a method it is a theatre that heals; as a technique it is an extended family.

2 THEORY AND METHOD

Psychodrama

Psychodrama is the spontaneous enacting of a situation. It aims to discover "truth" through dramatic means. The focus is directly on role playing: communication through action with insight for protagonist, group members and director. It centers on the individual whose session it is, and a problem or situation of particular interest to him. Its goals are to develop: interpersonal relations; attitudes and behavior by giving insight into their causes and effects; group participation, involvement and interest; spontaneity and creativity; inner conflicts and problems; research in human relations. Psychodrama usually consists of one protagonist, with two to four people playing roles, in front of a group, either for therapy or for demonstrating how problems can be solved.

This chapter will also describe multiple role plays where all the members become role players at the same time in smaller groups: members are given roles or written role playing assignments; the group plays are acted simultaneously. In the single psychodrama session, an individual may feel that he has been the only person benefiting from the session. But within multiple role play, all members participate.

Psychodrama is a disengagement from ordinary reality: a representation of the natural developmental processes which allow for a new synthesis based on mirroring. Thus we become receptive to novel thought formations and a restructuring of our perceptual world. It is an active, reflective methodology which clarifies the external stress of societal situations; it deals with the interlocking nature of cultural, ethnic, sexual, family and social class problems. Hopefully it begins to develop constructive attitudes to replace the use of alcohol and drugs. That is:

> God grant me the serenity to accept the things I cannot change;
> the courage to change the things I can; and the wisdom to know
> the difference. (*Serenity Prayer*)

Psychodrama as a life training tool can help develop serenity through an action inventory, *catharsis* and life training. The socialization aspects of psychodrama encourage reaching out and interpersonal relationships.

The Social Atom

Each individual has a social atom made up of all people who are important to him (his mother, father, sister, wife, neighbor, bus driver, minister, etc.) and with whom he has a daily, a long-standing, or just a casual relationship. The more effective he is within his social atom, the greater his personal reward.

Sociodrama

Sociodrama uses the same instruments and techniques as psychodrama; whereas psychodrama is concerned with one individual's difficulty in a situation, sociodrama concerns itself with the group problem.

Goals include assisting better intercultural relations; understanding and insight into social behavior; group exploration of a common problem or interesting situation and alternative ways of dealing with it; social research.

Some of the questions dealt with by sociodrama in a substance abuse setting could be: What do you tell a prospective employer about your drug abuse history after you have recovered? How are you going to deal with old friends and acquaintances when returning to the community?

Role Playing

Role playing can be either structured or spontaneous. It differs from psychodrama or sociodrama in that it focuses on the narrower framework of some specific area of life or role function that has to be explored. In general it helps to develop group feeling and understanding through its use of easy pace and informality; to render less threatening everyday situations or persons; to reduce the distance between group and leader (by allowing the director to participate occasionally); to serve as a common frame of reference for people of very different backgrounds.

When you role play, you are putting yourself into another person's *feeling*. When you encourage someone else to role play, you are helping him or her to *be* that other person. How can one human being put himself in the place of another? How can I, if I happen to be a white parole officer, put myself into the role of a black woman applying for a job? If you could do it easily you would not need role playing. If you had no common bond of humanity with the other person, you might not be able to do it. But you *do*. You have had related feelings to those of the person whose role you are trying to play. The effort and experience of playing that other person can lead to understanding them.

There are differences between forms of role playing. Structured role playing focuses on making the individual proficient in a particular area of his life. Its objectives are to assist: skills such as problem solving, or decision making; procedures such as counseling techniques or job instruction; attitudes related to interpersonal relations such as social or job role expectations; stereotyped roles of behavior commonly encountered in social or work situations.

Although the protagonist is permitted a degree of spontaneity, the session is usually pre-planned to deal only with specific subjects. The auxiliaries are given scripted roles or instructions on how to play the role before the action begins.

Spontaneous role playing focuses on helping the individual understand himself and others better, and on exploring new approaches to deal with problems of human relationships. Its objectives are to encourage: insight into the participants' own behavior and the feelings of others; attitudes related to job, family or social lives; new ways of dealing with problem situations; diagnostic information concerning the style and approaches of participants to certain types of problem situations; experience which may be helpful later, even if the participant is not aware that learning is taking place at the time of the occurrence.

Multiple Role Plays and Role Rotation

In training alcoholism counselors, a large group was broken into groups of four. Each group spontaneously acted how they felt when diagnosed as: (1) the alcoholic; (2) the spouse of the alcoholic; and (3) the employer and counselor. Each role play lasted about fifteen minutes. An observer assigned to each group reported to the larger group. Another variation was to break the group into sets of five: an alcoholic or drug addict, a counselor, a spouse or a significant other (an employer or a representative of the funding agency). After one participant dealt with the problem, the roles were rotated. Role rotation has been used to train union, management and labor in alcoholism grievance situations, as well as in teaching hospital administrators, professional personnel, and union employees in alcohol counseling. In addition, other creative expression modalities (such as poetry and "develop an alcoholic pattern person") were used to teach alcoholism counselors how to recognize and handle the problem employee.

Videotape and Therapeutic Motion Pictures

These have been employed to learn more about skill training and development, and also to understand the way things were in the past. For example: one scene was about what it was like to be the first person in the bar at 7:30 A.M.; another concerned projected job interviews. A two-hour session with one individual, who wanted the group to know who he really was and who wanted to find his identity, was videotaped. He edited this down to a fifteen minute representation of the man he wanted people to meet — a sort of action resumé. In another setting, we used videotape as a series of fifteen minute "my dramas": individuals acted out family scenes, past and future. These dramas were watched by the group who then criticized or agreed with what had been done.

PSYCHODRAMA & THEATRE

SOME DIFFERENCES

PSYCHODRAMA	THEATRE
Objectification of Problem	Reflection of Problem
Goal to free audience	Goal to capture audience
Explore alternatives that exist	Show that alternatives do exist
Discard cultural conserve for creative alternatives	Impose cultural conserve
Spontaneous	Structured
Participating Audience	Observing Audience
Concentration on development of multiple role repertoire and expansion of ability to play *many* roles well	Concentration on development of the personification and understanding of *one* particular role well
See through the role of the self to the player	See through the self of the player to the role
Spontaneous creation of present	Frozen creation of the past
Imagination creates sets	Pre-designed, physical sets
Re-enacted	Acted

(Chart continues)

PSYCHODRAMA	THEATRE
Feedback and sharing	No feedback or sharing
Brings self to play self (or resistance by self to play self)	Brings self to play another
Reverses roles with other actors	Strong identification with own role
Unlimited stage movement	Structured and limited stage movement
Audience permitted to create alternatives to observed enactment	Audience only observes cultural conserve created by others
Director must be spontaneous and responsive to "surprise" within the drama	Director can be slow and deliberate until enactment appeals to his sense of correctness
Director maintains direct contact with audience for feedback and can change or improve drama as it proceeds	Director acts in isolation from audience and faces only rejection or acceptance at time of final presentation when revision is not possible
Freedom of actor to choose between many roles and select the one(s) to keep according to what sensitivity the role brings to the person	Imposed role. Only choice is what kind of sensitivity to bring to the role
Focus on "What we are letting happen in life"	Focus on "What's happening in life if we would only let it"
Supportive doubling for actor	Role played alone with no doubles
Emphasis on "we"	Emphasis on "they"
Emphasis on seeing the person in in the role	Emphasis on seeing the role

3 OVERVIEW IN THE FIELD OF ALCOHOLISM

Alcoholism

Marty Mann, as Executive Director of the National Council on Alcoholism, has put forward three concepts:

(1) Alcoholism is a disease and the alcoholic a sick person.

(2) The alcoholic can be helped and is worth helping.

(3) Alcoholism is a public health problem, therefore a public responsibility.

Alcoholism is a disturbance of behavior with many determinants, social, psychological and physiochemical.[1] It is also an addiction: there is not only an emotional dependence on the drug but also a physiological one as well. This accounts, at least partly, for the craving to resume drinking when the blood level of alcohol begins to fall.

Drug Addiction

Drug addiction is a "state in which a person has lost the power of self-control with reference to a drug and abuses the drug to such an extent that the person or society is harmed."[2] Himmelsbach and Small have included three distinct, but related, phenomena: (1) tolerance; (2) physical dependence; and (3) habituation.[3] As Rasor states:

> The drug addict tries to reconcile his basic instinctual urges with the demands of reality through the use of an addicting drug. To reverse the process of addiction, the addict must marshal all his psychic energy on the side of his ego in abstaining from the use of narcotics, and reconcile his basic instinctual needs with the demands of reality.[4]

Dual Addiction

The statistics on the use of drugs-other-than-alcohol by women alcoholics echoes the national trend of women taking more psychoactive drugs than men. Dual addiction increases the problem because the substance abuser constantly blames one of the addictions and can use the "other" as a cop-out. An example of dual addiction is the housewife addict who started on Valium because of her "nerves" while, at the same time, having a serious drinking problem. She will use Valium or Librium to steady her hands early in the morning because she knows that "if you drink early in the morning you're an alcoholic." So she takes the pills until about 5

P.M. and then begins to drink. It is much harder to treat the dual-addicted woman as she will often slip back into taking the drugs after she stops drinking and say, "Well, at least I don't drink." Of course, she maintains no sobriety on the mental level but fools herself that she is indeed "sober." She will eventually slip back into drinking. She may be hard to reach because the use of sedative drugs is sometimes difficult to detect.

Aims of Treatment

Crises which cause alcoholics to come for help are varied. Most do so because of a family crisis. The husband of a woman who has a drinking problem for years has run through a gamut of reactions. He has denied and protested, felt rage, humiliation, guilt, and has often threatened to dissolve the marriage. Sometimes he is driven by concern for the children, their neglect, social ostracism, or an outright threat to remove them from her. With an unmarried alcoholic woman, it may be a response to the despair and anger of significant others in her life, like parents or siblings. Another set of crises is medical. Women with alcoholic problems are more likely to appear in physician's offices with medical and emotional symptoms. For women who are working, there are job pressures: some will quit work and go home to drink; if they are the sole support of their families there is a deep need for help.

The aims of therapy are not only total and complete sobriety, but a better functioning in all areas of life: to free the person from his fixed and destructive role, and to help him develop his potential—a move away from the egocentricity of addiction to a social sense and towards an ability to relate and share with others. As Cohen states:

"I am impressed how readily longstanding psychopaths and sociopaths become conformists and Establishment types when they are rid of their addiction, either in a therapeutic community or a maintenance program. Apparently we have been observing the addict's life style and calling him psychopathic when, in fact, it was his way to survive in a chaotic world. The psychiatric sick role may not be appropriate or useful for a number of alcoholics and addicts."[5]

Natural Child[6]

Alcoholics never had a 'childhood' that they enjoyed. They always lived the role of an adult on the outside with childish wants on the inside. When they get sober and drug free, unless they can have joy in their reality, they will not stay sober. During the first six months of my sobriety, I felt a newness and discovery like that of a newborn child (not a re-discovery but a new discovery). I was afraid that when it wore off I would slip back. Psychodrama really helped retain that sense of discovery until I found what I wanted to be and was not bored. You can never be an observer in psychodrama, even if you are resisting — you are simply being a participant who is playing the game of not participating. Psychodrama can appeal to the 'natural child,' the spontaneous child who says 'how wonderful and new everything is,' as opposed to the negative child who says 'I want what I want when I want it'.

It is appropriate here to mention the use of unusual co-therapists. In addition to patients becoming co-therapists, the Weiner-Fox group and the Kaufman-Weiner group employed a Yorkshire Terrier, Chadwick Chips, whose warm body supplied acceptance and rejection, whom patients could touch or yell at, and who also played the missing or lost animal in sessions set in the past. Youngsters (like Robert and Kim Bruce, Jonathan Moreno) and children from the age of four have acted as auxiliaries for adults, or as specialists on children's problems. Puppets and other creative forms such as dance, poetry, and art were also used.

Psychodrama should be employed early in the treatment of drug abuse, before the alcoholic can build up resistances. When the individual is in detox, he feels terrible. That is the best time to act — while he is feeling remorse, guilt, and is physically ill. The moment he starts feeling better physically, he begins to think, "Everything isn't so bad, I don't really have to do anything about my drinking." Psychodrama hits the individual at a gut level, a visual and physical level. The most effective treatment is in a group setting in the first throes of recovery. When the alcoholic is told at this stage to be honest with himself, he is usually willing as he is already "unzipped."

Psychodrama releases a sense of joy. It permits the feeling of childlike wonder, and it helps others by letting them see that joy. This joy is a key to lasting sobriety because it provides something to look forward to. It says, "Tomorrow I can have another whack at it." It touches off that wellspring that you must know you have in order to survive—that hope that keeps you going.

Children of Alcoholics

Psychodrama is beneficial in working with children of alcoholics. It helps them see and feel the alcoholic's deep sense of isolation, loneliness and feelings of inadequacy. Reversing roles with their own parents helps them "get inside" that person and their role. So often the children of alcoholics have themselves become isolated through the constant rejection by the alcoholic parent; and the preoccupation of the nonalcoholic parent with the alcoholic causes a double rejection. Sessions can be a relief for them, a place to go to be heard, to get support. Psychodrama also helps the therapist or counselor to understand the dynamics within the family and to aid the family explore their attitudes and values. It can show who steps outside the family value system (by occupation, marriage, etc.); predictable patterns of closeness and distance within the family and what the clusters of relationships will tend to be; who people are and in what way this is related to others; the boundaries that patterns within the family or family relationships will have.

Teenage Drinking

In a group at Resolve in New Jersey, teenage and adult drinking were examined in many sessions. Although the teenager might identify and understand the parent's drinking problems, he would choose to run away for the purposes of survival—then get caught—be sent home to live with the parents—then run away—then get caught. The question, of course, is: Who is the victim?

Two problems in recovery for teenage alcoholics are peer pressure and a sense of deprivation. The teenager feels emotionally deprived, less of a person, unable to have "fun." Psychodrama with teenagers is a good tool to release their sense of creativity and spontaneity; to help them recover their "envisioned loss" of "excitement;" and to become self-starting—to teach them how to have fun without a chemical starter.

Sexuality/Gender Identification

According to Silber[7] many alcoholics have confused gender identification, which leads to problems with sexuality. The guilt feelings of alcoholism can be dealt with in the group setting. Through verbalization in an atmosphere of suspended judgment, a *catharsis* is possible and "oneness within our individuality"[8] is experienced. In the Weiner-Fox group, we concentrated on individual choices for alternate life styles and a free choice of sexuality (lesbian, homosexual, heterosexual, bisexual). Various self-help groups were used at this time and the focus was on acquiring spontaneous living skills in the chosen role.

The alcoholic often becomes sexually active as an attempt to be in touch with some point of reality: trying to prove one's identity through another person. This often results in enormous guilt hangovers. Psychodrama can be useful in helping the alcoholic accept himself and assess how much of his conduct was a manifestation of the disease. Through role playing sessions we can uncover more meaningful choices of role and self identity, and we create a new world, a new reality.

Scenes

May I now ask you to be the audience spectator and join in the following scenes:

1. A handsome young black man of 24 has been released from Rikers Island. His life has changed. As he dresses, he is full of his new knowledge, gleaned from talk therapy and group therapy. He has been taught a skill, and his education was completed while in

jail. He owes some money to the pushers, but with his new job he knows he can handle that. He struts down the steps of his project, sees four of his stoned friends approaching him and greets them with, "Hey man, how ya doin'?" He wants to help them get rehabilitated, so he begins to talk. They "jive" him and offer him a "roach." He says "No," and they place one in his back pocket (he doesn't feel this). Police come over and the group scatters. He does not, because he has "nothing to hide." The police tell him to spread-eagle against the wall and they find the roach in his back pocket. His smile changes to astonishment and beads of perspiration appear on his forehead. He is speechless.

2. Imagine now a man 5'1", enthusiastic and open, secure in his newfound sobriety at a treatment center, telling about his wife and what he expects to be their first encounter since he has stopped drinking. He is participating in an exit test, designed to see whether he is ready to leave or not. Instead of asking him to tell us what his wife is like (since he has a voice that is barely audible), we ask him to *show us* his wife. In portraying her: he jumps on the table and stands very tall and, in a voice that could be heard outside the room, "she" introduces herself. She is an aggressive and controlling woman. When I ask "her" whether her husband is coming home today, she says "yes" with a sneer. The discussion that followed was about family support. By making an empty chair first his wife, then mother, then daughter, each man could make the most important statement he had to make without the fear of retaliation.

3. A well lit room in Washington, D.C., fairly large with high ceilings. There are three men in the front of the room. One smiles and begins to address the whole group. They each in turn talk about their alcoholism. We end by saying the Serenity Prayer and break for coffee. One of the women comes up to me in tears. I put my arm around her and she cries, "What is this, therapy?" I answer "maybe." She says, "Do you know what you've done to me? I've always hated alcoholics and now I know they are OK. This isn't like the movies or a play, there isn't any fade-out. I have to be involved with them there for two days and work on my feelings and prejudice." As you may have guessed, this was not a

play. It was a role played Alcoholics Anonymous session in a training program to teach employees how to understand and treat alcoholism.

These are but three scenes that developed into role training sessions. There really are not typical sessions, since each person is different. Some can be called recipe sessions. They deal with the area of detoxification, shame, and D.T.'s and are aimed at helping a person toward recovery. They may be geared toward care: to who you are and what you can do; to skills and survival; to alternate problem solving tools; to learning to take care of body needs; to teaching what alcoholism is; and to developing better choices in people, places and things. Sociodrama, role playing, situation tests, and laughter scenes (how to have fun though sober), are particularly effective. So is working with families and employers to help them understand substance abuse and how they can begin effective work on it.

4 DESCRIPTION OF GROUPS

The Weiner-Fox Group

Formed in the early 1950's, this group was a model of the use of psychodrama techniques. It was an upper middle-income group of various backgrounds and ages. Their common denominator was alcoholism or polydrugism. There were also spouse groups, and we would have joint meeting seminars or workshops. The warm-up was informal, and members could choose to attend one of three group sessions: didactic, education sessions on alcoholism; group therapy; or psychodrama. Most often they attended all groups and A.A. meetings as well.

Role reversal, future projection, doubling and mirroring were used. Sessions involved violence, family problems, decision making as to whether or not one was an alcoholic, whether to take Antabuse, go to A.A., Recovery, Weight Watchers or self-help groups exploring drinking, slips, personal inventories and Twelve Step skills.[9] Although the primary focus was therapy, it also became a group that was educational and informational.

Sessions on sexual explorations would often clarify the process of a loving relationship — not only by getting to the "root" of the feeling but also by supplying a support system in the acceptance of loving relationships. It was a family life education system for both the extended family and the substance abuser. Several members of the group became a traveling theatre known as "The Group of the Here and Now Players." They traveled to hospitals and schools to educate, and to explore the problems of alcoholism as a prevention and as a teaching modality, through action and sociodrama.

Phoenix House and Interim House

Working in a halfway house and a therapeutic community permitted the use of role rotation, multiple role plays, psychodramatic shock and all inclusive psychodrama. Because there was continued twenty-four hour knowledge about participants, sessions produced *catharsis*, new directions for living, life style changes and understanding of human identity. The total community would become involved, including staff. Here, and at Roosevelt Hospital, we concentrated on developing leadership skills in a life of sobriety and counselor training. As Weisman states:

> In discussing the respect in which the treatment of alcoholism and drug addiction are similar, one may well begin with the treating person rather than with the treated. They certainly experience similar frustrations in their attempts to be of help. Manipulation, lying, dishonesty, abuse, even assault are often problems in treatment in both groups of patients, and the treating persons must be trained in ways that transcend the traditional curriculum of the health professional.[10]

Roles, role relationships, expectations and enactments could be demonstrated, retained and understood. Both structured and unstructured sessions involved decision making as to whether to go home, whether it was possible to change life situations or, simply, how to live with other individuals. They involved religion, drinking, taking drugs and independence. Poetry, music and movement were high peak experiences. The warm-ups included games and structure (paper bags, photomontage or the Cup techniques) and sociometric families, male-female relationships, or discussion topics on trust, love, belonging or how to deal with new experiences; learning how to laugh and play; how to feel comfortable.

The South Oaks Foundation Experience

Bailey House is the alcoholism component of South Oaks Psychiatric Center. Hope House is their drug addiction treatment component. There is also an alcohol counselor training program. A six-month program of "on-the-spot training," weekly seminars and experiential sessions was designed for the entire staff, visitors, and patients. At other times, the alcoholic group reversed role and participated in discussions with visitors, staff, family and employers in dramatic interaction — environmental theatre at its best. We developed specific psychodrama techniques called Set-A-Scene or The Scene Shop. These would be situation tests of ten or fifteen minutes. They showed the impact of alcoholism in different phases of living, the alcoholic trying to live with the non-alcoholic, and scenes of perceptions. They often included costumes and masks. When the frustration test was incorporated in such scenes, the group chose to call the session "flashback and change." These were scenes of frustration, loss, mishandled moments or tragedies. They were first enacted as they actually were, and then acted as they could be, or as they were going to be. This kind of training produced the following findings: (1) Patients and staff preferred sociodramas (from which multi-psychodrama sessions grew and became an inclusive sharing experience) rather than a psychodrama session with one person who often experienced himself as a victim. (2) Psychodrama sessions in small groups were preferred to those in large groups. (3) Psychodramatic doubling on the spot (either in therapy sessions, interviews, around the dining room table or in family visits) produced almost immediate relearning, when the double acted either as a coach or as a burlesque. (4) Boasting was a favorite warm-up and was helpful to the therapist to discover whether or not, in ten boasts, the words "I am not drinking" or "I am sober today" were part of a new identity. (5) Sessions involving skill development and acceptance of human identity were most helpful. (6) Psychodrama could be used in detox as an educational, supportive, fear releasing technique.

5   SUMMARY

Psychodrama offers the possibility of fulfillment not permitted in the actual life of the individual. His lack of acceptance by mother or father can be lived through not only by acting in the role, but also by spontaneously presenting himself. Through centering on spontaneous actions, the individual learns to deal with unforeseen situations and to be productive in the session. There is a carry-over to all dimensions of living: he reacts to reality and not to distorted reality.

Psychodrama is particularly effective in substance abuse. It deepens the relation to the self and the other by providing an exchange of roles; a person does not remain what he was before, either in playing a role or becoming a member of a particular group. It gives an opportunity for demands of life in action: it provides insight and also rehearsal for living as well as therapeutic acting out. It leads to freedom from repressed hostilities and extortions because nonverbal memories and actions can be acted out. The remembered past is entirely present and may often create a psychodramatic shock. But by dealing with the "here and now" instead of the "now and then," we provide a time and space for all sorts of emotions in social interactions and struggles. It puts the individual in control of his own life by offering options, behavior modulation and role understanding. It encourages taking charge of rather than copping out on life. It develops spontaneity and creativity. Most important, it can train an individual in what is expected of him in different social settings. It provides an understanding of his fellow man. He learns how to feel him as well as understand him.

> All men are born to create
> No one shall have power
>   who does not create
> No one shall have more power
>   than he creates

You shall learn to create
You shall learn
to create me.[11]

APPENDIX

A variety of psychodrama techniques are used in substance abuse treatment groups, including the following:

Audience Analyst — A person in the group serves as audience analyst: as an observer to feed back to all participants his feelings regarding the audience reaction to the enactment.

Auto Drama — One person plays both or many roles in a given situation. He increases his flexibility by acting as himself and, a short time later, as his father. This technique is particularly useful in broadening the protagonist's perspective and ability to respond in new ways.

Auxiliary Chair — Using the chair as an auxiliary ego provides a number of roles without the embarrassment that may occur in shy or inhibited individuals. The chair has legs, arms, a back and can be moved about to represent the action of an individual or animal. It allows, in the absence of auxiliary egos, for unlimited auxiliaries to be presented in the form of different chairs. It is also less destructible than a human being and can be hit without fear of retaliation or injury.

Blackout — This is used when the area being explored is extremely painful for the protagonist (causing the scenario to become labored or slow), or is a problem which elicits shame or extreme shyness in front of the group. All the lights are shut off so that the group can no longer see the protagonist. This allows for the involvement of the group while respecting the need for solitude.

Cartoon-O-Drama — The group clips cartoons or messages from newspapers or magazines and acts them out. Or, very often with the use of water colors or felt pens, the group or individual will make a gigantic cartoon and can go as "mad" as possible, using all their zaniness.

Circle Warm-Up — The group sits in a circle. Each person thinks of something about himself that he likes; then thinks of another person he knows who likes the same thing about himself. He turns to the person next to him and talks about himself as if he were that person.

Coaching — Someone stands behind the subject and coaches him, telling him what to do in the situation. The audience may also act as coaches. On occasion, the protagonist is instructed to play the enactment not the way he feels it, but to play it according to the coach's instructions.

Comfort Circle — People from the group surround the protagonist to give him love and understanding—verbally and nonverbally. This is particularly useful after a scene of grief or despair. There is a great deal of hugging, kissing, and physical contact—real humanness.

Crib Scene — Volunteers take part as themselves as infants: they curl up on the floor as babies, taking a nap or a rest. "Mommies" and "Daddies" from other members of the group go around and check on their babies and give them lots of loving, tuck them in, pat them, make sure they are happy. The participant recaptures, or gains anew, vital parts of himself when he experiences or re-experiences universal love as a totally relaxed infant. It also offers training in accepting warmth and comfort.

Cup — This is used for groups of four to six. The cup may symbolize alcohol, sobriety, family, or any theme or institution to be discussed. The cup is passed around the small group(s) four times. The first time each member holds the cup in contemplation in silence, places into it his own feelings, attitudes, concerns, beliefs and disbeliefs (about the topic the cup symbolizes). At the second pass, each does something to the cup that symbolizes his own attitude, concern, fear, anxiety or acceptance of it. (Some people may drink from it, crumple it, tear it open petal-fashion, sit on it, etc.) The third pass is again in silence to re-evaluate one's concepts and try to think of one's own ability to change and develop. The fourth time the cup is placed in the center while each person in turn shares what the experience meant to him.

Double — This is an auxiliary ego who stands behind, or beside, the subject and verbalizes his inner feelings and thoughts. It helps an individual overcome a block and enter a formerly resisted area, or to verbalize some of the feelings he does not feel free enough to verbalize. Once the protagonist has identified his feelings, the auxiliary ego may ask him such questions as "Why am I feeling this way?" or "Why am I resisting so hard?" (The double should make movements and gestures and use his body in the same way the protagonist does.)

Ego Building — A member faces the group to hear them discuss him honestly — all the *positive* aspects of himself. The director must stop the discussion once he feels the audience has "run dry," and ascertain how the recipient feels (as well as how the group feels having said what they did). As many of the group as desire should be given the same opportunity.

*Family in Crisis (*or *Living Together)* — The question of returning home or to family court, separation, violence, drinking, child abuse, spouse abuse or financial indebtedness can be presented and role played in a concrete fashion through the following format: (1) the group on their own develop either a videotape role play or audiotape role play; (2) they present it to the group; (3) they have a shared, guided group interaction afterward.

Future Projection — The protagonist chooses a specific time and place in the future and acts out what he thinks will be happening to him at that time, first playing all the roles and then interacting with auxiliaries. It may be the best future, the worst future, the real future or as many futures until there is clarification.

First Experience — Developed by Ladeira, Weiner and Gottlieb, this focuses on first memories or contact with an alcoholic person, and how that experience has affected us. *Exercise 1*: Get in contact with the first word associated with alcoholism. Was it positive or negative? Were there any distinct physical characteristics? Focus on an image of an alcoholic in your mind and draw a diagram or picture that represents your idea of the alcoholic. Choose a partner and explain this picture. *Exercise 2*: Participants sit in a circle and close their eyes to relax. They recall their first drinking experience. When they are ready they share this information with the rest of the group.

Genogram — A sociometric chart of an individual's expanded family tree, this is a multi-generational history which emphasizes birth order, marriages, divorce, separations, sex, religions, occupations, deaths and communicational patterns within the family over several generations.

Genodrama — As developed by Barclay-Weiner, the protagonist chooses auxiliaries to play the parts of important family members (what a person's ancestors or progeny might be like). He then assigns characteristics to each auxiliary and interacts with them, either one at a time or simultaneously. At times he is permitted to say anything he wants to them and they are not permitted to respond. This relieves the individual of pent up rage and hostility, or permits him to say things he might not have had the opportunity to say while the person was within his social atom.

Group Role Reversal — The group counts off by ones and twos. All ones take a particular role (the alcoholic) and all twos take another role (the counselor). They have a dialogue for about five minutes. Then they "reverse roles," and the number twos become the alcoholic and the number ones become the counselors.

Magic Shop — Developed by Weiner, this is a diagnostic projective technique, often used as a warm-up with reluctant groups since it feels more like fun than reality. It is a place, feeling or dream that exists in the microcosm of the group. It is developed by individuals who project out loud what their "Magic Shop" would be like and what they would be like as the shopkeeper. The purchaser is encouraged to seek out something of value for himself and to leave, in a transaction or barter with the shopkeeper, those things of value he no longer can use.

Make a Person — Developed by Weiner, Drucker and Massi, the protagonist visits the "People Bank" which contains every imaginable physical and emotional characteristic which might be needed to construct a human being — eyes, smiles, frowns, good feelings, bad feelings, courage, shyness, etc. The protagonist chooses specific characteristics that he wants to construct the ideal person. It affords a feeling of safety since no definite positive or negative qualities have to be attributed to anyone chosen. It also readily involves the highly negative person and brings out alternatives.

Mirror — An auxiliary ego (the director or a group member) plays the role of an individual as the individual appeared to him, imitating his actions, responses and manners. This gives the individual the opportunity to "observe himself," somewhat like looking in a mirror. It helps objectivity in evaluating behavior and making a constructive change.

Mirror of the Self — The protagonist looks into an actual mirror and asks himself what he wants to do in a given situation, then takes the role of the face in the mirror and answers himself. (This is particularly helpful with individuals who talk in terms of "If I do this, then Mary or Sam will. . . I would like to. . . But the kids will. . .") It is also useful in separating oneself from "the caretaking of others" pattern because the process demands staying with yourself (one step removed), and demonstrates how much we use others as an excuse to prevent our own self-fulfillment.

Monodrama — Referred to as the self-presentation technique. The role player enacts all the roles in the scene; thus he conveys his impressions and may gain insight into playing all roles in an interaction. He discloses how others see his behavior, and the reasons why he received the reactions he did. When the role player shifts from one role to another, he is instructed to change his actions and mannerisms to fit the role of the other person. This technique is useful in broadening perspectives and increasing spontaneity.

Multiple Role Playing — The multiple role play post-enactment process is characterized by the following sequence: (1) A data round-up where each role playing group is asked to state the outcome of the role play (usually tallied on a blackboard as each group reports). (2) Questions such as: What decision was made? Were role players more or less satisfied than at the start? (3) A report from each group as to the reasons and/or the rationale for the outcome. (4) A class discussion in which the varying outcomes and their supporting reasons are compared and contrasted.

Nonverbal Role Playing — Situations are enacted completely

nonverbally. This technique is especially effective when the
subject expresses himself verbally, or is excessively talkative in
the session, or where the director feels there is a need for the
person to get more physically involved.

One Word Circle — Each group member gives one word which
explains how he is reacting at this moment. This is a good
warm-up technique. It gets individuals in touch with each
other both physically and emotionally by having them stand
with arms around each other in the circle and experience how
the other person is feeling.

Playback, Tape-O-Drama or *Replay* — These are forms of
structured role playing. The action is either taped or video
recorded; people may watch themselves in action, and in some
cases set up scenes in psycho-soap opera style; or reality testing
situations—playing them back and evaluating what happened.

Power Game — In this structured technique, each person in the
group writes his or her name on a piece of paper. The names
are placed in a hat, and the person whose name is drawn is
given absolute power over the group for an arbitrary length of
time: to request or do whatever he chooses, with cooperation of
the group being part of the contract. This exercise is useful for
individuals unwilling to take responsibility, and for making
clear self-limitations which individuals employ in self-denial.

Pressure Circle — The protagonist is encircled by other members
of the group who grasp arms and hands, and pressure the protagonist in the middle—trying to keep him there—not letting
him escape. He then tries to break out from the circle by any
method he sees fit. He may name his particular pressures as he
experiences them in life, or they may be "the" nebulous
pressure. If the individual finds this kind of interaction difficult with people, chairs may be used to symbolize the same
pressure circle, and he gets rid of them in any way he wishes. A
variation is the Plunging In Circle where the protagonist throws
himself spontaneously into a circle of people representing the
physical equivalent of his inner feelings.

Problem Clinic — This provides time for some introspection, as
well as some perception of dilemmas and attitudes, and can act

as an icebreaker. It is more successful in a large than a small group. Everyone reverses roles with his immediate supervisor and assumes his role; then chooses one, two or three other people in the room and sits down with them (either on the floor or around a table) and gives the following instructions: "We want you to imagine that this is a problem clinic where you have come to talk about the man you have sent to this workshop (in other words, yourself as seen through your supervisor's eyes). Explain what you would like him to obtain from the workshop and what you think your relationship with him is now. Discuss any problems he may have." Allow this to go for about fifteen minutes. Then each person tells his experience or asks the group to share the experience as they understand it. Typically the reports will indicate problem areas needing further role play. The original role playing therefore advances more easily into a psychodrama experience.

Progression Game — Developed by Ladeira, Weiner and Gottlieb, this is used to prepare patients for re-entry into the community from a hospitalized setting. On the premise that by purchasing alcohol a person also obtains illusions as to what he thinks will accompany that drink, this technique is set in a liquor store. The buyer makes purchases not with money, but with cards that represent items necessary for maintaining his present lifestyle. Roles are: Buyer, Seller and Rationalizer. The protagonist is then put into the following scenes which were chosen for their pressure value on the newly recovered alcoholic. *Scene one:* The Homecoming. The family prepares for the return of the alcoholic from his first hospitalization. After a few moments of interaction, the alcoholic walks in. Roles are: Alcoholic, Spouse, Oldest child, Youngest child. *Scene two:* The Do Drop Inn. The alcoholic's favorite "haunt" where he expects profuse congratulations from his former drinking buddies for returning on the scene sober. Instead, he unexpectedly receives indifference, ridicule and rejection from those he thought were his friends. He begins to experience the role shock that accompanies a major change in lifestyle. Roles are: Alcoholic, Bartender, Bar Fly, Drinking Buddies, Visitor. *Scene three:* The Job Interview.

The boss's office in the second week of the alcoholic employee's
return from the hospital. Roles are: Supervisor, Alcoholic.

Projection — The protagonist enacts the situation as he would
ideally like it to be, showing us how he would "wish" people
would act, or things would be in the situation. This acts as a
positive *catharsis*.

Psychodrama Dolls — People in the group have also made their
own psychodrama dolls. The reverse of having a baby doll, we
have "Mommy Dolls" and "Daddy Dolls;" a modern day
voodoo doll was also developed by Weiner in conjunction with
Gil Shay of the Fashion Institute of Technology.

Psychomime — A guest lecturer (Jacqueline Rouard, International Institute of Mime, New York City) at our alcoholism
counselor training group mimed a woman's struggle as to
whether or not to drink; in her silent enactment she poured her
drink away and received applause from the group. She had the
group break into smaller units and mime being at a party and
being offered a drink. The following reactions ensued: people
came to the director to report "she doesn't know what she is doing;" some left angry; others refused to take a drink in the
enactment; some decided not to go to the party; some asked for
a nonalcoholic drink; some liked being tested; some saw only
one alternative.

Recorder Technique — The group greet each other nonverbally
in their chosen manner (shaking hands, hugging, ignoring,
etc.) for two or three minutes. Everyone chooses one other person
(again nonverbally) with whom they feel they can communicate.
The pairs sit down in a comfortable place in the room. The
partners count off clockwise in ones and twos. All the number
ones tell the number twos what they wish them to know about
themselves (no longer than five minutes). The number twos act
as silent recorders and observe the number ones' movements,
tones of voice, overall presentation. At the end of the five
minutes, we ask who would like to see themselves as they appeared in the other person's eyes. The number twos show the
group what they think the number ones are like, mirroring
them. This technique is not only a good warm-up and fun, and

informative for the members of the group, but provides an abundance of material for the director to work with in the role playing session that follows.

Robot — Each assumes the position of a robot (arms folded across chest, body stiff, eyes closed). They have no feelings and can only follow instructions. The director instructs them to take small, shuffling steps forward and backward and, if bumping into another robot, change direction immediately; gradually they go in different directions (sideways, in a circle, moving faster and faster); then halt. Standing still, they are asked to realize that they want to be alive...feel the space around them, enjoy this space...explore their physical being and experience how their body feels...then to move around the room and if they bump into another person to shake hands...to shake as many hands as they can find...then to become more expansive and give each person they meet a hug...get as many hugs as they can from as many people as they can. To then open their eyes and look at where they are. Usually a great deal of laughter and sense of feeling alive pervades the room.

Role Reversal — Exchanging of roles where A takes the role of B and B takes the role of A, allows each a look at the other person's point of view. Distortions of perception regarding the other person's role may be exposed, dealt with and corrected. This and the mirror technique are most effective in teaching change of attitudes and behavior.

Role Rotation — This is similar to the single role play. When a number of persons rotate in one role, they tend to be more willing to participate in role playing. It is particularly effective for teaching the techniques related to various forms of interview involving discipline, grievance handling and communications. In writing a role play, the following points should be kept in mind: relevance to the trainee; comprehensibility; identifiability; role maneuverability; focus; conflict. Some of the areas that could be structured are: attempts to deny the problem, efforts to escape, how to seek outside help, loss of self-worth, and feelings of failure.

Self-presentation — The subject plays the roles of all the important people in the situation he presents. This is a most useful technique when in a one-to-one relationship with a protagonist. He can become his own auxiliary ego, leaving you free to be him or remain out of the action.

Silent Auxiliary Ego — Activities are suggested by gesture rather than by speech, similar to pantomime. Advantages are support, help for the uncooperative patient, and restoration of mental vitality.

Situation Test — Three people from the audience volunteer to leave the room for a few minutes and return to react to predetermined situations (set up in their absence). After the three have retired, the group think of a situation that might be of interest to all and could test the spontaneity of those people not in the room. The excluded individuals are brought into the room one at a time and put into the predetermined situation. Afterwards, the group and the protagonist discuss the different reactions and responses. This reveals the preparatory reactions of behavior, and the spontaneity reaction when behavior is undetermined in advance.

Social Atom Technique — The protagonist sets up and names chairs to represent the important others in his social atom — or parts of himself. He sits in each chair and plays these different parts (or chooses people from the group to represent these people, or different parts of himself and has them sit in respective chairs and respond). The protagonist places the chairs in proper relationship to himself as he sees them. He may show where he would ideally like them to be. He can tell each person what he wants them to know, but does not have the opportunity or the courage to tell them in reality.

Soliloquy — This is an aside from the action in which the role player expresses his covert feelings about the situation, such as "I feel nervous." It may either be a part of the enactment in a continuous flow, or the action may be stopped while the subject expresses his feelings.

Surplus Reality — This is an over-emphasis technique. To increase the impact of a given enactment, people are asked to overplay various roles. This increases tensions which were part of the original situation, and enables the participants to let them-

selves go and become more aware of interpersonal relations.
Telephone Therapy Technique — Sometimes in the middle of a psychodrama session, when individuals need to speak to significant others who were not present, we phone them, let the conversation take place, and role play it afterwards.
What I Like About Me — This is used in small groups (4-6 people each) or subgroups of this size in a larger group. Each person in the group goes around in turn and states: What I like about myself (no more than two, no less than one). What I want to change about myself or what I don't like (same number as above). What I like, or react positively to, in the person to my right (or, all relate to one person in the group until all have been talked about).

FOOTNOTES

1. Robert W. Rasor, "Drug Addiction: An Acting Out Problem," in *Acting Out*, eds. Lawrence Abt and Stuart Weisman (New York: Grune & Stratton, 1963).
2. V. H. Vogl, H. Isbell, and K. W. Chapman, "Present Status of Narcotic Addiction with Particular Reference to Medical Indications and Comparative Addiction Liability of the Newer and Older Analgesic Drugs," *J.A.M.A.* 138 (1948).
3. C. K. Himmelsbach and L. F. Small, "Clinical Studies of Drug Addiction," *Public Health Report Supplement* (1937): 125.
4. Rasor, "Drug Addiction," p. 110.
5. Sidney Cohen, unpublished paper on health care professionals and their training in the treatment of the alcoholic and drug addict.
6. These sections are the joint effort of Marilyn Middleton, protagonist and alcoholism counselor, and Hannah B. Weiner, Director, Center for Experiential Learning. The quoted passage is the personal statement of Ms. Middleton.
7. A. Silber, "Psychotherapy with Alcoholics," *Journal of Nervous and Mental Disorders* 129 (1959): 447–85.
8. D. A. Hofrichter, "The Experience of Community in the Psychodramatic Technique of Sharing: An Existential-Phenomenological Investigation," *Group Psychotherapy and Psychodrama* 26, no. 304 (1973): 88–100.
9. One of the steps is the A. A. program, where members try to help other alcoholics take steps toward sobriety.
10. Maxwell N. Weisman, "Treatment of Alcoholism and Drug Abuse," unpublished paper, 1973.
11. Jacob L. Moreno, *Who Shall Survive?*, 2d ed. (New York: Beacon, 1953).

R. E. SHUTTLEWORTH is principal family therapist at The Family Institute, Cardiff, Wales. Actively involved in training workshops in Britain and Europe, he has had extensive clinical experience in group therapy, including drama therapy, and is chairman of the British Association for Dramatherapy.

Chapter 11

ADOLESCENT DRAMA THERAPY

R. E. Shuttleworth

1 INTRODUCTION

In this chapter, I wish to show how drama therapy can be adapted to meet the special demands of disturbed adolescents in a modified therapeutic community.

At Long Grove Hospital, Epsom, Surrey, we have twenty in-patients and ten day patients who attend our own special school and take part in an extensive therapeutic program.

We deal with the whole gamut of psychiatric complaints: psychotics, depressives, all forms of neurosis and organic brain damage. School refusal is a major problem of a large proportion of our clients. While we take some clients with behavior disorders, we limit them to those with heavy neurotic overlay as we seem to have less success with the more straightforward delinquent. This is probably because we have such an open system with limited controls.

Three years ago I wrote about my drama sessions at the Adolescent Unit.[1] At that time there was very little formal therapy, and the therapeutic atmosphere was in the very early stage of development. That period was characterized by great anxiety, suspicion and, sometimes, hostility by both staff and adolescents to my form of formal treatment, including drama therapy. The anxiety was illustrated by the frequent flight from sessions by some members of the group when the tension became too great. I had little opportunity to work directly on an individual group problem. I therefore devised more indirect ways. Each session was primarily an entity in

157

itself with little chance of relating it to an integrated community program. It should be said that many of our clients did resolve their difficulties, but slowly and painfully.

Our present community has evolved a much more integrated and elaborate treatment program. While medication is used to relieve excessive anxiety, depression and psychotic symptoms, the keystone to treatment is psychotherapy. Each adolescent gets compulsory weekly individual supportive therapy, small talking groups twice weekly, and family therapy. First thing each morning, there is a community meeting chaired by an adolescent. This meeting concentrates upon the day to day problems arising in the community. Some of the adolescents attend a social skills group as well, where appropriate ways of expressing feelings are encouraged and learned. This group is designed "for the more socially constipated" individual.

Unlike the above, the drama therapy group is voluntary and is attended by an average of ten adolescents weekly for one hour. We attempt to plug in to the existing therapeutic milieu, and use the unique characteristics of drama therapy to explore, elaborate and, hopefully, resolve some of the material which arises.

Our model for the therapeutic community is that set up by Maxwell Jones.[2] To the best of my knowledge, he was the earliest practitioner of drama therapy techniques in Britain. He used a form of sociodrama to rehabilitate ex-prisoners of war. Our small groups tend to be group analytic; that is, we try to concentrate on intragroup events and regard as secondary any material brought in from outside.[3] Family therapy is also group analytic, and in this field our great source of inspiration has been Robin Skynner.[4] With the development of the therapeutic community, there has been considerable emphasis on the doctrine of the multidisciplinary team. This approach has allowed us to speed up the treatment. Each adolescent stays on average four months, which gives greater job satisfaction to the staff and helps to create a positive therapeutic milieu. This is reflected in drama therapy where problems can be looked at directly; also the group feels secure, and individuals do not have to resort to leaving the group frequently.

My approach to drama therapy is eclectic. There has been increasing enthusiasm for group techniques in Britain over the last ten years, but there are few rigid schools of thought.[5] I received my training at Foulkes' Institute of Group Analysis, and I was introduced to action techniques by Sue Jennings. At her Remedial Drama Centre, we experimented with different techniques, and Moreno's psychodrama was particularly valuable. Veronica Sherbourne's movement work was also used, together with aspects of encounter, Gestalt, Transactional Analysis and behavior therapy. I feel that any drama therapy should incorporate the best of the other movements in a drama context.

Drama therapy has many advantages over the conventional talking group. This becomes particularly evident with less verbal clients, such as disturbed adolescents and chronic patients. It is often easier to act out conflicts and so initiate new ways of coping than it is to talk about them.

The major difficulty with drama therapy is that it makes great demands upon the therapist's creativity, and there is the danger of the therapist being drained of his energies. I find, therefore, that I can only use drama therapy sparingly and that now and then I need to retreat to the relative tranquility of a talking group for my own state of mind.

I use drama therapy: (a) as part of the inpatient therapeutic media; (b) in staff training sessions; (c) in small talking groups, particularly in open-ended outpatient groups; and (d) as an adjunct to family therapy with outpatients and inpatients.

2 DRAMA THERAPY IN THE ADOLESCENT THERAPEUTIC COMMUNITY

The group processes in a community are always multi-dimensional, and it is difficult to perceive specific themes and answers to these without seeming overly simplistic. However, occasionally events do seem clear. The following description of a recent two week period in our community will illustrate the inter-relationships of our therapeutic program and the special contribution of drama therapy.

The compulsory, small, weekly talking group had two primary

therapists, myself and a psychiatrist (John), supported by at least two female co-therapists.

Many of the group members shared either an absent or poor father figure. For example: Mike, 13, came to us with depression, uncontrollable tempers and delinquency, and his father was a chronic paranoid schizophrenic who showed great inconsistency in the handling of his son; Richard, 14, lived with his divorced mother and two sisters, and was a cross dresser with encopresis; Hazel, 15, also lived with her divorced mother, came to us with severe depression following an abortion, and had many confused feelings about men; Colin, 14, suffered from mania which was partially controlled by medication — at the time, he lived with his aunt because his divorced mother was herself manic-depressive and had had another breakdown; Clare, 15, and David, 13, were both school refusers with weak fathers and very anxious mothers; Dick, 16, was a schizophrenic whose father was chronically disabled with the same condition and treated him very inconsistently; Nick, 16, a school refuser with an alcoholic father; and finally, Piers, 15, a psychopathic boy with the genetically based Klinefelter's syndrome.

This small talking group had been going through a relatively quiet period when John, my co-therapist, went on holiday for three weeks. The first session after his departure was full of hostility, largely directed against me, and led by Mike, Richard and David. It started mainly as castrating aggression: "you're weak," "you're a poof" (homosexual), "you're not as good a therapist as John." In the next session, the attack developed into a struggle for power, with Mike as the major protagonist demanding that the group alter its structure by having a changeover of group members and therapists. I saw this behavior as an attempt to test my strength and consistency. By the third session, the relatively good humor of much of the aggression had turned sour, and there was a lot of depressive anger with long uncomfortable silences. Periods of shared group feeling like this are magical moments in therapy. I felt the time had come to relate the group's feelings about the absent group "father" to their own home situation by trying to verbalize for them their anger, depression, frustration and confusion about controls. I feel that interpretations with adolescents should be kept to a minimum, be straight-forward and made at the "right" moment. The group fell into a depressed silence punctuated by occasional short angry outbursts. Many were close to tears. At the end of the session Mike, Richard and David came up to me and pushed and kicked me in a semi-playful way.

Over this same period, the adolescents had shown various disturbances within the community. Clare, Hazel and Piers had absconded for a night, David refused several times to attend the Unit school, Colin had multiple psychosomatic symptoms, while Richard and Mike went to a local pub and returned drunk. The most disturbed behavior was shown by Robin, a 12 year old, who was in another small talking group, and who had come to us following a number of fire-raising incidents. Robin had been rejected by both his parents who live separately, and he was expecting to have his future decided at a family session straight after the drama therapy group.

That day, before drama therapy, there was a community meeting attended by the consultant psychiatrist in charge of the Unit. The law was heavily laid down, with the threat of suspension for further wrong doing. This was met with angry bravado by a number of the boys.

By the time of the drama therapy session, the adolescents were feeling a great deal of anger and showing a lot of acting out that tested the limits of our control. This was related to two factors: the feeling of rejection raised by John's departure on holiday; and to their identification with Robin and his impending family meeting. While the verbal group had allowed some opportunity to examine the emerging feelings there was still much that had not been resolved.

Somewhat to my surprise, virtually all my small talking group came to the drama therapy session. I had thought, with all the negative feelings in the community, largely directed at myself, that they might stay away.

As the group arrived, there was much hyperactivity with verbal and physical aggression being expressed to each other and the staff. It was obvious that they were not in a psychological state for a direct look at what was troubling them. My co-therapist suggested that we should do some physical containment work. The group readily agreed to this, and Mike insisted that he be first. He lay on his back, and the group knelt beside him to press him down while he tried to get up. Each member of the group took turns, and then they insisted that they should do it to me. Remembering the physical attack of a few days ago, I felt rather vulnerable and so discreetly asked a staff member to supervise. They used a lot of extra effort to keep me down, and expressed great glee when I did not succeed in moving; however, no harm came to me. Then we did some standing containment, with the group surrounding one individual with his shoes off; he tried to get out without using his feet or hands. Again, all the group took turns. After these exercises, which lasted about ten minutes, there was a more relaxed mood. As there was still some residual excessive energy despite the strenuous beginning, we played the "catch and bounce game": the group forms two lines and pairs off with hands linked; they try to catch an individual who runs up the line, jumps onto the arms forming a passage, and is then bounced along the line.

The group was now tired and contained, and ready for some trust work. One member asked for the "caring" exercise which he had done in the past. In complying I tried to pair an adolescent with an adult because it is easy for this exercise to be ruined with horse-play. One of the pair sat on the ground and was supported by his partner who knelt behind him, and gently manipulated his arms and head. The pair then changed places and repeated the exercise. (This is one of a number of trust-inducing exercises that I use. I feel that basic trust is a pre-verbal phenomenon and can be most easily established through nonverbal means.)

The group then asked for a game. Dick, who was not very popular and often bullied others, offered to show us one. The group accepted, and Dick put us into a circle for a "suggestibility" game where he "talked" a member of the group (with his eyes shut) off the end of a diving board, with the rest of us there to catch him. The circular shape of the group demonstrated their increased cooperation: we were now standing and working together. It is also interesting to note that the spontaneous theme of the game had to do with control.

I was now ready to let the group relax and let them leave with good feelings. But, to my surprise, Robin asked if he could dramatize his family meeting which was to follow this session. He gave members of the group the roles of his rejecting father, stepmother, social worker and, after he had decided to play one of the family therapists (a much safer position), he asked me to play his role. The rest of the group was invited to represent one of the characters if they felt they could say what they were thinking — that is, by placing their hand on the shoulder of the character and speaking in the first person in the classic psychodramatic way. Hazel, David and Michael were particularly active, concentrating upon Robin's feelings towards his father. They expressed a lot of aggression towards Robin's father for being so rejecting. Some group members found this too emotive and left the group. Robin (in his role of therapist) was able to say, however, that his father probably had many problems himself and that this explained his behavior, rather than because Robin was unlovable and rightfully rejected. He said that Robin should learn to accept this and live his own independent life.

We had only a few minutes left at the end of the session. The group looked very thoughtful, and we all were rather exhausted. Of course, the events just described were only part of what will hopefully be the resolution of some of the group members' conflicts, and this process will take years. What I hope has emerged from the description is not only the way in which drama therapy has been used in conjunction with other therapies but also its unique contribution. At an individual level, we were able to work in some depth with a basically nonverbal and highly defensive boy and, because the situation fitted in with the shared group feeling, our work was able to partially resolve their conflicts. After the session, the community seemed much quieter, and most of the acting out stopped. At other times, when the community is more relaxed, we can move straight away into a direct approach.

3 SCULPTURING

An effective way of learning how the adolescent sees his world is to use sculpturing techniques. He is invited to schematically set out "my life," using either inanimate objects in the room or other

group members. He is asked to place elements around a chair
that represents himself. He uses the spatial distances to indicate
emotional stress — that is, the stronger the positive emotional feeling the closer the element is to him. Wastepaper bins are used as
the rubbish in "my life," while ashtrays on radiators may indicate
people he would like to burn in hell. Large chairs represent fat or
powerful people. When people are used as elements, they are
positioned and manipulated so that they show their feelings nonverbally — that is, anger by the waving of a fist, love by holding,
rejection by pushing away or turning the back. Besides allowing
the sculptor to work through some of his unresolved conflicts, this
exercise also supplies material for both the adolescent and the
therapist to take into his next family therapy session.

For example, Colin, the manic boy, normally found it difficult
to verbalize his confusions, particularly over whom he should live
with. He moved to his relatives whenever his mother was ill, and
back to her when she had recovered. This was very unsettling. His
sculpture consisted of a small cushion with a football (his favorite
pastime) sitting on top of it to represent himself. Close to his left
was a single chair representing his mother. To his right, and only
a little further away than his mother, were two chairs representing his uncle and aunt with whom he now lived. Far away to the
right, facing the wall, was a single chair indicating his absent
father whom he had not seen for several years. Colin was invited
to sit in the different positions and become the various characters.
Through these improvisations he was able to experience some of
their feelings, as well as to work on his conflict over whether he
should live with his vulnerable mother or his healthier relatives.
He was then asked to rearrange his sculpture to show us how he
would like his life to be. He opted to push his relatives well away
so that his close tie was with his mother whose illness he had
banished. His father was brought closer because he would like to
see more of him and forgive him for going away. Other members
of the group also rearranged the sculpture, some opting to push
the mother away and have him stay with the relatives, because
they felt it was unrealistic to expect Colin's mother ever to be well.
Eventually Colin accepted this position if time was to prove that
his mother's condition could not be stabilized.

The group therapist may sculpt the individual's life as the group members have observed him in the community, or he may take some part of the sculpture and psychodramatize it. With an individual who is reluctant to sculpt his life because of shyness, we get one of the group to fantasize his life with a sculpture. This not only gives that individual some feedback on the impression he makes, but invariably leads him to rearrange the sculpture to fit his perceived reality.

4   COMMUNITY EXERCISE

In teaching professional groups some elements of group dynamics, I have found drama therapy techniques very useful in speeding up the process. Even in a short two hour session, a lot can be explored. I developed exercises which allow the whole group to participate and also build up trust so that the group allows the social defenses, particularly their fixed roles, to be lowered. There is some irony, I feel, in the (sometimes) heavily defensive nature of verbalization, particularly with a group in its early stages of development, when this is a major tool of a talking group.

Usually, I start these groups with an action warm-up, follow it with some nonverbal trust work of the sort described earlier, and then devise a "community" game. Mostly I get the group to play the game without verbal communication. Later, some limited verbalization may be permitted. Finally, in the sharing segment, we use group sculptures and see what has happened.

In a two hour session with a group of sixty social workers, who had already been divided into five ad hoc groups three days previously, I turned the groups into tribes. Then I asked them to establish their villages and do whatever they felt like for the next hour (except to verbalize). What emerged (to be examined in the feedback) were many aspects that normally take a long time to crystallize in verbal groups, such as leadership struggles, sexual and other stereotypes, group defenses against anxiety, and the individual's way of coping with his personal space.

I have been able to use modifications of this "community" exercise with adolescents by limiting their nonverbalization to just a few minutes. They have created separate communities with limited verbalization (e.g. communication limited to one-word statements) so that the individual has to think carefully about what he wants to say and does not drown us in defensive verbiage. On occasions, when a group is very unsettled, we may just verbally fantasize a community. For example, one group was very angry and negative after one of the community had had feces placed in his bed. For the first twenty minutes of drama therapy, the group had just copped out — telling dirty jokes and not responding to any direction. I suggested that we should escape by going to a desert island. The rest of the session was spent discussing what we would take with us, who we would live with, who would lead us, and what rules we would follow. Despite the verbalization, the group was able to look in a safe way at many of the aspects that can be more directly examined in an adult group.

There are some problems with troubled adolescents which are often difficult to tackle directly even in a good therapeutic situation. Two of the more prominent are the re-emerging oedipal complex (used in this context as a general term for both males and females) and death.

While my background has taught me to have an open mind about classic psychoanalytic theory, I find the oedipal concept a good model to explain what I have often seen in different therapy groups, particularly in family therapy. Even if we do not accept the more poetic theories of Freud, it seems natural that the parents should be used as a model and sounding board for sexual feelings. While these usually unconscious sexual needs for the parent of the opposite sex are common to all adolescents, in the disturbed adolescent there may be imbalancing forces in the family which make the resolution of this difficulty more acute. These forces could be a weak, seductive, ill or overly dependent parent, or the one parent family. In the therapeutic community, these oedipal feelings will often be displaced onto one or more members of the staff in their role of surrogate parent. If this relationship is better balanced and less ambiguous than their home relationships, the disturbed adolescent is often able, at least partly, to resolve his feelings.

This is one area which, in my experience, it is virtually impossible to interpret directly. Yet, apart from the natural informal resolution that comes about through the community relationships within the family therapy session, attempts will be made to ease ambiguous relationships and restore the parent to the parental role. Case histories show that drama therapy techniques can also help to resolve this conflict. Linda (15) was a girl who had lived in children's homes from the age of eleven. She could not be contained at home because of her extreme hostility towards her mother. Linda's father was rather ambiguously, and probably unconsciously, seductive toward Linda, and a form of oedipal confusion was one way of construing Linda's difficulties. Linda attended the formal drama therapy session in her first few weeks at the Adolescent Unit, but played a relatively passive role. She was in my small talking group and, from the way she behaved towards me, had developed a strong positive transference. This attitude towards male figures had been characteristic during all her placements away from home, whilst she had often shown strong negative transference towards adult female figures. Indeed, her admission to our Unit had been precipitated by a physical attack upon the headmistress of her school. Linda had been benefitting from the social skills group where appropriate ways of showing feelings were being explored. Following one such session, Linda attended the small talking group and turned it into a drama therapy group. She began by separating me off from the rest of the group and announcing that we were married, that she was pregnant, and she needed money to buy clothes for the baby. The group allowed the fantasy to continue but with some rather anxious giggling. Linda showed great affection towards me and elaborated on our domestic life. My co-therapist (Pam) was ignored during this fantasy and then, suddenly, Linda turned on her saying that Pam had hurt her earlier that day. Pam protested that she had gently tugged her hair as a sign of greeting. Linda would not accept this explanation, but she calmed down when Pam said gently that she had no reason to hurt Linda because she liked her. Gary, one of the more hard-headed boys, then brought Linda back to the fantasy, and injected some reality by saying that I was married, Linda was too young and yielding to daydreams.

We were thus able to play out a form of oedipal relationship within the safety of the group. While Linda had enjoyed the fantasy of pairing off with the father figure, and tried aggressively to push away the mother figure, she had been treated with warmth and understanding by this mother figure (unlike the usual negative response from her real mother) which increased her anxiety and guilt. This session provided the groundwork for attempting to work on her family relationships.

Linda's first family session followed soon after this, and we used a conventional talking group format. (I use drama therapy sparingly in family therapy because it can, on occasion, create too much tension for clients in an already high anxiety state.) I tried to adapt her experience in the "oedipal drama" to this session. A start was made by making Linda's father show his feelings towards her in a less ambiguous and seductive way. We also reinforced the more realistic and positive aspects of a relationship between father and daughter. As Linda had worked through some of her guilt and anxiety towards her mother, she no longer needed to react in an aggressive way. She was able tearfully to show warmth towards her, and apologize for her past behavior. In a subsequent small talking group, a lot of angry feelings were expressed towards me which suggested that some re-alignment was taking place.

I hope this description shows (1) that the adolescent who is used to drama therapy technique can spontaneously bring it into another setting, in this case, a small talking group; (2) that he can test out an important conflict — in this case, an oedipal need without the therapist directly interpreting the action, which might only lead to the mobilization of a massive defense system. The essential reality testing was provided by another adolescent, and this same message will be extrapolated to the family setting, usually with the adolescent himself making the cognitive jump; and (3) that those members who are, in a sense, mere spectators to the drama will, perhaps, see something of themselves and, therefore work through some of their own oedipal needs.

Death is a subject most of us find difficult to cope with, and the adolescent perhaps more so. He or she often needs to work through it indirectly. During a recent drama therapy session, I had a professional visitor and used her as the protagonist. The group took turns to fantasize about her by doubling. I used one of the group's fantasies of our visitor to build up a family. The visitor was made the wife, I the husband, and an unpopular boy, Marcus, the dead grandfather (buried under some cushions) and the rest of the group various children. I then invited them to put some life into the characters, and the drama developed into a situation involving rebellious children. After about ten minutes, I was feeling uncomfortable about Marcus' isolation. When I remarked about poor grandfather, one of the group said that I could die as well and join him. This I did. From my position on the floor under the cushions, it suddenly struck me, perhaps partly from the comments being directed my way, that both the two major participants were having to cope with the problem of death. One was Andrew, 16, a long term school refuser who, after the recent death of his father, had become depressed and suicidal. He had not come to terms with his loss. Robert, 15, had parents who were still alive, but both suffered severe illnesses which could lead to their deaths at any time.

Robert reacted to this appalling situation by stealing and hyperactive behavior in an attempt to thinly disguise a severe depression. Neither had been able to directly talk about his feelings. From my position on the floor I directed the group's attention towards us. Andrew and Robert were able to express many of their own feelings about death, in particular the anger they felt both in regard to the loss, the feelings of rejection and their impotence to do anything about it. This was expressed verbally and sometimes non-verbally by kicking at us (usually hitting the cushions). Some affectionate feelings were expressed too. This came out of the aggression where an attack would lead to wrestling which would lead to holding (a safe way for boys with anxieties about their sexual identities to experience physical affection from males).

During the feedback I tried to relate more directly their own dilemmas to the drama and was met with denials that it had concerned them. I felt they were rather unconvincing in their answers and that they had partly worked on some of their feelings and that maybe a start had been made on an eventual resolution.

I have tried to describe just some of the drama therapy techniques that can be used with disturbed adolescents. While I have
found many ideas in the writings of authors like Sue Jennings[6]
and Howard Blatner,[7] I found with increasing experience that I
was more able to allow the group to draw on its own creativity, to
come up with themes to work on — to a point that some of the
group may become better drama therapists than the group leaders. Certainly they are expert critics and are not slow to let us
know when we have failed them and, more rarely, they can be
fulsome in their praise.

5   STAFF GROUPS

Once a week, available staff attends a drama therapy session
primarily to examine the groups. We concentrate on sculpturing.
Initially, the objects are very concrete: for example, the individuals in family therapy are placed in chairs with some attention to
their spacing and physical posture. Later, we try to extend our
perception and sculpt more creatively — for example, with a dom-
inant mother sitting literally on top of the person playing the
adolescent. After the sculptor has placed the elements in the
sculpture, the persons representing the elements are asked to tell
us how they feel in their roles. Particular attention is paid to any
strain or tension from their postural stance. The co-therapist will
then make modifications to the sculpture. There are often quite
surprising variations in the co-therapist's perceptions. To look at
group process, the therapist walks into the center of the sculpture
and tries spontaneously to tell us what atmosphere he feels. Finally, the sculpture will be re-arranged to show us what the therapist
is aiming for in his sessions.

An important aspect of these sessions is to encourage staff communication. Where tensions exist between therapists, the group
will consciously or unconsciously use these to defend themselves
against working off their own difficulties. Action techniques
facilitate this feedback by allowing the individual who has difficulty in expressing his feelings to show them directly by nonverbal means (e.g. if the co-therapist is placed on a chair towering
over the group, a very clear statement is made about his domi-

nance); or, by having the individual talk through another, he may be able to verbalize much more freely. In my experience, this has always been positive and supportive to the team.

6 OUTPATIENT DRAMA THERAPY

With our community nurse, I run an open-ended group for adolescents whose disturbance is not severe enough to merit treatment in our inpatient community. Our clients stay in the group for about six months, and decide for themselves when they want to leave. Because we have a small room in a crowded clinic, the opportunities for very active drama therapy are limited, so it is basically a talking group with a group analytic bias. Some drama therapy techniques, however, are used at times. Two of these are:

(1) The "button" technique. This is a modification of group sculpting. The individual sculpts his life using buttons (or other small objects) as elements in his life. The size of the buttons, the special relationships and general shape of his sculpture are all looked at. As new people are continually coming into the group, it is a very effective method of getting to know them without having to resort to excessive verbalization which they may find difficult because of shyness or poor verbal ability.

(2) We use simple role reversal with people in the group, or ask each person to become a member of their family and continue in the group within that role. This task may be facilitated by masks which can easily be made with scraps of paper, quickly drawing a face, pushing out the eyes and holding it up to the face.

7 CONCLUSION

I have described drama therapy as an important adjunct to other, more verbal therapies in the treatment of disturbed adolescents and their families, as well as having an important function in staff training and communication. It could be argued that drama therapy, because it works directly on the many aspects of communication including the verbal, is an essential treatment for those groups which, because of poorly developed ego structure, find verbal expression difficult.

FOOTNOTES

1. R. E. Shuttleworth, "Psychodrama with Disturbed Adolescents," in *Creative Therapy*, ed. Sue Jennings (London: Pitman, 1975), pp. 157–80.

2. Maxwell Jones, *Social Psychiatry in Practice* (Harmondsworth: Penguin, 1968); idem, "The Working of an Industrial Neurosis Unit, Preliminary Report," *Occupational Therapy and Rehabilitation* 26, no. 4 (1947): 213–21.

3. S. H. Foulkes and E. J. Anthony, *Group Psychotherapy: The Psychoanalytic Approach* (Harmondsworth: Penguin, 1957).

4. A. C. R. Skynner, "A Group Analytic Approach to Conjoint Family Therapy," *The Journal of Child Psychology and Psychiatry* 10 (1969): 81–106.

5. John Rowan, *Ordinary Ecstasy: Humanistic Psychology in Action* (London: Routledge & Kegan Paul, 1976).

6. Sue Jennings, *Remedial Drama* (London: Pitman, 1973).

7. Howard A. Blatner, *Psychodrama Role Playing and Action Methods* (New York: Beacon, 1973).

CLAIRE MICHAELS was a founding member of the Circle in the Square Theatre, New York City, and is a performer, painter, and an author. She has taught creative drama and Geriadrama in the United States and Canada. In 1976 she was awarded the American Theatre Association's Special Recognition Citation for drama with the elderly. Geriadrama is a trademark of Claire Michaels.

Chapter 12

GERIADRAMA®

Claire Michaels

"Imagination is the outreaching of minds . . . By the creative act . . . we are able to reach beyond our own death." —Rollo May

1 INTRODUCTION

Geriadrama is a name which has been coined to identify my work in drama presently being developed in nursing homes and recreation centers for senior citizens. It incorporates pantomime, kinesics, improvisation, body movement, transformation games, verbal, nonverbal and physical games in conjunction with poetry, music, scenes from plays and topical newspaper articles of interest to the elderly. Memory recalls are an important part of the work and are used to create imaginative scenes from the individual's past.

Geriadrama workshops are chiefly designed to help individuals and groups become oriented to more creative, constructive and satisfying lives. Whether the members are sick, senile, disabled, or severely deprived in some way through the aging process, the leader attempts to construct situations which offer enjoyment, ego reinforcement and, ultimately, the opportunity to build a stronger self-image. Frequently, the elderly underestimate their ability to do anything worthwhile, especially after arriving at a nursing home or rehabilitative institution. It is the function of Geriadrama to offer the supportive and educative environment that will make use of each individual's unique talents, however limited and minimal these may be. It is the leader's goal to help make the institution rehabilitative not debilitative.

175

The workshops do not have finished productions as a primary goal. The true value of Geriadrama lies in its participatory process. Though eventually a group may choose to perform for an audience, it is unnecessary to achieve the essential goals of Geriadrama. This does not preclude the possibility that the group, or several individuals in it, will wish to engage in a finished, improvisational product. This, too, can help to build a positive self-image for those who want to engage in dramatic play but have never had the opportunity to do so. Nevertheless, this is not the major focus of Geriadrama. Rather, it is the aim of the workshop to allow individuals, without fear of criticism or failure, to become freely involved in creative activities.

Geriadrama takes into account the fact that the elderly are no longer concerned with their previous daily life problems, but with making satisfactory adjustments to their limited future. This future is often accompanied by the loss of physical, mental and sexual power as a result of illness, bodily breakdown and the frequent rejection of the aged by a youth-oriented society. Geriadrama, therefore, does not seek primarily to teach for the future, but for the present — to involve all people regardless of their state of physical and mental health. It is a process of re-education and, thus, can be distinguished from creative dramatics for the young person which does seek to teach future life preparation.

The aged in nursing homes have a number of physical or mental deficiencies which limit their participation in the group to various degrees. The leader will, as a consequence, relate requests for movement and speech to the capacities of the participants. This applies whether group members need walkers, are confined to wheelchairs, or have suffered severe impairments in speech, hearing or sight. The leader makes it possible for these individuals to understand and follow simple directions. In the case of senior citizens' centers where people are usually more ambulatory and alert, there is much greater participation, with less dependence on the leader's guidance. However, in both nursing homes and recreation centers, the purpose of the workshops is to alleviate frustrations and tensions, while implementing dramatic activities which have therapeutic, recreational and experiential value.

As a therapeutic agent, the Geriadrama leader must help the aged rediscover and place their past in the context of their present. "Where has it all gone?" "What do I do now?" "Who cares?" they ask. And the answer must be that the retelling of their personal histories and memories makes them vital and alive human beings, and then they can find meaning and self-esteem. Simone de Beauvoir says:

> . . .each person in his heart preserves the conviction of having remained unalterable; when they summon their memories they justify this assertion. . .tirelessly they tell stories of this being that they were, this being that lives on inside them. . .they are a perpetual ex-service man. . .an adored, run-after woman, or a wonderful mother. . .they bring the bloom of their adolescent years to life again, their childhood. All their life, whether they are thirty or fifty or even eighty, they have escaped age.[1]

In this process of making, of sharing the history of their memories, wishes and dreams, of working with the magic of make-believe and dramatic play, the Geriadrama leader offers the aged a constructive outlet and the opportunity, as Rollo May has said, of "actualizing themselves."[2] There is much self-importance to be gained by listening and sharing one's own life history with others. There is also pride and joy and awareness to be gained. These are necessary for any human being. Thus, it is through drama—the key that unlocks the closed door of the past and gives meaning to the present—that the Geriadrama leader can attempt to reconstruct and rehabilitate the aged. By bringing more expression into their daily lives, he can tap the inner but dormant resources they may have believed long dead and past. Drama acts as the artistic agent to bring life to art and art to life.

2 WORK PROCEDURES

Rules

In order for the work to proceed smoothly, some necessary rules are explained to the group.

(1) There are to be no private conversations during the sessions—

except with a staff assistant who is aiding someone in the work, or if the patient is not well and in need of help.

(2) No personal hostilities are to occur in criticizing a fellow member's work. It is always more important to stress what is good than to find out what is "wrong."

(3) Each member of the group is asked to make a personal commitment (barring unforeseen emergencies) of spending at least one hour with the group, arriving on time, and being ready for work on arrival. (In the nursing home, staff should be informed of the workshop schedule so that people are medicated, dressed and on time.)

(4) Attendance in the workshop is not compulsory since it is essentially a recreational activity. There are times when a patient is urged by the staff to give the workshop a trial visit. If, after consultation with the leader, the patient and the recreation administrator, it is felt that no benefit is to be gained by the person's attendance, he will leave. At some future time, it may be suggested that he try again.

Materials

Generally materials are kept to a minimum since the work is of an improvisational nature. At each session, various devices are introduced for audiovisual aids: large, hand-printed, multi-colored posters (describing the themes of the day, poems, or body movement instructions), sound and music tapes, rhythm instruments and even children's toys. Other properties may include items that may be tasted, smelled or touched, photographs and bits of colored paper or cloth. Stage settings, lights, costumes and scripts are unnecessary but may be introduced to a senior citizens' group wishing to do a more formalized theatrical production.

Ideal Working Conditions

The time of day is optional, but mid-morning or early afternoon after rest time (in the nursing home after nursing care) when the person is freshest is preferable. It is stressed that all people attending should have had some previous exposure or orientation before entering an ongoing group. Sessions must be scheduled regularly for a satisfactory level of progress and interest in the work to be maintained. Ideally, the size of the group should not exceed fifteen members, with twenty as the maximum. If there are more, then time spent in going around the circle for individual responses tends to drag, and members fail to maintain their attention span and energy level.

Physical Needs

(1) Adequate space for a circle of chairs and wheelchairs.

(2) A tape recorder for record keeping, and for playing of sound and music tapes, should be provided at every session.

(3) There should be no interruptions, loudspeakers or telephone calls, and a sign should be posted stating that a session is in progress.

(4) A regular staff member is helpful and necessary in the event of any emergencies, to give out materials, and to participate in the demonstrations with the members or the leader. This person should have had previous knowledge of the objectives of the workshops and be given some training and orientation apart from the group. This frees the staff member from any misconceptions or inhibitions he or she may have about working in front of the group.

(5) The taking of photographs should be explained to the group as necessary and useful for reviewing what has taken place from time to time. It is also useful for record keeping, teaching and training purposes, and permission to take them should be obtained in advance.

3 SPECIAL APPROACHES

Warm-Up

At the beginning of the session, the leader and the participants exchange personal remarks, greetings and handshakes with each other. As the leader goes around the circle, he pins tags with first names on all the members of the group for easier identification.

Since there is the need for fullest concentration before beginning, a specific signal such as a clear bell is suggested. This type of device should also be used to get the attention of the group, to signal for silence and to help make transitions during the workshop. This ritual reinforces memory and establishes the mood for the work that follows.

If the group is fairly new, some introductory name games may help to "warm-up" the group to the leader and to each other. One example might be for the group to tell their names and any nickname they may have once had, adding some personal piece of information, such as: where they were born, what jobs they had before coming to the home, and so on. It is valuable for the leader to have a repertoire of such "ice breakers." They are a means of helping the group to overcome their inhibitions and reservations about performing and working with each other. At times, the day's session may begin unexpectedly from some chance remark or bit of information given during the warming-up period. It is the leader's initiative and ingenuity that will turn this "accidental" beginning into a productive and enjoyable result.

Later workshops always begin with a review of the contents of the previous ones. Significant events that may have occurred between the sessions, such as holidays, trips or some interesting news from someone in the group, are discussed and reviewed before continuing with the new work. Procedures of the workshop are also gone over each week. If the past work has evoked pleasure, released energy and stimulated their minds, they may go on to discuss or debate a particular point. Heated and animated opinions may be given. Here, it becomes the leader's task to provide help and support for any member needing it. If the conversation becomes too overwhelming or threatening, the leader should step in and redirect it into another area. Thus the "stuck" person can be extricated without loss of face. This may be done without fear of becoming too manipulative. Frequently the new direction is an exciting and constructive outlet to explore.

Pantomime

This helps the group to find some original ways of using their bodies to communicate such messages as "Hello" or show "How I feel right now . . ." It is the most rudimentary form of imaginative movement, using any part of the body which is not impaired. A variation of this activity is to show "What I like," or "What I dislike doing," or "What I did before I came to the nursing home." This calls upon any number of past activities, sports, hobbies, professions or skills. When this exercise is done at the beginning, it is considered a warm-up activity.

Movement

The free and expressive use of space plays a somewhat minimal role in Geriadrama because of the limited physical abilities of the aged. The leader and any staff member assisting should be prepared to make up for the group's limitation of movement: by the group directing the leader to do what they can no longer physically do for themselves. The leader is likely to be quite physically involved in the activity — playing different roles, directing others, and even asking for indications from the group members in certain movements. "Show me how to do that," or "Let's all try doing that," he may suggest as everyone mimes life roles and professions such as a house painter, artist, cook, waiter, musician, railroad worker, sewing machine operator, carpenter, and many others. In the case of those confined to wheelchairs or with other physical impediments, simple movements may still be done, even if they are only with the hands or the head. If this group can do little else, they can at least wave colorful scarves (or even paper napkins) expressively to the music, or sing songs from an earlier era, beat time to basic rhythms, or simply listen to their favorite music.

If there is some difficulty in carrying out a movement due to a physical or mental handicap, the leader will give directions for each specific movement to be followed, step by step, participating with the group. "Look at the ceiling." "Find a spot on the floor." "Move just your eyes and not your head, and look suspiciously at your neighbor on your right." "Look surprised at the leader, raising your eyebrows and your shoulders." "Look up, down, left, right — just moving your head." "Make circles with your hands . . . fingers . . . shoulders . . . eyes . . . mouth . . ." "Paint your name on the wall in red paint using your hand as though it were a brush."

"Paint your name on the ceiling." "Dip your hand into a bucket of yellow paint, and make your finger prints all over the wall." "Say 'oh,' 'oooh,' and 'owwww'!" "Make eye contact with me and tell me what color you think my eyes are." "Leading with your head (or chin, hands or shoulders) push away the space in front of you as though it was a brick wall." "Now, with both arms, gather in all the love you can and hug yourself." "Take the hand of the person nearest you, look into his or her eyes and say 'hello'." All these directions must be given slowly and clearly to avoid confusion.

One significant movement activity, briefly touched upon above and related to pantomime, is the making of facial expressions. It is customary to ask the group to express such moods as anger, surprise, fear, joy, sadness, puzzlement and ugliness in a game called, "Make a Face!" These expressions are helpful for toning, getting energy to flow again, and releasing tension. They are of particular use in communicating with those who may be hard of hearing or deaf. If the group is slow in responding, or has difficulty in making the appropriate facial expression, the leader may associate a particular emotion with a specific event or situation. That is, for joy he may say, "You have just won the lottery;" for sadness, "You have just lost a great deal of money;" for surprise, "It's Christmas (or your birthday) and you open a present to find something you've always wanted. Try to imagine that you see something real . . . now take it out and use it." The group tries to guess what it is. The leader may act as a mirror, duplicating what-ever expression the person is trying to make and, thereby, helping him to arrive at the one required. Each person enters into the fun and tries to do better each turn he takes. The leader calls out each new expression, proceeding round the circle.

Sounds or words are added to movements, such as yelling out "Ow!" (as if you were hit in the stomach), or "No! I won't go," or "Yes, I feel terrific!" or "We want more love!" and so on. "Stop!" for example, might be accompanied by the clenching of fists, and "No!" by the stamping of feet or shaking of heads. All are urged to use as much energy as possible before proceeding on to the next phase of the session. In fact, the group may end this phase by shouting out their own names in unison. It is hoped that the more energy that is used, the more tensions will be released and the better the person will feel.

Language Arts

Narratives and scenes from well-known plays, poems, and other literature can be introduced and even read to the group. These are sometimes a stimulus for those who enjoy writing to bring in their own material for use in workshops. In one group of senior citizens, a man who had been a lawyer before he retired wrote a very impressive poem after attending five sessions. Originally, he had been shy and inarticulate in the group, insisting that he could never perform as an actor. Finally, he did participate and volunteered many times, without fear, happily creating improvisational scenes that did not threaten his self-image.

In another group of seniors, a woman brought in her own short story hoping we could re-enact it. I suggested that she turn it into a scenario for the group to act while she narrated it. Although she had never before written a play, she quickly became interested in solving the many problems of playwriting, and later sent me an outline for the scenario explaining how she thought it might be done.

In a nursing home, a group read a scene between the mother and son from *The Glass Menagerie* by Tennessee Williams. I then asked them what alternative behavior the mother might have used in order to keep her son from leaving home. Quite excited, they made such suggestions as: "She would have gone out and gotten a job," "She could have gone on welfare," "She could get married," "She should have made friends outside her home," "She should let her son go," and more. Afterwards, we discussed the relationships between parents and children initiated by reading Langston Hughes' poem, "Mother to Son." When I asked them, "If I came to you for advice, what could you (as an older and wiser person) tell me that might help me to live a good life?" every one of the thirty people had some pithy suggestion. These included: "Work hard for as long as you can, and only stop when you can't go on," "Give out as much as you can, and don't give up," "Pray every day, and thank God you're alive every morning," "Advice is cheap, and

I can't tell you how to live," and one woman's surprising remark: "As Polonius said to his son, 'Neither a borrower nor a lender be. . . .'." This same woman outside the group, so I was told, had always been disruptive and difficult, but in the group she had many interesting comments to contribute.

Acting Techniques

These consist mainly of improvisations arising out of literature, problems of family life, ambitions, dreams, wishes, or from the leader's suggestions. People freely take on the character of a parent or child, portraying any person required for an improvisation. Time, setting and mood, in addition to roles, vary. This helps the members to adopt new faces to suit a new situation. The leader uses any acting technique, from Stanislavski to Spolin, as long as the group's interest is engaged. A trained leader should also be able to incorporate creative dramatic techniques, always adapting them to the specific elderly persons.

The use of the exercise, "Costumes and Properties"[3] to stimulate characterizations, helps improvisations with the elderly. Hats, shawls, utensils, tools, or whatever items or memorabilia the leader may find, can spark an interesting group scene. Questions are asked, such as: "Who might have used this tool?" "What is the job of a person who uses this object?" (or wears this costume piece?) "Take this prop: who might you be? and what might you do for a living?"

The game "Body Talk"[4] uses a form of role playing to deal with a person's pain or illness. The leader begins by asking someone "How do you feel today?" He or she may respond with a particular complaint and locating the body part that is hurting. The person then tries to assume the role of another part of the body that is not hurting. The leader plays the part of the person's body that is in pain. Or the leader may ask the person to play a part of the leader's body (that is free from pain) while the leader takes on the role of the person's body part that is hurting. In any case, the leader and the person will switch roles—alternately playing the healthy or painful body part in an improvised dialogue. For example, a patient with a severely arthritic shoulder may be asked to play that shoulder, while the leader acts the person's toe (which is free from pain) and attempts to make the person's shoulder feel better than the toe:

TOE: Shoulder, you're so lucky to be up there where it's so warm and you can see things like the blue sky, the spring flowers, the falling rain. I don't get to see much down here where people are always stepping on me. I never get to see anything, or hear anything, in this old shoe. Gee, it must be great to be a shoulder . . .

SHOULDER: Well, I never thought about it that way before. I guess things aren't so bad. Maybe I shouldn't complain so much — things are never perfect anyway. I'll try to remember that . . . the sky is blue and my toe is cold . . . (laughs).

In playing this game, the patient may accomplish several objectives: release his pain by expressing it dramatically instead of merely complaining about it; find a part of his body that is free from pain; derive pleasure and enjoyment from acting it out in front of the group; and relate to his body in a new way. Each person is encouraged to try to play this game. Though it is stressed that it is a game, that the pain is real and may still be there afterwards, it is emphasized that the pain, or the organ in pain, is not the total person. After this brief encounter, the person who may have originally been reluctant to participate because of being unwell may be more able to engage in the rest of the day's activities. Not only being able to talk about pain but also being able to "play it out" is an important factor in gaining relief.

Getting into the Picture

Paintings, prints, and photographs of different types of people are stimuli for improvisation. The group explores what is happening, who the people in the picture are, and what they may be saying or doing. The leader then asks the members to "Put yourself in the picture, and try to take on the mood or personality of the character(s) you see." If there is more than one role, the leader may assume one and members of the group will be asked to

play the others. In some instances, the entire group may be incorporated into the improvisation pictorially, through dialogue, or
by shouting out individual comments. With the players placed in
the center of the circle, a short scene can evolve.

The Senses and Recall

> There is a kind of magic in recollection . . . a magic that one feels at
> every age . . . it is above all the old who love to call the past to
> mind . . . This delight in former days is characteristic of most old
> people.[5]

Recall, perhaps the central focus of Geriadrama, attempts to
utilize what every elderly person has: a past life filled with memories. The leader uses any activity that will recall that unique past.
By reminiscing about and reviving the past, the individual can
receive a bolstered self-image, an opportunity to expand himself
creatively, alleviating previous conflicts. In the course of sharing
his knowledge, feelings and common humanity, a sense of wholeness and oneness with the group is experienced.

The leader may initiate the process of recall in any number of
ways. He may use a photograph, newspaper clippings, song,
stuffed animal, brooch, and so on. Or he may suggest themes
from life, using such topics as selecting a mate, starting a family,
choosing an occupation, finding a new friend, a childhood experience, moving out or leaving home, an important wish, fantasy or
dream. All can stimulate memories which can then be worked into
a scenario. Questions, as well as objects, can have the same effect.
Participants may be guided to talk about a past way of life by such
questions as "What did you do during the depression?" and
"Where were you the day World War I (or II) ended?"

Recall can begin simply through the senses: touching, seeing,
listening, smelling and tasting. For example, objects can be passed
round the circle to activate the sense of touch: shells, stones,
pieces of cloth, fur, materials, metal, glass, and so on. These may
be explored for their particular texture, weight, temperature,
and other characteristics. Colors are often used for expressing certain moods or emotions. For example, "What kind of person

would be red (holding up a red cloth)? Someone angry, like a parent or policeman?" "What do you feel when you are yellow? Happy, sad, lonely?" Music may be played in conjunction with the color and appropriate adjectives can be added to describe specific feelings. Spices and foods can be brought in to elicit personal taste memories and sensations. Ginger, cinnamon, curry, vanilla, and so on, may remind the participants of certain dishes from a particular occasion and, thereby, evoke a whole string of memories. Taste, however, is one of the weakest senses in the elderly, and very sharp stimuli must be introduced and explored.

Giving the people my furry teddy bear to hold, examine and stroke, usually evokes childhood memories of a favorite toy or pet of their own. Sometimes the long forgotten name of the pet may even be recalled. One partially blind patient, upon feeling the bear, said "He impresses me with his silence. . . he is a thought provoker!" The group was greatly touched by this. Later, I learned that this man was usually considered anti-social and uncooperative in group activities. Yet the tiny bear had acted as a catalyst to trigger an important moment between us and create a bond of friendship.

In another group, a stroke patient named Lossie recalled the day when "those girls" had stolen her own teddy bear from her. She remembered she was in school and how much she loved it. Now she wished aloud that she had one of her own. Suddenly, as the group watched, she established a short dialogue with the bear. Later, as a direct result of her little "play," each person felt freer to stroke, fondle, talk to, and even hug the teddy. At the last session, Lossie asked to hold the bear again. The group unanimously agreed that she needed the tiny toy the most and should, indeed, have him for that session. I have seen this reaction to him time and time again. It is clear that the elderly, as much as any other group, have a strong need for someone or something to hold and to love. This need can be embodied in a stuffed animal, given the proper surroundings and audience, and the freedom from criticism and ridicule.

In the case of Lossie, her initial remark about the bear was that she was "too old for a teddy bear." I had reassured her that "we

are never too old" and that "if I thought that, I wouldn't be able
to do half the things I enjoyed in my life." With the leader's
patience and understanding, as well as the group's cooperation
and compassion, a very painful memory in Lossie's life was
replaced by a joyful one which she would treasure. With a more
inhibited or reserved group, the teddy bear may just be passed
around to elicit a tactile response without any other reactions.

The leader works not from a planned script but from his imagination and intuition. He fits his ideas and activities to the
group, often spontaneously and to his own surprise. It is valid to
try out unexpected ideas, because this is the way that new techniques can grow. Perhaps the leader's greatest reward lies in the
joy of discovering a new stimulus to pry open the unique but dormant imagination.

One example also indicates the balance the leader must strike
between patience and understanding on the one hand, and "push
and shove" on the other. The theme chosen for this session was
"Changes: Leaving the Old and Beginning the New" and was suggested by the Passover from the Exodus. The ideas proposed to
the group, with their accompanying key questions, were: moving
to a new country or a new home (where and when?); starting a
new family, or a new relationship (whom was it with, a friend or
lover?); finding a new job, or taking on a new role in life; and
discovering a new part of yourself (can you describe what it was?).

Five of the six women in the group responded with a specific
memory sparked by the theme. One had a new mother at age six
and moved to another home in a different city. Another remembered going from Germany to Switzerland, and being thrilled at
seeing the Alps for the first time. A third told of a move from the
city to a new house near the seashore, of seeing the water and the
beach for the first time, and of her mother's fears as she watched
her play from a top floor window. ("I used to wave to her, and she
would wave back.") Finally, the sixth member of the group,
Gertrude, a quiet and sad woman, insisted she had "nothing
good" to tell the group. She refused to believe that there was an
important memory about "change" that all could share with her.
"I have nothing like those stories to tell you," she reiterated. I ex-

plained that it was *her* memory of some special event that we wanted, and that I was certain she had one. At last, the word "exodus" triggered her memory. She became more and more excited as she recounted her move from Europe with her sister, her dreadful sickness on the boat, her landing in New York and journey to Baltimore to meet her brother whom she had not seen for many years. "How did I know that the man who spoke to me was my brother?" she said. "After all, I had heard stories of men in America...I was afraid. Then I asked him to take off his hat and there was the mark I was told he had," as she pointed to her forehead. "We threw our arms about each other..." By this time, she was radiating joy, and the whole group was caught up in one of the golden moments of her life. Each detail, each feeling, each sensory memory (even of a smell from long ago) was recounted by Gertrude and her companions. Little had they known that these facts were still stored within, to be brought forth at the touch of a button.

In describing the different types of memory, Simone de Beauvoir categorizes them as follows:

> Sensory-motor memory, in which recognition is a matter of action and not of thought; it is made up of...forms of behavior that obey the laws of habit and normally remain intact in old age.
> Autistic memory, which is governed by the unconscious and which actualizes the past in dream and delirium...the subject is not made aware of remembering but re-lives past impressions in the present...(this is what psychoanalysis attempts to do).
> Social memory, an intellectual operation that reconstructs and localizes past facts, basing itself upon physiological data, images and...knowledge...this is the only one that allows us...to tell ourselves our own history.[6]

In Geriadrama, we are concerned with the social memory which we attempt to bring forth. It allows the aged to retrieve their lives. As de Beauvoir says, "the people whose old age is most favored are those whose interests are many sided," and retrieval is easier for this group.

One final example of a memory recall which brought great joy to the creator and the group alike, will suffice. Sister Mary Beatrice remembered the day she was "allowed to receive the holy sacrament." She was only five years old and lived on Prince Edward Island. The church she described was "St. Anne's, a white wooden building with eaves and green shuttered windows of stained glass." The entire group was asked to close their eyes and imagine the little girl in a pure white communion dress with orange blossoms in her hair. It was a moving experience for all, but especially gratifying for the little softspoken nun who was now bound to a wheelchair.

Geriadrama uses all the arts at its disposal. Music, art, dance, literature, drama or poetry are all fair game if they help to facilitate memory recall, but none are used for creating final products. The hope is that they will help the individuals concerned to rediscover those aspects of themselves that they have long forgotten; that they will salvage that part of themselves that is still vital and alive. Ultimately, the goal of all workshops is (to paraphrase de Beauvoir) for the elderly to recapture "the child" in themselves so that they may remain eternally young.

Post Session Reviews

After about five sessions with a single group, meeting once a week, these are the general observable results:

(1) The group members work together more cohesively and productively in other activities, in addition to the Geriadrama workshop, and even in cases where they may have previously resisted integration.

(2) They do remember what occurs from one session to the next. In many instances, they anticipate the following week's session, voicing disappointment if one is missed.

(3) They make such statements as "the workshops help us to forget the cares and burdens we carry around with us."

(4) They appear to display more energy, vitality and good feelings after each session. At times, there is kissing, hugging and handclasping, indicating that there has been experience of pleasure.

(5) The profuse thanks and many letters from members attest to the fact that it is an important activity in their lives and one not soon forgotten.

4 CONCLUSION

...in our age there is occurring a new valuation of spontaneity and a strong reaction against rigidity. This goes along with a rediscovery of the values of the child-like capacity to play... People must recover the 'lost' aspects of their personalities, lost under a pile of inhibitions, if they are to become integrated in any effective sense. [7]

The purpose of Geriadrama, as it is presently used, is to help the elderly recover those "lost aspects of their personality" and reconnect themselves to the outside world which has for too long shut them out. Drama is also able to provide a unique form of relief for those who daily feel the anguish of physical and mental deterioration. Through drama, the aged are able to leave their problems, at least for a short while, and think, feel and respond once more. They are not deadened to the harsh realities of old age by such artificial means as drugs, or further removed from reality by what Carl Rogers has described as "making belts and wallets...usually in silence." [8] Instead, they are aroused to an aesthetic reappraisal of their past and of its continuing meaning for their present. And they have pleasure doing it. Geriadrama places a major emphasis upon play because, as D. W. Winnicott notes, "Only in playing is communication possible." Thus:

It is creative apperception more than anything else that makes the individual feel that life is worth living...living creatively is a healthy state...on the basis of playing is built the whole of man's experiential existence. [9]

It is important to understand what the Geriadrama leader can and cannot do. He does not attempt to solve life's social problems; nor does he delve deeply into psychological areas that are best left to trained personnel. He is, of course, sensitive to both these areas, for he believes that it is through the development of self-confidence and self-worth that the aged can achieve a better adjustment both to themselves and to the world. In a recent session with a group of elderly ladies, the song patterned after the well-known quotation from Ecclesiastes was read: "There is a season for everything and a time for every purpose under heaven . . . a time for knocking down, a time for building." The ladies were asked, "And what are you now building in your lives?" They responded eagerly with the following thoughts: "We are adjusting to our old age . . . studying to carry on our lives . . . maintaining our self-esteem . . . building ourselves . . . we are hoping to be remembered and valued." Perhaps these are the best answers of all as to what Geriadrama is, and what it can do.

FOOTNOTES

1. Simone de Beauvoir, *Coming of Age* (New York: Putnam, 1973), p. 538.
2. Rollo May, *The Courage to Create* (New York: Norton, 1975), p. 40.
3. Viola Spolin, *Improvisation for the Theater*, rev. ed. (Evanston, Ill.: Northwestern University Press, 1969), p. 380.
4. I am grateful to my colleague, Allen Stern, who suggested the basic format of this game.
5. de Beauvoir, *Coming of Age*, p. 537.
6. *Ibid.*, p. 539.
7. May, *The Courage to Create*, p. 116.
8. Carl Rogers, *The Therapeutic Relationship with Schizophrenics* (Madison, Wis.: University of Wisconsin Press, 1967).
9. D. W. Winnicott, *Playing and Reality* (New York: Basic Books, 1971), p. 54.

Part 3
RELATED
TECHNIQUES

Spontaneous drama can lead with ease to the other creative arts therapies. Drama therapy, therefore, as well as being mainly concerned with enactment, includes creation in many media.

There is a very close liaison between drama and movement therapy, as Judith Koltai shows (Chapter 13). From a very open and patient-oriented approach, she concludes that the unique potential of drama therapy is that it can "unite the intuitive/expressive instinct of the artist, the precise and controlled skill of the therapist, and the ritualistic and spiritual yearning of the religious man."

Viola Spolin presents an overview of her theatre games and their relationship to drama therapy (Chapter 14). Her work has had a deep effect upon improvisation in many fields—drama therapy, education, rehabilitation, as well as the theatre—and in this chapter she usefully summarizes her position.

Jack J. Leedy and Sherry Reiter demonstrate the links between poetry, drama and therapy (Chapter 15). Like dance and drama, poetry is an ancient healing method, and the writers hinge their approach upon *catharsis* and identification, providing examples of a variety of situations.

The first three chapters in this part deal with the three key media of drama therapy—drama, movement and sound. Connie E. Naitove, however, draws many media together in her work with adolescents (Chapter 16). From a multi-media approach, she indicates approaches from sound, movement, mime, visual art, masks and puppetry.

Finally, Hugh James Lurie provides a unique paper on the role of an actress in a program for the psychiatric education of nonpsychiatric physicians and nurses (Chapter 17). This original method of training in drama therapy is demonstrated as effective and, being controversial, should provide much food for thought.

The reader should note that Part 3 of Volume I includes related techniques of drama therapy with children. Many of these, with minimal adaptions, can be very useful with adults.

JUDITH KOLTAI has taught drama and movement in many educational, mental health, and personal growth settings. She now trains students in theatre, social services, special care, and early childhood education at Camosun College, Victoria, B. C., Canada.

Chapter 13

MOVEMENT, DRAMA, AND THERAPY

Judith Koltai

"No one is separate from another;
how difficult
That is. I move, and the movement
goes from life
To life all around me. And yet I have
to be
Myself . . ."
　　　　—Christopher Fry

1 EPIDAUROS: A SYMBOL AND ITS LESSONS

About ten kilometers from the coast of the Saronic Gulf in Greece lies Epidauros, known as the site of the most famous theatre in antiquity. Epidauros is also known as the symbol of one of the highest levels in the Western world in art, culture, and education. Few people realize that this blossom of culture grew out of, and because of, man's eternal and most basic desire to purify and heal himself and to strive for spiritual, intellectual, and physical wholeness. The roots of medicine and psychotherapy of our times in the West can be traced back to the same seed.

The healer disciples of Asclepius, the god of healing in ancient Greece, knew that disease is always a functionally interactive disturbance in the body, spirit, and mind, and that meaningful treatment has to look at man in his wholeness of being on every level rather than as a mechanism of isolated elements.

197

An integral part of the healing process was to create beauty
and harmony around and inside the person, and to enable him
not just to be a passive spectator but to experience and understand himself as creator and participant in the living process of
beauty and harmony. That is how the arts, artists, and culture
came to flourish at Epidauros. The artist attempted to heal
himself and others through his act of creation, and those who
were ill engaged in the act of creation as part of their effort to
heal themselves.

What are the lessons Epidauros can teach those of us who, today, are involved in facilitating the healing/integrating process in
others? First, we must realize that we have overemphasized classi-
fication, methodology, and technique. We have gradually lost
our grasp of the vital, transcendent nature of human beings as
whole entities and, thus, betrayed the founders of our art in spirit
and in deed.

Epidauros reminds us that the arts, particularly those of the
theatre and dance, grew out of man's natural instinct to exist in
harmony with the universe, to heal and rejuvenate himself. They
are not separate external or "fringe" techniques applied to the art
of healing.

The healers of the Asclepia did not see a dichotomy between
the educative and the therapeutic processes. People were healed,
and they were also informed and taught what to do in order to
heal themselves and to remain healthy in body and spirit. Today,
too, good education produces health in body and spirit, and good
therapy creates openness to learning and growth.

Scientific knowledge and precision was not contradictory to intuition and spirituality. The healers at Epidauros were good
scientists and keen observers. They looked at the whole person,
assessed the need and only then did they apply or suggest a
method. Surgery, prescriptions, miracles, dreams, "shock" treatment, song, mime, poetry, exercise, and martial arts coexisted as
compatible approaches to treatment.[1] Today, in our work, we
must rediscover the true meaning of eclecticism and team approach in therapy.

At Epidauros "the healer himself was healed, first and most important step in the development of the art, which is not medical but religious."[2] As therapists today, we must cease to see ourselves simply as engineers engaged in repairing broken mechanisms. Recovering the transcending creator in ourselves, we can enhance our ability to reach and awaken the creative spark in others. We can then enter the healing dance together, kindle and support the creative flame, and emerge together at the end mutually healed, purified, and edified.

To heal and integrate within the act of creative expression is:

> to carry the ego to its last summit and to deliver it triumphantly . . .
> then: To know peace is total: it is the moment after, when sur-
> render is complete, when there is no longer even the consciousness
> of surrender. Peace is at the center and when it is attained the
> voice issues forth in praise and benediction. Then the voice carries
> far and wide, to the outermost limits of the universe. Then it heals,
> because it brings light and the warmth of compassion.[3]

Today, as Miller points out for us, Epidauros is merely a symbol. The real place is in the heart, soul, and body of every one of us if we wish to find it.

2 PRACTICAL IMPLICATIONS

Having described the symbol, I wish now to examine the practical implications of its lessons as a therapist and educator working primarily in the nonverbal and self-expressive modes of movement, dance, and drama.

To educate is to awaken and "lead out" the potential of people for knowledge, understanding, and creative action in the world. The Greek word *therapeutes* means "servant" or "attendant." In the act of expression the person encounters his own limits and resistance. In a supportive environment, the healthy individual can master limits and obstacles with confidence and joy. When the person is incapacitated and distraught, the resistance becomes impenetrable; attempting to overcome it causes suffering and a feeling of defeat. Life, then, becomes worthless and unbearable.[4] An educator is primarily responsible for providing an environment which supports learning and expression. In the therapeutic setting, one's role becomes that of the attendant/servant aiding another person to gain, or regain, his ability to overcome resistances and limits in living and learning. The primary focus in the two roles is different; the essential goal, it seems to me, is the same. It is my firm belief that a good educator needs to possess some therapeutic skills just as the effective therapist has to be able to teach when necessary. Here, inevitably, we return to the by now classic "begin from where you are"[5]: when psychological and emotional obstacles prevent learning, we have first to work on the elimination of those obstacles; when readiness to learn emerges, we should be able to provide opportunity for it.

The word drama means "action" or "a thing done." The earliest form of therapeutic procedure was the dramatic act of a priestly man who recited his magic charm and engaged the sick in ritual interaction. Our nonverbal physical mode of being is the truest, most significant reflection of our experience in the world and of our relationship to it. Therefore nonverbal physical and expressive modes of diagnosis and therapy need to work hand in hand with other modes in order to address human beings as the thinking, speaking, feeling, moving, breathing, digesting, blood-pumping creatures they are.

Drama, particularly in the therapeutic mode, is an extension of life. The body *is* man's form and life. It is not merely an "anatomical corpus" but an all-encompassing manifestation of all vital functions in man. The body is the incorporation of the lived past and present of the organic being. As a guide in understanding the existential problems of living, the body is a rich, clear, and comprehensible phenomenon permitting precise observation and revealing an enormous multiplicity of information. It is, therefore, "methodically prior" to other forms of assessment and expression.[6]

3   PRACTICAL APPLICATION

My work is based on the assumption that the person as a physical phenomenon (with his appearance and mode of action) is the most clearly observable and accurate diagnosis of the problem. Often physical behavior can also become the most organic and reliable indication of the desirable approach to solving the problem. In a group, for example, the spatial and directional relationships are reflections of the participants' ability to relate and interact with the environment and other people.

In the dramatic and nonverbal therapeutic interaction several progressive stages are essential. First, one has to observe keenly, objectively, and without preconceived plans or ideas of methodology. If my decision about method precedes my observation, my assessment of the problem is likely to be colored by my intention of approach, rather than the true need of the person or group. In order to see individuals as they are, not as they fit arbitrarily defined professional categories, I must (at least temporarily) suspend my knowledge or expertise and be open to any and all possibilities. In addition to being a good observer, I must exercise what Shunryu Suzuki calls an open and ready mind:

> In the beginner's mind there are many possibilities, but in the expert's there are few.[7]

Understanding gained through uncritical observation then needs to be communicated with acceptance and empathy. Often this requires active participation through mirroring, responding, reflecting, taking part. I need to assimilate the client's experience into my own intellectual, emotional, and body language in order for mutual trust, acceptance, and genuine identification to occur. Only then am I in the position to exercise my skill as a therapist, to initiate changes and to propose alternatives. When it comes to particular techniques at this stage, for me, true eclecticism is the key. The important thing is that the changes grow naturally out of the experience rather than being externally superimposed solutions. The only limits here are those of my skill, knowledge, and judgment. We must be keenly aware of the limits of our competence and remain within them; we must also maintain our openness to expanding those limits through constant self-evaluation and exposure to new learning. In our eagerness to be flexible and eclectic we must not forget caution and professional accountability.

As the individual or group begins to accept and try out changed

behaviors, it also becomes my task to provide responses to these
behaviors, so that there is opportunity for practice and assessment
of success. At this stage it is important to watch alertly for the
creative spark: the moments when new ways of behaving emerge
which are initiated by the individual or group independently of
the therapist. Those moments are the signs of health, the
emergence of strength, and ability to cope. To watch these
moments appear and to nurture them into growth is the most
rewarding and joyful part of the therapist's work.

An excellent and moving illustration of this process in movement therapy is the film *Looking For Me* by Janet Adler demonstrating sessions with autistic and psychotic children.[8] Another illustration is a description of the movement therapist's work by
Mitchell L. Dratman at the Second Annual Conference of the
American Dance Therapy Association:

> She (the dance therapist) takes the child where she finds him and
> tries to become one with him. She mirrors and imitates what he
> does until the child is comfortable with her — and she attempts to
> be his body double — with all his disturbance and his with-
> drawal — his autism. She practices blendmanship, to coin a phrase.
> Then slowly she changes just one small part of the child's
> movements. She attempts to become part of the space and rhythm
> around him. Where he ends and she starts he doesn't know and
> after many weeks or months she slowly disentangles herself — very
> slowly and hopefully. Gradually he recognizes her as an entity, sees
> where he begins and she starts.[9]

4   SOME ILLUSTRATIONS OF
THERAPEUTIC FUNCTION

Out of the basic working assumption and steps of approach
described above, some specific elements of therapeutic function
can be illustrated. In order to do so, it is often necessary to
describe what may look like success stories in a therapist's work.
For the layman or student this can sometimes be misleading or
even discouraging: it seems the therapist has to be perfect, his
skills foolproof. Yet most professionals know that in the reality of
day-to-day work this is not so. The truth is that sometimes at-

tempts are not successful and goals are not achieved by even the most skillful and well-meaning therapists. We all feel discouraged and self-doubting at times. It is an important part of the therapist's personal art and creativity to be able to forgive himself and to go on to the next task having learned from past failures and grown in wisdom, humility, and practical skill.

In drama therapy, much of the focus of my attention is the nonverbal physical behavior of the person. It is, however, important to keep in mind that in most cases there is no structural division between movement and drama, and that verbal and nonverbal enactment alternate freely according to what is the most appropriate mode of expression for the therapeutic process.

In the initial stages I try to assess the content and range of actions by paying attention to such elements as breath, muscular tension, quality and effort in motion, relationship to gravity, spatial and directional behavior, etc. I watch to see whether there is a coherence in the body or lack of it: does this person utilize his body as a harmonious cooperative unit or is there a sense of fragmentation in the movements? As missing links and deficiencies of the person's range and vocabulary of movement emerge, I attempt to bring about opportunities to try out new ways. Sometimes these get initiated through suggestion and/or participation. For example, if someone shows predominantly heavy motion, which is mostly downward directed and passively giving into gravity, I will gradually encourage experimentation with lightness and reaching upwards. This can happen in many different ways. If I am working with a small child, I may lift him and ask him to "help." I might use light chiffon cloth or balloons and imitate, "become," or dance with these objects. If the person is ready to work with images, I will suggest becoming the wind, birds, clouds, a kite in the air, etc. I will also allow opportunity for the person to experience his familiar habitual mode of relating to gravity, as well as to begin to appreciate the contrast and change between "lightness" and "heaviness." This tells the person that I am not trying to change him or take away his familiar mode of behaving; my aim is to increase his possibilities, to expand his limits.

Without jumping to diagnostic conclusions, I also try to be aware of the theories and research findings of others. For example, as a result of observations of the movement characteristics of psychiatric patients, Davis[10] found that diffused, flaccid, and limp features in movement related to strong depression and possible suicidal behavior. If my observation indicates that the person consistently shows these characteristics in drama or movement sessions, I will alert myself and others involved in the therapeutic process. Utilized appropriately and with caution, such information provided through movement observations can be valuable contributions to diagnosis, treatment, and prevention.

In drama and movement I also watch for double messages or contradictions between verbal and nonverbal behavior as well as within the nonverbal elements of behavior. The therapist receives an important message when words express command and confidence while the body looks shrunken and defeated; or when a smiling face appears in a person with a tense, defiant body and tightly held fists.

As an example of contradiction between verbal and nonverbal message, the case of a young woman, Joan, comes to mind. Her words expressed confidence and willingness to go ahead with plans she made in consultation with her psychiatrist and family. These plans were oriented towards increasing her independence and self-reliance. She maintained that she had considered and understood what lay ahead of her. When Joan moved, her body orientation was consistently backwards or sideways, her movements lacked directness and purpose. When watching her walk forward, one had the feeling that something was pulling her back. She seldom looked in the direction she was moving in. When asked what she could remember visually of the room she was crossing, she knew exactly what was behind her and at the two sides; she could not remember seeing anything in front of her. When she received feedback about this (both verbally from me and watching on videotape), she became willing to admit and discuss her fears, resistances, and resentments about becoming self-reliant. She thus allowed opportunity to deal with these feelings practically and therapeutically. Since she expressed a desire to enhance her strength and ability in "moving forward," some of her movement therapy aimed at improving her directional ability and clarity of focus in movement. We would practice walking toward each other with directness and keeping eye contact; we would move spontaneously and call out loud what we saw in front of us as we moved; we would explore the contrast between advancing and retreating, practice movements requiring directness. Dramatic enactment often included moving forward with fear, encountering obstacles, sometimes overcoming them, sometimes having to retreat in defeat.

Occasionally hidden causes of problems emerge spontaneously and unexpectedly through movement experiences. Recent psychological work in *felt* experience distinguishes two basic levels. The more direct and implicit one is what a person knows through sensory, kinesthetic, and internal emotional sensations:

> A body sense of a problem or situation is preverbal and preconceptual
> . . . Experiential body process is carried forward by action. . . .[11]

As one acts and receives feedback from therapists and others, further clarification occurs. The person is enabled to perceive his behavior, reflect upon it, verbalize, and conceptualize about it, which then allows for further growth.

A young woman, Mary, undergoing verbal psychotherapy was referred for simultaneous movement and drama therapy. She considered herself a sexual failure and was unable to "let go" physically and emotionally. She was tall, slim, almost skinny looking, and appeared very tense. For a while, much of our work was concentrated around muscular relaxation and release of spontaneous expression. Although she achieved some success in these areas during the sessions, Mary's problem outside the therapeutic setting showed no improvement. Then, during one of our sessions, we explored some forms of trust exercises; these required her to allow me to support some or all of her weight. Since she was a slender woman, this was easily possible for me. Her reaction, however, was, "Oh no, you can't possibly hold me up. I'm so heavy." As we examined this reaction verbally and nonverbally, a new clarification of her tenseness and holding back behavior emerged. Mary was, in fact, considerably overweight until approximately a year before her entering therapy. She went on a crash diet and quickly reduced to the slim appearance she now had. However, she had a slow metabolism and had to keep very strict control over her diet. Any lapse into indulgence or letting go of this control meant that she would "go wild over food" with the result of having to diet even more strictly afterwards. This extreme need for control gradually spilled over to all other areas of her life, including the sexual. In addition, in spite of what she could see in the mirror now, her felt experience and body image had not changed. Subjectively she still knew and experienced herself as fat and heavy. Once this clarification occurred, the goal was to put her in touch with her present body image and to incorporate this reality into both her sensory/kinesthetic and conceptual/verbal awareness. The issue of having to hold back from food could be dealt with in the verbal part of her therapy. Her attempts to release physical tension and spontaneous response now became more lasting and self-directed.

"The spontaneity of the moment is not a gift from heaven, but the outcome of lifelong practice. . . ".[12] Often, as a therapist, I encounter individuals who are used to withholding their spontaneity of the moment. In the beginning stages this may have come about through restraint from a feared authority. Later the repression becomes an unconscious pattern of life. On the physical level the person has built a muscular armor around his spontaneity of which he may not be aware and which separates him from the source of his own creativity. Since breathing encompasses both the conscious and unconscious, its function often is a reflection of the psychosomatic organism.[13] When a person is restrained in spontaneity, the free flow of breath is blocked and vocal freedom becomes restricted.

The case of Sam, a young acting student, illustrates this process. He had a pleasant and warm personality and a sturdy looking, healthy, strong body. He had spent considerable time outdoors and in physical activity. He was quite flexible, athletic, and he progressed well in structured movement exercises. In his acting work, he learned and executed the blocking in scenes with ease and control. However, in improvised movement and free vocalization, Sam appeared incapacitated to a large degree. His motions were repetitious and one dimensional, his vocal production very limited. Although he made a good willed attempt each time, he soon became frustrated and often withdrew from the activity. At these times his eyes looked somewhat hazy, as if holding back tears; he swallowed frequently and his body showed a defiant and tense attitude. Movement classes normally began with concentration, relaxation, and breathing exercises. Punctuality, therefore, was a strict requirement. While otherwise reliable and cooperative, Sam was regularly late (thus missing the initial work) and openly hostile and defiant of my insistence that he be there on time. I recommended some sessions of individual tutoring and he agreed willingly. Work on relaxation and breathing progressed slowly and was accompanied by unusually frequent swallowing. Being an intelligent and sensitive person, it quickly became apparent to Sam that he was "holding back something," although he could not articulate the experience very well. However, we did make some progress and, while we were working on maintaining relaxed deep breathing during standing and walking, I became aware of a protrusion, the size of a small lump, which appeared in the scapular region of his back each time he exhaled. This was not, as I first feared, a tumor, but a muscular contraction. After some careful work, while previously totally unaware of its existence, Sam was now able to tell whether the lump was appearing in his back or not. After achieving several consecutive exhalations without the contraction, he broke down in heavy sobbing. In the conversation which followed he said he felt "good" and "cleansed" but was puzzled as to what he was crying about. That night he had a dream which brought back a painful memory from his childhood. He remembered that as a little boy he was punished for crying and used to run away and hide in order to be able to shed some tears.

In the sessions which followed his willingness and ability to work with expressive images increased. Many of these were directed towards overcoming something that held him down and his attempts at escaping to freedom. Later he began to initiate open encounter and defiance of the "depressor" who, in the reality of his young life, was his father. Some of this imagery was also explored during movement classes with fellow students in drama improvisations. It is important to note that as Sam's comfort and confidence with free expression increased, he also became better able and spontaneously willing to improvise around themes of love and tenderness.

The fully functioning human being is available to himself simultaneously on two levels of consciousness: "healthy fantasy and healthy rationality."[14] This can often be observed in drama work with healthy children where unrestricted flow of imagination combines with control and confidence of voice, body, thought, and feeling. In the therapeutic situation, the opposite of extreme control is behavior which is almost (and sometimes entirely) at the mercy of unconscious chaotic impulses. Movement tends to be erratic, disorganized, and, often, the person lacks ability to exercise judgment in matters of bodily safety for himself and others. This causes disruption and prevents dramatic interaction in a group, and therapy on a one-to-one basis is necessary.

Within boundaries of safety precautions, the function of the therapist in the beginning is to allow, observe, accept, and identify behavior. Careful and uncritical observation might provide the therapist with clues which can lead to the discovery of an underlying thread in the seemingly irrational behavior. In movement, for example, this can emerge as some physical action or pattern which the person repeats from time to time in the midst of the erratic behavior. At this point the therapist needs to utilize his skill to encourage and help the person in the creation of a more appropriate and controlled form of expression, and to enable him to clarify underlying feelings and problems.

The above described chaotic behavior was exhibited by Paul, a six year old boy in a residential treatment center. Paul appeared hyperactive, constantly "on the move," and frequently involved in accidents of varying degrees of severity in which he hurt himself and/or others. He often collided accidentally with people and objects. He seemed to move around randomly with no awareness of his environment. Paul's previous history was not well known. Until his arrival at the center at five years of age, he was brought up as a foster child and changed homes several times. Diagnosis did not indicate brain damage or other organic cause for his behavior. Paul was referred to movement and drama therapy to improve his coordination and to enhance his awareness of himself and his environment.

In the initial stages of therapy, Paul was allowed to move freely in the room, but was helped to learn about the differences between dangerous and safe parts of the room. He was also encouraged to begin to adapt his movement behavior in the different areas of the room according to their degree of safety (no sharp corners, carpeted open floor areas, etc.). After a few sessions, he began to spontaneously utilize pillows and cushions to build a safe area in which he could abandon himself freely. He began to verbalize about this activity and to give me direction as to his preference of my participation ("Catch me;" "Don't catch me;" "Don't look when I'm falling,"etc.). At this point it became clear that Paul was extremely preoccupied with getting hurt himself, and his own reactions to other people getting hurt. This was further explored through play therapy and drama methods in which we interacted in various roles. We also dramatized events and environments using stuffed animals, pillows, and mats. The emerging picture during these sessions showed that Paul's understanding of relationships, and people's dislike or care for one another, was limited to the context of "getting hurt." If he got hurt, he could test how much others cared for him according to their reactions. He himself showed his feelings by either walking away from, and laughing at, the victim of an accident, or showing concern and attempting to comfort and help. Although we did not know much about the attitudes of Paul's various foster parents, it is most likely that the only times Paul was held, carried, and given close physical contact as a baby and toddler were when he had an accident and got hurt. Through his spontaneous actions, Paul showed us what the real goal of his therapy needed to be: to enable him to learn new and appropriate ways of testing relationships; to learn how to directly ask for, and give affection and care; to realize that he could elicit praise and warm response from others by showing that he could be responsible for his own safety.

Time, patience, and the understanding cooperation of the entire therapeutic team was required. At the end of six months Paul still was involved in many accidents. But he began to show signs of change and an understanding of his own behavior ("I hurt myself because I want you to hold me"). During his drama/movement sessions he would simply sit on my lap and ask to be held or carried instead of acting out an accident. In his play he sometimes saved the stuffed animals from being hurt, or taught them how not to get into danger, while in the early sessions he had always hurt and then comforted them. It was reported that during a visit to a crowded department store Paul asked his worker to pick him up and hold him because there were too many people. His previous behavior pattern in similar situations was to run away from the worker and get involved in some mishap.

5   A PERSONAL CONCLUSION

The successful and appropriate blending of who we are, and what we have learned through training and practice, seems to me essential if we wish to remain true to the lesson handed down to us by the healer/artists of Epidauros.

The unique potential of drama therapy is that it can, in one coherent process, unite the intuitive/expressive instinct of the artist, the precise and controlled skill of the therapist, and the ritualistic and spiritual yearning of religious man. Drama gives man the vision of what he can be in his full splendor: artist, scientist, and priest blended in one harmonious being. In the process both therapist and client are called upon to resonate and respond with the whole of their organic self. If healing occurs in this way, the need for lucidity, reason, and social rationality does not conflict with recognition of the intuitive, spontaneous, and spiritual aspects of the person. Then, we do not demand the soul to deny the body, nor the intellect to defy the creative spirit.

For too long, fragmentation of the self has been the destructive fate of adult and child in a technocratic, scientific, and materialist world. The orientation of therapy in this world has been to reduce intuition and creative spontaneity to a repressed bundle of evil and antisocial instincts.

In the therapeutic process of drama, the client is not the passive subject but a fellow creator. Healing is a shared journey and common struggle towards the goals of better life and health. Instead of imposing arbitrary norms of behavior, drama aids the client and the therapist to reorganize experience into forms of reality which are more personally and socially fulfilling. Therapy, thus, becomes a vehicle by means of which human beings are freed from forces which oppress and alienate, and are enabled to find their true and whole selves.

FOOTNOTES

1. E. J. Edelstein and L. Edelstein, *Asclepius: A Collection and Interpretation of the Testimonies* (New York: Arno Press, 1976; reprint of 1945 edition).
2. Henry Miller, *The Colossus of Maroussi* (New York: New Directions, 1941), p. 77.
3. *Ibid.*, p. 80.
4. Lama Anagarika Govinda, *Creative Meditation and Multi-dimensional Consciousness* (Wheaton, Ill.: Theosophical, 1976), p. 225.
5. Brian Way, *Development through Drama* (London: Longman, 1968), p. 28.
6. Karl Jaspers, *Nietzsche: An Introduction to the Understanding of his Philosophical Activity* (Chicago: H. Regnery, 1965), p. 314.
7. Shunryu Suzuki, *Zen Mind, Beginner's Mind* (New York: J. Weatherhill, 1975), p. 21.
8. Virginia Bartlett and Norris Brock, producers, *Looking For Me* (1970). Film available at Extension Media Center, University of California, Berkeley.
9. Mitchell L. Dratman, "Reorganization of Psychic Structures in Autism: A Study Using Body Movement Therapy," *Proceedings of the Second Annual Conference of the American Dance Therapy Association* (1967): 44.
10. Martha Davis, "Movement Characteristics of Hospitalized Psychiatric Patients," *Proceedings of the Fifth Annual Conference of the American Dance Therapy Association* (1970): 25–45.
11. E. T. Gendlin, "Focusing," *Psychotherapy: Theory, Research and Practice* 6, no. 1 (Winter 1969): 8.
12. Govinda, *Creative Meditation* p. 224.
13. *Ibid.*, pp. 114–15.
14. A. Maslow, *The Farther Reaches of Human Nature* (New York: Viking, 1972), p. 91.

VIOLA SPOLIN, D. Litt., author of *Improvisation for the Theater* and *Theater Game File*, is director of the Spolin Theater Game Center, Los Angeles. A leading innovator in improvisational theatre, she is now focusing her efforts on the use of theatre games in education, mental health, and other extra-theatrical fields.

MARY ANN BRANDT has worked closely with Viola Spolin in many capacities—as secretary, student, editorial assistant, apprentice, and teacher of the Spolin Theater Games.

Chapter 14

THEATER GAMES

Viola Spolin
(with Mary Ann Brandt)

1 OVERVIEW

It is widely recognized that theater games have had a great impact on drama training, and have been instrumental in exciting a
mushroom growth of improvisational theatres throughout the
United States, Canada, England, and elsewhere. In appreciation
of the structure and function of this body of work, one enthusiast
has proclaimed, ''Theater games are to theatre what calculus is to
mathematics.''

Theater games were initially developed as problems to solve
problems related to theatrical needs. When players showed needs
in listening, moving, working with fellow players, or contacting the
onstage environment, a problem — in the form of a game or an exercise — was presented to them. These problems, now called
theater games, are play (operational) structures, and each evolved
its own name: the Where Game, the Who Game, Give and Take,
Exits and Entrances, Audience Directs, Silent Scream, Rocking the
Boat, Excursions into the Intuitive, Sight-Lines (Transformation of
Stage Picture), Part of a Whole (often called "Machine" by other
users), Contrapuntal Argument, the Multiple Stimuli series,
Verbalizing the Where, Seeing the Word, the Gibberish series,
and the Mirror series, to name a few.

Over the years it has been my pleasure to see that the many
dimensions of the exercises — both theatrical and extra-theatrical —
have inspired their introduction into the fields of art, dance,

music, psychology, recreation, sports, prison work, and mental health. Although used extensively by many therapists to help people with emotional, mental, or physical handicaps, please understand that, even in the therapeutic situation, theater games are a process (play) and should be entered into for the joy of playing, without interpretation, while they are taking place.

The theater game approach is off-the-subject: indirect and lateral. It is a two-part process providing for reflection during action. Rather than isolate the individual's "problem," theater games give the group of players a problem to solve. In the course of playing the game or exercise a door is opened and the player's "problem" dissolves as a new action (insight) emerges.

Theater games embody group agreement and allow for individual freedom. The games are played in a workshop setting on a bare playing area. The agreed reality is created out of the space between the players. The chosen on-stage environment (the "where"), the accepted relations between the players (the "who"), and the group decision of the activity (the "what"), all develop in the moment of playing the game or exercise.

Each of the more than 250 published games and exercises[1] involves all workshop participants, either as on-stage or audience players. The workshop leader, called the "side coach," facilitates the playing by coaching from the sidelines as the playing proceeds. The side coach assists the players in maintaining the structure (rules) and staying on focus.

Focus, a key element in theater games, channels the energy of the participants to playing the game or exercise. Focus acts as a meditation (reflection) around and through which the action (playing) is laced: "Keep your eye on the ball!" Consciousness! Consciousness—wherever, however, whenever achieved— becomes a part of the player's life:

> The specific objective upon which the player must constantly focus and towards which every action must be directed provokes spontaneity. In this spontaneity, personal freedom is released and the total person, physically, intellectually, and intuitively is awakened. The energy released to solve the problem, being restricted by the

rules of the game and bound by group decision, creates an explosion—or spontaneity—and as is the nature of explosions, everything is torn apart, rearranged, unblocked. The ear alerts the feet, and the eye throws the ball. Every part of the person functions together as a working unit...one small organic whole within the larger organic whole of the agreed environment, which is the game structure. Out of the integrated experience, then, a total self in a total environment, comes a support and thus trust, which allows the individual to open up and develop any skills that may be needed for the communication within the game.[2]

Theater games lead players to the focus, rather than to their own subjectivity. Subjectivity is the personal, usually past frame of reference, consisting in part of the individual's feelings, attitudes, prejudices, beliefs, and reasons. This is the conditioned response and acts as a censoring mechanism. In playing theater games, the full, whole body attention of all players (side coach, on-stage, and audience players) is guided away from subjectivity and directed to the stated focus of the game or exercise being played.

Thus, with Focus between all, dignity and privacy are maintained and true peerage can evolve.[3] As we are working in an art form, the personal emotions of the players must be distilled and rechanneled through the form in which they are working. An art form insists upon this objectivity.[4]

The power of the games springs forth during play when all strive to stay on focus, when the invisible becomes visible, when players reflect what they see, not what they think they saw, and when events are out of the head and in the space between players.

2 THEATER GAMES—A KEY TO TRANSFORMATION

All of us have known moments when we did "exactly the right thing without thinking." Sometimes at such moments, usually precipitated by crises, danger or shock, the "average" person has been known to transcend the limitations of the familiar, courageously enter the area of the unknown and release momentary genius within himself.[5]

Theater games are a safe harbor and a simple way to bring players to this state of crisis or imbalance. This aspect of theater games builds self-trust and is useful to therapists. From years of observing people of all ages and backgrounds playing theater games, it would seem that in crises, players enter the moment (present time); an energy source opens up that can transform itself into a visible event. Feelings, relationships, objects, whole environments appear or arise spontaneously in the empty space when players stay on focus within the established structure of the chosen game. The invisible (hidden) becomes visible. Such transformations are theater magic and an intrinsic part of most theater games.

Psychiatrist Dr. K. Frederick Nystrom — after observing theater game workshops with his young charges in a boys' home — recognized this transforming power and writes, "Without the capacity to free present time, people are chained to past identities, whether the role is that of a businessman, a country club matron, a neurotic, a young thug, or a psychotic. The capacity to create or to find a new reality (for oneself) within the existing reality is a penetrating power."

While dramatizing anti-social behavior might bring understanding and even change, simple change is not enough. In change there often rests just the other side of the coin, a residual of the old (good/bad, better/worse, past labels/future goals). Theater games seek more: Transformation! In the moment of playing, a path to body, mind, and intuition is opened. A cleansing, a dissolving of past attitudes (approval/disapproval, excuses, reasons, "I can't," "I won't," "I should have," roles, soap operas) takes place, which allows a space for the real communication and the person/the hidden self to emerge. In that dissolve there is no returning to past limitations (roles). The butterfly does not become the caterpillar again. That past moment (life) is exhausted. Transformation!

3   DO ONLY WHAT YOU ARE ABLE TO DO — NO MORE! NO LESS!

The infant moves from kicking to crawling to walking. The enlarged capacity found in the new moment — the breakthrough — dissolves the limitations of the preceding capacity. (At the same time, of course, a new limitation/capacity appears and emerges.) The preceding capacity is not dissolved, only its limitations. We can always crawl, but we will never need to become the crawling baby. The infant cannot be made to walk. External obstacles can be removed, support can be tendered, the breakthrough is witnessed and the joy shared. But the new step belongs to the infant alone.

> We learn through experience and experiencing and no one teaches anyone anything. If the environment permits it, anyone can learn whatever he chooses to learn; and if the individual permits it, the environment will teach him everything it has to teach.[6]

Before playing theater games, the therapist should go through the book (*Improvisation for the Theater*) or file (*Theater Game File*) and select those exercises and games that the group will or can play and that may bring the leap we seek. Adaptations should be made to get or keep the players playing. Most of the early ground work in both publications offers games and exercises that will bring participants together as fellow players. This is the first stage of workshop activity. Other experiences, more geared toward creating and communicating through the theatre form, follow in later sections. The book and, especially, the *File* offer concrete suggestions on how to design workshop formats and how to adapt games and exercises for specific needs.

The therapist, as side coach, becomes a fellow player, drops roles, attitudes, and judgments, puts aside immediate goals of performance, social adjustment, or rehabilitation, and becomes a support to the players, lends eyes and ears to the playing, and, in turn, is supported by the players. Theater games seek to address the person, not the role, the label, the handicap or the cover-up. Seek not the cause, nor the effect! Look for what the players need to keep playing. In this way, the therapist, by becoming a fellow player and not working directly on the patient's "problem," avoids the role of the do-gooder by seeking to remain in process (playing) together with the "patient." Hence both the therapist/patient and the patient/therapist have within themselves the probability of transformation. In theater games, this is the role of the diagnostician.

Playing games and exercises will open players to one another, their environments and the exploration of feelings. It is present-time playing that sparks spontaneity and that will, in time, spill over into the areas of players' lives labeled problematic. Writing about her workshop experience, one high school-aged participant states, "Through theater games I am becoming more comfortable with myself when with other people. I am dropping the image of what I perceive 'me' to be and letting it show itself. And I am discovering how much fun it is." Another comments, "I am seeing things about myself and others beyond the workshop, in my school, in my home, and in my relationships, in subtle ways. Learning is growth, neither ever ends." The reserved and aloof teacher who spontaneously leaps into the air during a moment of joyous excitement in a game, the domineering child who allows his fellow player the opportunity to play, the businessman who learns the meaning of give and take, and the actor who reflects what he sees have all discovered in the moment of play the mutuality of experience which is theirs to create.

This work accepts as a given that all of us long for extension and growth, to see and be seen, to use and be used. *Reaching out is reaching in.* Theater games do not endeavor to inspire "proper" moral behavior (good/bad), but rather seek to free each individual to feel his or her own true nature and that of fellow players—hopefully, out of which a felt/experienced/actual "love of neighbor" will appear.

Players are asked to do only what they are able to do—no more! No less! Individual differences are to be accepted and respected. Focusing on differences and problems creates differences and problems. Nobody is sick/well. All are sick/well. (How else do we recognize one another?) In playing theater games we are momentarily relieved of the burden of our lives; hurtled into the present, we have the opportunity to become masters of our own fate, even if only for fifteen minutes.

Find problems to solve problems. This task is not easy. It is simple, elusive, and challenging. Let this search through the material begin your excursions into the intuitive for the expressive, alive, being/person/genius — no matter where it is hidden — under whatever guise, physical or mental. Theater games call forth the person.

Come out! Come out! Wherever you are!

FOOTNOTES

1. Viola Spolin, *Improvisation for the Theater* (Evanston, Ill.: Northwestern University Press, 1963); idem, *Theater Game File* (St. Louis: CEMREL, 1975).
2. Spolin, *Improvisation for the Theater*, pp. 4–5.
3. Spolin, *Theater Game File*, p. 12.
4. Spolin, *Improvisation for the Theater*, p. 248.
5. *Ibid.*, pp. 3–4.
6. *Ibid.*, p. 3.

JACK J. LEEDY, M.D., is in private psychiatric practice in New York City, where he is also director of the Poetry Therapy Center. Founder and director of the Association for Poetry Therapy, he is the editor of *Poetry Therapy* and *Poetry the Healer* and co-author of *Psyching Up For Tennis*.

SHERRY REITER, M.A., a certified poetry therapist, is vice president and director of training for the Association for Poetry Therapy. She has conducted workshops for the Postgraduate Center for Mental Health and the New York City Department of Social Services.

Chapter 15

POETRY IN DRAMA THERAPY

Jack J. Leedy
Sherry Reiter

1 INTRODUCTION

The first poetry therapist on record was Soranus, a Roman physician of the first century A.D., who treated the mentally disturbed in the Roman temple by having his patients enact scripts in poetic form.[1] Soranus found tragedy helpful in the treatment of mania, and recommended comedy for depressives.

Written accounts trace poetry as far back as the fourth millennium B.C., when Egyptian chants were written on papyrus. The words were dissolved into a solution which was then physically ingested, so that the power of the words would take healing effect immediately. The Bible records the use of music and poetry therapy to soothe the savage breast of King Saul when a fit of distemper was upon him; the psalms of David are as effective today as they were then.

Still earlier in time, in different parts of the world, the witch-doctors, high priests, and shamans used healing potions on the sick of their tribes.[2] However, their magic was incomplete without drama, poetry, music, and movement in the healing ritual.

It should be remembered that we have been making the distinction between the forms of the musical, the drama, the dance, and the opera only for the past few hundred years. Similarly, the fields of drama therapy, music therapy, poetry therapy, dance therapy, and art therapy have achieved recogni-

221

tion as separate ancillary therapies only within the past few decades.

At the Poetry Therapy Center in New York City, and at Cumberland Hospital in Brooklyn, we have been using the techniques of drama and poetry therapy since 1959. They have proved to be of immense value to our patients, who suffer from a variety of emotional problems. Sessions which combine music, movement, and drama with poetry are often more dynamic and fruitful than those using poetry alone. Whenever the elements of drama can enhance the therapeutic process, they should be used. This chapter will explore the specific uses of poetry within the field of drama therapy.

2 THEORY

Principles of Poetry Therapy

Poetry therapy may be loosely defined as the expression and release of emotion through poetry and other forms of creative writing (including prose, allegory, and the dramatic script) in order to attain greater insight and understanding of the self. By identifying with the feelings of the poet, the patient knows he is not alone, and is able to acknowledge and release emotions which have been previously repressed or denied. This process of identification is crucial to the therapeutic process.

Freud pointed to identification as a highly important factor in the mechanism of hysterical symptoms: "By this means patients are enabled in their symptoms to represent not merely their own experiences of a great number of other persons, and can suffer, as it were, for a whole mass of people, and fill all the parts of a drama by means of their own personalities alone."[3] In drama and dreams, characters enact scenes and express feelings we repress in everyday living. In poetry, the identification takes place with the character and spirit of the poet through his written words. Nevertheless, the process is almost identical.

For example, one young woman, Judy, depressed and ashamed after a broken love affair, was able to express her feelings with far greater ease after one of Shakespeare's sonnets had been read aloud in group:

When in disgrace with fortune and men's eyes
I all alone beweep my outcast state,
And trouble deaf heaven with my bootless cries,
And look upon myself, and curse my fate . . .

At the end of the session Judy's response was one of renewed hope when she reflected, "Gee, you mean Shakespeare felt that way — just as bad as me. And he got over it. So will I."[4]

An important consideration in the choice of the poems is the isoprinciple, which has been used in music therapy by Dr. Ira Altshuler of Eloise, Michigan: music is used which is identical to the mood or mental tempo of the patient. In poetry therapy the isoprinciple, or the principle of using poetry similar to the mood of the patient, has also been found to be helpful. In Judy's case the Shakespearean sonnet was chosen to match her feelings of despondency and shame.

Eli Greifer, a volunteer who introduced poetry therapy at Cumberland Hospital in 1959, advocated memorizing inspirational poetry for a kind of "bloodless psychosurgery." The patient is actually borrowing ego-strength from a poet. He writes:

We have here no less than a psychograft-by-memorization in the inmost reaches of the brain, where the soul can allow the soul-stuff of stalwart poet-prophets to "take" and to become one with the spirit of the patient. Here is insight. Here is introjection. Here is ennoblement of the spirit of man. . . by blood transfusing the personality with the greatest insights of all the greatest-souled poets of all ages. . . The hypnotism of beautiful figures of speech, the melody of rhythm and meter and assonance. . . painted scenes. . . dramatic espisodes, love's pervasiveness — all are consecrated by the master poets to gently enter and transfuse the ailing subconscious, the abraded and suffering personality.[5]

Poetry does not necessarily have to be great to foster identification. Indeed, a patient will often identify with a poem of mediocre quality written by another group member. For poetry therapy, the standard is not whether or not the work is good or great poetry, but whether it will help the sick. Nevertheless, we are more likely to draw effective therapeutic poetry from great poetry than bad poetry. Great poetry has withstood the test of time because of its universality which breaks down barriers and fosters identification. The endurance of the work of Kahlil Gibran, Keats, Longfellow, and Dickinson are testaments to this fact.

Advantages

Of all the arts, poetry is the one which comes closest to Freud's "talking cure." One advantage in drama and poetry therapy is its focus upon the spoken word. Verbalization is the life blood of most forms of psychotherapy, including psychoanalysis. The type of patient who never expresses emotions is liable to suffer from psychosomatic illnesses. The patient is encouraged to think of his ulcer as a poem struggling to be born. When he learns to express himself in a poetic rather than physical form, it is far less painful and far more gratifying.

Freud called the poet the "professional daydreamer" and noted the similarities between poetry, drama, and dreams. The mechanisms used in dreaming — condensation, symbolization, and displacement — are the same elements used by the poet to transform the threatening emotions of the unconscious into an acceptable form during the waking hours.[6] During the sleeping hours the dream takes on the form of dramatization. "The waking mind produces ideas and thoughts in verbal images and in speech (and poetry and drama) but in dreams it does so in true sensory images."[7]

The psychiatrist who has a poem in hand to interpret has certain advantages over the psychiatrist who attempts to elicit dream material from a patient with hazy recall. The poem is concrete and physically available for examination. Its completeness will not be at the mercy of the patient's memory. In addition, the poem becomes an entity outside of the patient, which is less threatening to him than examining his thoughts and feelings directly. Instead, we become intent on examining the thoughts and feelings in the poem.

The principles and techniques of poetry therapy are now used in individual and group psychotherapy. The patients write poems about their symptoms, fantasies, dreams, conflicts, and relationships with others. Learning to write poetry gives the patient a sense of mastery, as he gives outer form to inner conflict. Hopefully, this will lead to mastery of feelings and orient the patient to new and meaningful goals.

The poetry therapy group is especially valuable when used in conjunction with one-to-one counseling. Information which could not have been extracted during an ordinary conversation becomes available to the therapist. Seeing the patient interact within a group gives additional clues to the individual's behavior patterns. The therapist can take mental notes of reactions or statements elicited during a group session and bring them up in individual sessions where there is a better opportunity to focus on specific problems.

Population

Most of the clients at the Poetry Therapy Center are former addicts, alcoholics, and offenders who have tried to escape from their emotional problems by acting out in ways unacceptable to society. For them, poetry therapy is a new way to be honest with themselves and others. When someone with an addictive personality disorder first comes to the center, he is helped to write a poem. Rather than escape from problems by turning to outside stimuli, the client is encouraged to look within himself.

Only after the client has expressed his feelings in writing will the doctor consider prescribing medication. This technique is especially effective in breaking the habit of the addictive personality who is a "taker" but not a "giver." Sharing one's thoughts and feelings is a gift of one's self which results in the reward of receiving. In addition to learning the art of giving, the client begins to develop discipline and a sense of responsibility which has previously been lacking. This sophisticated blackmail is initially met with incredulity and much resistance. But even though the patient may at first respond to this technique with hostility, in time many of our clients become "hooked" on writing as a new "high." And since no one ever died of an overdose of poetry, this is one kind of addiction we encourage.

The patients are conditioned to ask for paper and pen and are helped to express feelings either alone or with assistance. If they are only able to vocalize their feelings, the poetry therapist will write it down for them. The participants receive recognition from the group and become proud of a poem they have done by themselves. Many of our clients, who have had no previous contact with poetry, are exhilarated and astounded to find success and praise in an "academic" area which, to them, has formerly symbolized failure.

Once again, the patterns of expectation are broken. Rather than being rebuffed and rejected as outcasts in society, they are accepted by the group. Writing poetry becomes a form of acting out along with the fellow offenders. However, the competition which takes place is healthy, as each participant strives to outdo and give more than his peers. Drama and poetry tap the previously misdirected creative energy of clients and result in a sharing experience which is new and satisfying.

The experience is just as exhilarating for the therapist. An observer may be surprised to see a hardened criminal fumble in his pocket and unfold a dirty scrap of paper on which he has written about flowers and the beauty of nature. But if the individual can get in touch with the beauty within himself, he can triumph over the ugliness of his past.

The patients attend a weekly group session of poetry therapy in conjunction with counseling sessions held individually. Ideally, there are no more than six to eight participants for a one and a half to two hour period. Whenever possible the group is led by two therapists, preferably of both sexes. Manifestations of transference indicate that patients tend to identify differently with each of the therapists.

As an added dimension to the total treatment plan, poetry and drama therapy can be used in any and all types of emotional as well as physical disorders with all age groups. Successful groups have been conducted with various populations, including adolescents in six hundred schools, retarded children, nursing home residents, the physically handicapped, and prisoners. Of course, methods and techniques will vary according to their particular needs.

3 METHODS

Basically, drama is used in three ways: (1) Oral interpretation in which either the poetry therapist brings in a poem and recites it as a catalyst for group discussion, or the group members will recite their work after writing on a given theme. In either case, the art of oral interpretation plays an integral role in the poetry therapy session. (2) Physicalization and pantomime may be added to the written form to elicit greater involvement. (3) Song, movement, and theatre games are valuable as tools for warm-up and closure.

On occasion we combine all the elements of drama—music, movement, art, and poetry—in the same session. For example, the session might begin with the playing of atmospheric music. Edward Macdowell's *Woodland Sketches* and Johann Strauss' *The Blue Danube* have proven effective. The music relaxes the participants and helps to develop the senses. Once the group is absorbed in the music, the leader might suggest that each person moves to the music in his own space. After a few minutes participants find a partner and respond to each other's movements. In silence, partners begin to have a conversation in "body talk." Sounds, grunts, and words may be added. Or, one person may participate through body movement while his partner responds only verbally. Partners may choose to proceed in gibberish. Once the partners have become completely engrossed, the suggestion can be given to form groups of four.

At this point, creative writing may be introduced. Either one person may be appointed as "scribe," or papers and pens may be distributed. The leader can call out a word—love, childhood, memory, etc., as the groups spontaneously give their word associations. One-word associations eventually grow into full sentences. When the works are complete, the scribes of each group share the resulting creative expression. Individuals communicate the feelings which they have experienced during the session. If crayons have been used, art works are also shared at this time. To conclude the session, music may again be used, with a group circle moving in unison.

We may divide a session into three phases: (1) Warm-up, (2) Sharing, and (3) Closure. In the above example, music and movement were used in the warm-up phase, poetry and drama during the sharing phase, and music, once again, for closure. The use of drama during warm-up and closure is optional, but it is always used in the form of oral interpretation during the main body of the session, the sharing.

Oral Interpretation

The sharing of the written word, either by group participants or the leader, is basic to the session. Reading aloud allows the poem to be heard and experienced word for word within the mind. Some of the world's greatest poetry was written by dramatists with the express purpose of performing in the theatre. Upon introducing a drama workshop on a psychiatric ward, it is possible that one of the group members will lapse into a rendition of Hamlet's "To be or not to be." This is an excellent opportunity to point out the close ties between poetry and drama, and introduce poetry into the session.

One may be inspired by the thoughts of a poem or play to emulate the behavior of a noble character. Through identification with words and characters, a patient may incorporate other objects and ideals into his own ego system. In all likelihood, the patient who memorizes the words of Hamlet identifies strongly with the plight of the character; he is a man whose power of action is paralyzed by his intellect, "sicklied o'er with the pale cast of thought." On one level or another, when the patient read or saw the play, part of him cried out, "I am Hamlet." This statement is not necessarily a conscious one. As Freud writes, "The dramatist can, indeed, during the representation, overwhelm us by his art and paralyze our powers of reflection."[8] "It is, however, a subtle economy of art in the poet not to permit his hero to give complete expression to all his secret springs of action. By this means he obliges us to supplement, he engages our intellectual activity, diverts it from critical reflections, and keeps us closely identified with his hero."[9]

When introducing poetry into a drama session, the point can be made that Shakespeare's work is most alive and moving when we hear rather than silently read it. Only when poetry is vocalized can we completely enjoy the elements of sound which give poetry its power—rhythm, rhyme, meter, alliteration, and onomatopoeia.

The importance of truthful and effective interpretation of the chosen work must not be underestimated. Gwynneth Thurburn has written, "Beauty depends, in speech as in every other art, on the truthfulness with which the mind is presented, and this truthfulness depends upon the mastery of the instrument."[10] All poetry therapists should be trained in the basic techniques of oral interpretation, a course generally offered within the speech or drama departments of colleges and universities.

If the poetry therapist has inadequate training as an interpreter, he may lose the attention and respect of the group. Volume, speed, pitch, tonal quality, and emotional affect all contribute to the effectiveness of the interpretation. If these factors alienate the listeners, they will not be able to identify with the feelings of the poet and, conclusively, will be unable to share any of their own feelings. Since honest sharing of feelings is our prime goal, an ineffective interpretation can kill a session from the very beginning. Certainly the reader need not be a professional actor, but insufficient volume, clarity, and insincere affectation should be carefully avoided.

There are exceptions to this general rule when a therapist may exaggerate one of these elements for a particular effect. For example, psychiatrist Dr. Smiley Blanton found that he was able to relieve one patient's anxiety by reading a poem, "Uphill" by Christina Rossetti, in a whining, exaggerated manner.[11] This poem proved to be reassuring to the patient, a fifty-five year old man who was afraid he would not be able to continue performing well in the work world because he was getting older.

> Does the road wind uphill all the way?
> Yes, to the very end.
> Will the day's journey take the whole long day?
> From morn to night, my friend.

But is there for the night a resting-place?
A roof for when the slow dark hours begin.
May not the darkness hide it from my face?
You cannot miss that inn.

Shall I meet other wayfarers at night?
Those who have gone before.
Then must I knock, or call when just in sight?
They will not keep you standing at that door.

Shall I find comfort, travel-sore and weak?
Of labor you shall find the sum.
Will there be beds for me and all who seek?
Yea, beds for all who come.

In this case, the therapist acted out the role of the traveler, and, by his dramatic interpretation, fostered the identification of the patient with the character he portrayed. However, an alternate method would be having the patient, rather than the therapist, act out the poem through oral interpretation. Or, the poem could be used as source material to create an improvisation or playlet between a traveler and the people he meets along the road. Any one of these three methods can be effective in changing the emotions and perceptions of the client.

If the therapist is working with a client who lacks spontaneity or is not ready or able to take part physically, the first method is preferable. Otherwise, unless the client is resistant, direct involvement as interpreter/actor is likely to produce more rapid results.

At times one may ask a client who is very angry, but withholding his emotions by reading in a soft voice, to repeat his poem in the loudest voice he can muster. Or, the therapist may ask a reader who is letting his words run away with his emotions to read aloud in slow motion, or vice-versa. In any case, such exercises must be chosen at the discretion of the therapist in the best interests of the individual with whom he is working.

When participants in a poetry therapy group write their own poetry, the sharing process of reading aloud is often met with resistance. Occasionally a client must be coaxed and weaned

gently from writing to reading and further encouraged to interpret dramatically. However, once the client has taken the initial
and most important step of acknowledging his feelings to himself,
the far more threatening phase of sharing them with others is
usually not far behind.

James, a young man in a mental health clinic, could not always
control his jaw in speech. When sharing time came, for the first
few months James would ask the poetry therapist or a group
member to read his work for him. Finally the group took it upon
itself to encourage James to read his own work. James tried, pushed
the paper away more than once, but finally succeeded. Week
after week his attempts led to eventual mastery. This success
helped James to develop self-confidence and to strengthen his
interpersonal skills.

The readiness of participants to share and acknowledge their
feelings varies greatly. Some clients will resist involvement with
such comments as, "This is silly," "How boring," or "I'm really not
interested." Other clients may be so in touch with their feelings
that the therapist should be prepared to handle sudden emotional
outbursts. The therapist must be sensitive to this factor of "readiness" and use careful judgment as to when to provoke the client, or
leave him alone.

A word of caution here. Stress on oral interpretation can
enhance the therapeutic process, but when urged upon the participant who is *not* ready for it, can hamper and destroy progress
already made. The therapist must always remember that his
prime goal is concern with the patient, and not the product,
which is incidental. Too great a stress on product will produce
"performance anxiety." The participant will protest that he is not
a writer and not an actor and will not share his work for fear of a
negative judgment. Confusion of this kind can be eliminated with
repeated validation. For example: "You may not think of yourself
as a writer, but you are a human being who thinks and feels. Let's
put our thoughts and feelings on paper. Let your pen do the
talking."

When the time for sharing comes, clients can be reminded,
"Don't underestimate the importance of what you've written.

What you write is yours alone. Focus in on your ideas and do them justice by the way you speak them." Viola Spolin advocates this same technique of focusing in on the problem or task to be performed to eliminate self-consciousness of the actor.[12]

The result is an ego-building process. What the therapist is actually saying is, "What you think and feel is valid. We are giving those feelings a space in time, and listening to them, because they are an important part of you. And you are important."

As we have stressed, confusion between performance and content of material should be avoided. A participant should never fear that an inadequate rendition invalidates the contents of his thoughts. In an ideal situation group members can join in a double workshop, one stressing the dramatic interpretation and the other devoted to its written creation. Monthly poetry readings, with invited audiences, can greatly add to the enthusiasm of the participants.

Group reciting is another technique suggested for decreasing anxiety and increasing ego-strength. Suggested poems for this purpose are: "Jabberwocky" by Lewis Carroll, "The Congo" by Vachel Lindsay, and the psalm, "The Lord Is My Shepherd."

Physicalization

When physicalization is added to poetry, the resulting therapy (drama) is beneficial for three reasons: (1) it encourages unification of psyche (mind) and soma (body); (2) it increases involvement and group participation; and (3) it minimizes an intellectual approach, which clients often use to resist dealing with their emotional problems. Clients should be told to park their "thinking brain" at the door and come in with their "feeling brain."

Poems may be purposely chosen for dramatization. Or, a poem may be written by a group member which is particularly well-suited for dramatization. For example, the following poem, "Before the Storm":

> Once I stood
>   tall and straight
> Before the storm.

And then one day
         the wind came weaving,
      winding,
            wearing me down.
And my leaves were torn off
My branches were bent
And my trunk gnarled and knotted.
But still my head did not bow down.

This poem affords the opportunity for total group involvement. Using the principles of creative dramatics, each participant may choose his/her role. The writer may wish to choose a dramatic interpreter as he recites his poem, or vice-versa. Other group members may choose to be the wind, the leaves, and the branches. Additional elements — the sun, a lover, a friend, lightning, etc. — may be added, as the group's imagination dictates. The group may use the poem as a catalyst for improvising a story which may hardly resemble the original poem.

Fairy tales, fables, and allegories have been used with great success in drama therapy. Mel Yosso, whose allegories have been presented at the Church Center for the United Nations and at the Jungian Institute, has created several allegories which are extremely effective in therapy because of their universality and use of unconscious symbols. Patients acting out scripts distance themselves from their immediate situations and then associate with varying personal degrees of intensity. Immersed in neutrality, clients do not feel threatened by specific personal involvement. Roles easily reverse, moods change, and problems gain perspective.

These allegories may be called "transcultural" since patients of whatever socioeconomic level can create new and more healthy scripts beyond the shared, neurotic scripts of their specific culture and individual situation. For example, the following, "Transcultural Allegory Example"[13] by Mel Yosso, was used with great success at the Poetry Therapy Center in New York City:

Man and Woman sit by fireplace.

Man: It's not very bright just now.
Woman: What do you expect?

Man: More flames!
Woman: It's been burning for ages. You expect too much.
Man: I do not!
Woman: *(Sadly)* You do.
Man: *(Apprehensively)* It's getting dimmer.
Woman: Yes, it is.
Man: What should we do?
Woman: Keep it going.
Man: You think we can?
Woman: Possibly.
Man: We have to.
Woman: But can we? That's the question.
Man: We've done it so far.
Woman: *(Points to the fire)* We've had lots of help.
Man: *(Dismayed)* You don't think we can expect more?
Woman: I wish I knew. All we can do is wait.
Man: *(Lights candle from fire)* We can keep it alive till then.
Woman: Until when?
Man: *(Raises candle)* Whenever . . .
Woman: *(Lights another candle from his)* Till then . . .

They embrace. Both fondly nurture the candle flames.

The group can stop the reading at any time if they have any
particular associations they wish to share with the rest of the
group. The flame may be interpreted as a symbol of joy and
hope, whereas depression has often been likened to a dark cloud
constricting the brain. Participants should be given the understanding that there are no right or wrong interpretations. Group
members then have the freedom to choose their own interpretations, create original variations of the script, and act them out.

Poetry and drama as twin techniques in therapy have been
extensively used by the psychotherapist Dorothy Kobak and the
dramatic coach Evelyn Neinken. In their approach the group
reads, writes, and acts out feelings from poems purposely chosen
to stimulate the senses and relate to physical activity. Clinical
aspects are guarded by the psychotherapist who interprets, inter-
venes in stress, and supervises the emotional involvement. The
dramatic partaking is guided by the drama coach, who assists the

participants in acting out in words, pantomime, or body language those feelings elicited by the poems. The following examples illustrate the technique:

A poem about old worn-out shoes that will be thrown away[14] is used with the invitation to "be an old shoe." Dialogue is then encouraged in which participants speak as if they were an old shoe. This is conducive to sharing feelings of abandonment, lack of self-worth, insecurity, and repressed anger. Following dialogue, a playlet is improvised between an old shoe and a new shoe, in which the old shoe can express its immediate pain as well as project for the future.

Another poem, "Bursting Out" by James D. Freeman, deals with a bird breaking out of its shell. Participants may be asked to experience breaking out of their own shell through movement. They can then verbalize what their individual "shell" is and what they need to do in order to free themselves. In subsequent playlets they can act out the new roles which are possible without the confines of their present shells.

"Going to Sleep," a poem by Dorothy Aldis, deals with the recall of falling asleep as a child and hearing the voices of the parents in the next room. Participants may be asked to curl up in their imaginary blankets and simulate sleep, recalling fragments of overheard conversation. They are encouraged to share these conversations aloud one at a time and then their reactions to the recall. They may act out new playlets in which they participate in the conversation or are given the freedom to select "new parents" and create new scripts. In all of these encounters poetry and drama is followed by dialogue with the psychotherapist to enhance the insight of the experience for the person and the group.

Warm-Up and Closure

Warm-ups are valuable in bringing the group to a point of readiness so that the identification process can occur. Physical exercise, group singing, or theatre games are suggested as openers to the session to relax group members and bring them closer. These same exercises may be used for closure.

Eli Greifer usually began his sessions with five minutes of group singing. Some of his favorites were "Que-Sera-Sera," "America," "Count Your Blessings," "Always," and "Silver Threads Among the Gold." Greifer maintained that "the real magic of verse is the ideal combination of feeling, thought and music; by the mixture of long and short vowels, in addition to rhythm and rhyme, music is blended to poetry."[15] Using music is helpful in tuning participants in to the elements of rhythm and sound in poetry. Poems with regular rhythms, which approximate the beat of the human heart, seem to affect clients most deeply.

Warm-ups act as bridges to allow the participant time to adjust from the outside world to the intimate circle of close interaction. They include sensory stimulation exercises which can affect the "feeling part" of the brain. For example, once music hits the thalamus it relaxes the "feeling brain" and pleasure predominates. The "feeling brain" unlocks the twelve billion brain cells which have been imprisoned, and the "thinking brain" is affected. The individual is then more apt to express and act out his finer thoughts, and the thinking process will be more efficient and creative.[16]

The following exercises are suggested as tools for warm-up and closure. They relax and unite the group. They also begin a sharing process which continues through the main body of the session to closure. Each theatre game carries its own message, often on an unconscious level.

THE MIRROR GAME

Two parallel lines, divided into pairs, take turns in reflecting the movement and facial expressions of their partners. Each couple work so closely together that an observer would not be able to tell which partner is initiating the movement, and which is reflecting it. The Mirror Game helps a person to see himself and others as they really are. As one sees oneself, one becomes aware of problems and improves those traits that cause discomfort. The individual becomes stronger as he sees both the positive and negative traits. On a more conscious level, mimicry is a favorite childhood game and enables the individual to laugh at himself with others. Reflection of movement and facial expressions give the initiator a different view of himself. It should be noted that it is easier to make contact with one person before establishing trust with a group of people.

THE MAGIC BOX

The group sits comfortably in a circle. The leader holds an invisible magic box from which he extracts an imaginary object. He shows how to use this object and passes it to the person next to him. After using the same imaginary object, the second person changes it into a new object, uses it, and passes it on to the next person, etc. Once again the theme of giving and sharing appears, as each person gives his object to the next. Using raw materials (one's self and one's imagination) the individual is encouraged to "make it what you want it to be." In therapy we try to give the client incentive and offer the hope of new beginnings. On an unconscious level he is being given the chance to start new beginnings. He can convert apparent failure into success. The difference between failure and success is a little more effort. The Magic Box also deepens the appreciation and awareness of simple objects we use daily. This exercise captures the essence of what poetry is—a conversion of the commonplace into the unique and memorable.

THE HUMAN KNOT

A volunteer leaves the room as the other members of the group create a human knot by joining hands and/or feet. The volunteer, returning to the room, must untangle the knot without breaking the clasp of hands. This exercise develops an awareness of tradition, structure, and order. The structure of the circle is unconsciously perceived as a symbol of the family or community. In certain primitive cultures, if a person was inside a circular structure it was considered sanctuary; even enemies respected this unwritten rule. The holding of hands is in accord with Gestalt philosophy, encouraging touch in order to build trust and confidence. Participants are urged to obey the rules of the game. Hopefully, this respect of rules will carry over into everyday life. The volunteer who disentangles the knot has the satisfaction of bringing order out of disorder. This is a prime goal of many patients whose personal lives are confused. Concentration, discipline, and hard work create order where none has previously existed.

THE HUMAN MACHINE

Using sound and movement the leader and a volunteer create an imaginary machine of moving parts. Group members are invited to join in with their own sound and movement until everyone is working together in a mass of moving parts. It is necessary for each moving part to make physical contact with another moving part. Touching is giving part of yourself to share. Because the feeling part of the brain is the most archaic, touch satisfies a primitive need which is often ignored in the Western culture. As in The Human Knot, physical contact is extremely effective in breaking down barriers and unifying group members. Cooperation with each other is stressed, as the machine is most successful when participants work with each other. The task demands building and working closely with each other. Nevertheless, each participant retains his individuality by contributing a unique movement and sound to blend with the whole. In society one also must find a place for oneself in the large scheme of things without losing a sense of identity.

These theatre and movement games are spontaneous fun and instantly establish a link between members. Theatre games, group singing, or exercise may also be used as a unifying device in closure. Especially following an emotionally charged session, members need to relax and know that their fellow members still accept them despite new information which may have been revealed during the session. These group activities help to provide this reassurance when necessary.

4 CONCLUSION

Dr. J. Rof Carballo once remarked, "In every one of us there is a bit of the physician, the poet, and the madman."[17] Poetry is *poiesis*, which is Greek for "creation." In order to restore the client to health, the therapist must reawaken the poetic, life preserving faculty which has been imprisoned by emotional conflicts.

When poetry and drama are used as therapeutic tools, this method offers infinite possibilities for increased insight through emotional release and self-expression. The process is a dynamic, safe, and ultimately joyful one, tapping our artistic creativity as well as our intellect. These effective tools are becoming recognized within the field of psychiatric medicine as well as recreational therapy, counseling, and education.

FOOTNOTES

1. Alfred M. Freedman and Harold I. Kaplan, *The Comprehensive Textbook of Psychiatry* (Baltimore: Williams & Wilkens, 1967), p. 11.
2. Abraham Blinderman, "Shamans, Witchdoctors, Medicine Men, and Poetry," in *Poetry the Healer*, ed. Jack J. Leedy (Philadelphia: J.B. Lippincott, 1973), p. 127.
3. Sigmund Freud, *Dream Psychology* (New York: James A. McCann, 1921), p. 84.
4. Jack J. Leedy, "Poetry Therapy: What It Can Do For You," *Pageant Magazine* 28, no. 7 (February 1973): 108.
5. Eli Greifer, *Principles of Poetry Therapy* (New York: Poetry Therapy Center, 1963), p. 2.
6. Sue Robinson and Jean K. Mowbray, "Why Poetry?" in *Poetry Therapy*, ed. Jack J. Leedy (Philadelphia: J.B. Lippincott, 1969), p. 193.
7. Sigmund Freud, *The Interpretation of Dreams* (New York: Basic Books, 1955), p. 51.
8. Sigmund Freud, *Character and Culture*, ed. Philip Reif (New York: Macmillan, 1963), p. 170.
9. *Ibid.*, pp. 161–62.
10. Gwynneth Thurburn, "Speech, Voice and Sound," in *The Uses of Drama*, ed. John Hodgson (London: Eyre Methuen, 1972), p. 87.
11. Smiley Blanton, "The Use of Poetry in Individual Psychotherapy," in *Poetry Therapy*, ed. Jack J. Leedy (Philadelphia: J.B. Lippincott, 1969), p. 178.
12. Viola Spolin, *Improvisation for the Theater* (Evanston, Ill.: Northwestern University Press, 1963), pp. 20–26.
13. Reprinted by courtesy of Melvin L. Yosso, copyright 1976.
14. Dorothy Aldis, "The Sad Shoes," in *The Secret Place and Other Poems* (New York: Scholastic Book Services, 1972).

15. Jack J. Leedy, "Some Principles of Poetry Therapy," in *Poetry Therapy, A New Ancillary Therapy in Psychiatry*, ed. Rolland S. Parker (New York: Poetry Therapy Center, 1966), p. 10.

16. This has support from findings in modern research into the left and right hemispheres of the brain. See Robert Ornstein, *The Psychology of Consciousness* (Harmondsworth: Penguin, 1974).

17. Felix Marti-Ibañez, "Bronze and Dream," *M.D., The Medical News-magazine* (July 1964): 16.

CONNIE E. NAITOVE, M.A.L.S., is president and founder of the
National Educational Council of Creative Therapists, Hanover,
New Hampshire (formerly the New England Council of Creative
Therapies). She practices and teaches an interdisciplinary
approach to therapy and is the author of several research articles
on the subject.

Chapter 16

A MULTI-ARTS APPROACH TO DRAMA THERAPY WITH ADOLESCENTS AND YOUNG ADULTS

Connie E. Naitove

1 INTRODUCTION

Most of the creative arts are recognized as basic forms of communication. However, the potential for the therapeutic application of these modes of expression is not so well appreciated or understood. This, in part, is due to the tendency to equate creative expression with talent. In the therapeutic application of the arts it must be stressed that talent is not the issue since the emphasis is placed upon the creative process and not the product.

Therapists and clients unfamiliar with arts practices may be unsure of how to invoke the creative process. Inhibition concerning the use of the arts in therapy arises from a common ignorance of, and an inability to appreciate and utilize the artistic and creative experiences available to all of us in our everyday life. We tend to lose sight of the components of form, texture, sound, rhythm and spatial relationships that fill our environment. The reader who feels that s/he has no sense of rhythm may have forgot-

243

ten or be unaware that in utero s/he existed in a point/counter-
point environment of two heart beats; that we all move to the
natural rhythms of our breathing and, thus, that there is no one
alive who lacks a sense of rhythm.

2   PREMISES

The premises upon which all of my work in the expressive
therapies is based are the following:

1. Emotional problems which are not due to chemical imbalances commonly arise from inadequate or inappropriate
   responses to stimuli.
2. Among the least threatening and most satisfying approaches
   to self-awareness and creativity are the ones which are innate:
   sensory impression and bodily expression.
3. Verbal and nonverbal behaviors are related to each other and
   are expressive of responses to sensory impression.
4. Each individual has a repertoire of symbolic expressions, and
   being cognizant of that unique repertoire reinforces the sense
   of identity.
5. The more ways that new information or awareness is syn-
   thesized, the more complete is the understanding. The more
   complete the understanding, the greater the sense of self-
   assurance. The more assured the individual, the more willing
   and able s/he is to deal with sensitive areas which have led
   into problematic behaviors.
6. A multi-media or multi-arts approach to therapy is one of the
   most satisfying educational approaches to expanding sensory
   awareness while enhancing communication skills. Repetition
   or translation of material from one arts medium to another
   leads to a better understanding of the overt synthesizing process.
7. An emphasis upon the creative process, rather than product,
   reduces apprehensions about talent and skill, allowing hes-
   itancy and inhibition concerning the use of arts in therapy to
   be overcome. The understanding of this process is applicable
   to other areas of overt behavior.

3   APPROACH

My approach to clients is to inform them that everything we think, do or experience is a unique and individual response to something (thus reaffirming the individuality of the client). I define this as innate creativity, and my purpose in utilizing arts media is to provide a means for the client to learn more about him/herself. I explain that the emphasis will be upon the creative process rather than the development of artistic skills. I then reinforce this vital aspect of my work by the use of uncommon or unfamiliar media or techniques which I call "equalizers": e.g. writing your own name in the air with your shoulder or nose effectively neutralizes any concern with skill; no one can write your name in the air with your nose better than you yourself can.

I try to keep my explanations and instructions as simple, direct and clear as I can while being as undirective as possible. My purpose is to assist the clients in tapping their own creative resources rather than replicating my own. I have found a simple vocabulary of terms to be appropriate to a multitude of media, and readily comprehensible: e.g., up, down, long, short, heavy, light, strong, weak, etc. I try to select media which allow for rapid, unrestricted movement and a range of gratification from immediate to long term. On occasion, I use themes to facilitate work on goals or expression in a new medium. I frequently employ music as a facilitator of activity, a dictionary of pattern and rhythm or a means to correlate the uses of volume and mass, repetitions, etc. with expression in other media.

Sound

I use sound because it is a part of our environment. It is the first instrument of communication, expression and power the infant learns. When the infant cries, an adult responds. Sound is also a source of pleasure, as when the adult soothes, sings, chants, or in the child's own squeals and screams of apparent delight. The qualities of sound with which I work are: duration, pitch, volume, rhythm, emphasis and relationships to silence and each other. The types of sound with which I work are: abstract, creative, verbal and nonverbal, internal, external and creative.[1]

An abstract verbal sound is like a gesture (indeed, I often urge the coordination of sound and movement in such exercises). It is usually colloquial in origin, such as a cheer or a "raspberry." A creative verbal sound might be a unique descriptive communication such as the following, from Lewis Carroll's *Through the Looking Glass*:

> *'Twas brillig, and the slithy toves*
> *Did gyre and gimble in the wabe . . .*

An abstract nonverbal sound is one which is derived from mimicry of an external, nonanimal source, such as a squeaky door. Other nonverbal sounds (such as drumming, clicking, whistling and yodeling) are still used in various parts of the world as a form of communication and these may also be explored. Internal sounds are remembered sounds while external sounds are heard but not made by the listener.

In practice, I will often use recorded sounds and chants as well as poems and mini-dramas in foreign languages, either to facilitate activities (as example of some of the potentials of the human voice) or to demonstrate the elements of continuity, pattern, mood, change and counterpoint. I point out to the client or group that the voice of an instrument, or the human voice, may be correlated to the volume of space it occupies (much as a composer might orchestrate a piece of music), that the rhythms can be depicted by the pattern and number of repetitions, silences or spaces, and changes in pitch, volume or duration correlated to color and linear movements.

Mundane verbal language is explored in terms of its symbolic content and relationship to behaviors. Verbal communications are often colorful and dynamic, suggesting a variety of approaches to activities. For example, a client may say that he is "going around in circles." We may explore this concept first in movement, then in art, etc. In each instance I would ask the client if he felt that there were any options and, if so, we would

then explore those options in terms of avoiding or altering the un-
desired patterns of behavior.

Movement

My purpose for using movement is that it is inherent in us.
When we breathe, we move; and we cannot escape our bodies.
Movement is healthful and relaxing, and I find it useful for
enhancing body awareness and mobility. Several of the movement exercises deal with becoming more aware of the articulation
of body parts frequently ignored, such as elbows or ankles; others
deal with extension and relaxation, such as reaching for
something (an imaginary rope or fruit) which remains continually
out of reach or, once grasped, is used to lift the body off the
ground. When full extension has been achieved, clients are then
asked to very slowly "melt" down to the ground, much as the
Wicked Witch of the West was "melted" by water thrown on her
by Dorothy, in *The Wizard of Oz*. [2] Movement exercises may also
be used to familiarize the clients with their own natural rhythmic
patterns of breath and heartbeat. In addition, we may explore
favored dances for purposes of uncovering the essential qualities
of these movements and their significance for the client.

Mime

When using mime, I emphasize that we do not live or move in a
vacuum; each act is a phrase, a personal communication, while
gagged or oversimplified acting is either inappropriate or inadequate to the communication intended (a client behaving in such a
manner would be encouraged to explore this behavior in terms of
other social interactions). The premise for using movement and
mime in drama therapy is that many people are kinesthetic
learners (i.e. these activities reinforce learning via physical awareness acquired through enactment). Verbal dramatizations are
contraindicated as these people may be distracted by verbalization
and thus confuse the issues involved.

Mime is a verb and implies action, and therefore I rarely
distinguish it from movement exercises. Mime examines innate,
natural and acquired movements and gestures. Its characteristics

are: (a) "the art or technique of conveying emotions, actions, feelings, etc., by mute gestures . . . "[3]; (b) mimicry or imitation; and (c) the use of unlimited movement and accommodation to space. It deals primarily with observation and attention to detail in kinesics (body language), recall and response. Mime is the study of gesture, style, the placing and manipulation of imaginary objects. It is a thinking activity and, because of this, can be used to extend concentration, improve coordination and body awareness as well as improve communication and socialization. By tradition, mime is an activity which involves minimal physical contact between individuals and, because of this, it is also nonthreatening.

There are at least five basic types of mime, and within these categories are numerous subclassifications.[4] Some of these are:

(1) *Personification:* Characterization, demonstrating occupations, clowning, impersonation of animals and solo mime (as in the performance of classical mime).
(2) *Pantomime Blanche:* Setting a scene by "drawing" an object or objects in the air and then utilizing these "objects" in the course of portraying an incident.
(3) *Abstract Mime:* The embodiment of emotions, feelings, forces, and life cycles.
(4) *Traditional Mime:* Using traditional gestures, stories and characterizations from the commedia dell'arte, such as Harlequin or Pantaloon.
(5) *Modern Pantomime:* Complete vignettes, with one or more performers who fully develop characterization, having a conflict or dichotomy at the apex of the tale.

Movement, mime and sound exercises involve the immediate and the intangible. Emphasis upon awareness of these aspects of those media underscores the uniqueness of individual perception. However, because of these very characteristics, it may seem difficult to relate them to such tangible expressions as art or poetry. Clients often wish to have their perceptions validated. This can be accomplished either by translation of the experience into graphic media or, if available, by videotaping of sessions.

Art and Related Media

The rationale for using graphic and plastic media is that color and form fill our environment. Such media lend themselves to correcting patterns of speech, movement and sound, as well as the use of projective and subjective interpretive techniques. For example, the scribble, a graphic form of the "equalizer" concept, can be viewed for suggested images which might then be explored in other media. One form of artistic expression is particularly applicable to drama therapy, and that is the creation and use of masks.

I subscribe to the opinion of Peter Slade, who suggests that masks which do *not* obscure the entire face or head are more popular and effective than those which do.[5] They are also less expensive in time, energy, materials and comfort. Partial masks are more applicable to therapeutic use than full masks because vocal and facial nuances are not inhibited or obscured by them. I have evolved a series of partial masks of a simple eyeglass variety, as well as one I refer to as an Etruscan mask (which resembles a pair of half-glasses or half-rims — the top half — some with noses attached, some without). I provide a firm material, like oaktag, a variety of found materials and colors, doublestick tape and glue, some stencils and scissors. I usually suggest the creation of several masks: a monster; something elaborate or elegant; someone you'd like to talk to or someone you'd like to be; and an animal you might like to pretend to be. A client might be asked to select someone from the group to wear a mask of Someone-To-Talk-To and proceed to have a dialogue. The same client might then don the idealized mask, and the conversation might continue.

Another activity involving the use of arts media in drama therapy is the creation and interaction of puppets. Some of the intrinsic therapeutic values of puppetry are: role and situation exploration; enhancement of concentration; responsiveness and spontaneity; manual coordination; development of communication skills; an opportunity for depersonalization or sublimation of problems through projection; its appeal and, therefore, applicability to a variety of groups and individuals of various ages as well as a variety of physical and social disabilities.

Puppetry can be used to develop insight and promote *catharsis* in conjunction with behavior modification techniques. Because of the properties inherent in projection, it is an effective medium for the reduction of fearfulness when dealing with emotional issues. Symbols can also be objectified and identified through this non-threatening medium. Fantasy can be explored by reaching deep into internalized experiences. Abstract concepts can be objectified and made more comprehensible. Techniques for character development may deal with self and body awareness while encouraging a respect for the identity of others. Techniques of creative drama, improvisation and psychodrama can be explored through puppetry in a manner which is less confrontational. The various skills developed in the process of puppet making and manipulation, as well as performance — whether for an audience of strangers or within the group or institution — can enhance self-image and social integration.

Many of the basic characteristics of puppetry can be related to behavioral difficulties, offering client and therapist an alternative approach to such awareness. The use of verbal skills such as diction, enunciation, voice projection, consistency, listening and reacting are emphasized. Nonverbal skills such as observation and mimicry of body language and gesture are also encouraged. Manual dexterity and the enhancement of both large and small muscle activity can be encouraged or inhibited depending upon the types of puppets selected.

Besides marionettes and string puppets, there are rod puppets, hand puppets and shadow puppets. Within each of these categories there are several other types. Rod puppets have a main support and may have additional rods attached to body parts to be articulated. These are frequently used in silhouette with back lighting, as with other shadow puppets. Features and costumes for these shadow puppets are usually defined by cut-outs or intricate patterns of slashes and holes made in the puppets themselves. Characters can be defined by size relationships, by association with a sound or musical instrument which accompanies their appearance, or by speech.

Hand puppets of the sleeve or mitten variety are simpler to manipulate than three-finger or fist types of puppets. As with all forms of puppetry, it is important to remember that puppets are a form of doll and should not be used to replace dolls, nor should they be over-used, allowing the client to become arrested in this doll stage of play and interaction. The use of puppets should not be restricted to one place or theatre. Because they are an excellent medium for working through themes of violence and trauma, puppets should be made of relatively sturdy materials in order not to compound any guilt inspired by a puppet broken during a therapy session.

It has been the experience of the author and others[5] that the use of puppetry during the adolescent years of 10 to 13 may reflect regression to the doll stage mentioned. It may be that the client has not previously had such an opportunity, has been isolated from siblings or peers, or has been severely withdrawn and needs to work through this stage. However, if such is not the case, then it is better to focus the interest in puppetry on an aspect of craftsmanship commensurate with the child's capabilities.

Groups

A good deal of my group work centers about the concept that cultural creativity serves to foster group solidarity; that cultural creations educate, reconcile past and present, and provide clues to solutions of current social and survival conflicts. My premise is that our culture is a means of knowing ourselves, providing understanding and perspective of where we have been and where we are going. I have devised several exercises which involve the education or training of the group by individual members through mimed instruction of a new game, or a movement/dance sequence. Other exercises refer to concepts of mythology, religion and drama, and the differences in approach to these areas of cultural expression. In the mythological exercise, the group may be asked to quickly evolve and perform a mime on the theme of creation. In the religious adaptation of this exercise, the group may be asked to create a mime based upon the significance of a sculpture which they have created from their shoes. Other dramatizations may be based upon life experiences, or the group may devise scripts from a series of words, nouns, verbs and adjectives (some of which suggest a season, time of day and place where the action is to take place) which they have contributed and which are written down for all to see and refer to. Each group is counseled to select one word from each category in order to devise their dramatization. Aside from the satisfaction which the group derives once the mystique of creativity is swept aside, scripts tend to proliferate, and life experiences are explored more freely, even when the group is of mixed age levels.

Many of the group drama and mime activities are first worked through in clay medium, without verbal exchange. I have found that concepts and roles are crystallized much more quickly, and the resulting dramatizations are much more clear and succinct than those arrived at by group discussion.

Before the session concludes, we will discuss the aspects of group dynamics and creative process experienced during the exercises. This, in turn, will suggest the direction and areas of exploration to be dealt with in future sessions.

4   TECHNIQUES

I begin each session with activities designed to relax physical and emotional tensions and acquaint the individual or group with the therapist, each other and the techniques and media available. We then progress to a core activity which is therapeutically direc-tive, but which is often based upon material expressed in the warm-up activities. (Therefore it is essential that the therapist have a thorough grounding in observation and sensitivity to group and individual dynamics.) Subsequent to the core activity, the session usually concludes with a restorative activity designed to give personal satisfaction to the client. This may then be followed by a general discussion and explication.

An example of a simple progression might begin with a warm-up activity designed to loosen and stretch large muscle groups, often to the rhythmical accompaniment of music or sounds made by the participants. The next step might be a simple mime exer-cise in the dynamics of movement: e.g., participants may be asked to carry a heavy load of wash through a variety of environmental textures such as deep snow, hardening cement or a field of tickling fingers. The burden is put down and various pieces of laundry hung upon the line in such a way that any observer might recognize the objects. Keeping in context, the group might be asked to relax after such heavy work and enjoy the warmth of the sun. They might be encouraged to imagine that they are somewhere special, a place they have visited in the past, or hoped to visit, or even hoped existed. This becomes a sort of guided fantasy in sensory awareness of this imaginary or remembered place. They may be asked to use any real or magical means to bring back something special to them from this place, an object which can be large as a house or as small as a sunbeam, or as indefinable as a mood. When the clients have been restored to an active state, they may then be requested to mime or draw or, in some personally directed nonverbal manner, depict what they brought back and why, what they saw and did, whom they met, or how they felt in that special place.

This sequence might be followed by a dramatization using a conductor: e.g., a scene from a client's childhood might be enacted by other members of the group cast in their roles by the client/director/conductor. These actors create a spontaneous improvisation based upon information provided by the director/conductor.

The preceding guided fantasy has attuned the group to sensory impressions while the improvisation has provided the client/conductor with an opportunity to relive a possibly threatening occurrence as an observer. In addition, the client/conductor may derive insight into his own interpretations or recollected fantasy of what actually occurred.

A concluding exercise for such a session might be to have the group or client reconstruct the scene and environment in such a way as to provide an idealization of the depicted circumstances. This final creation may be the result of a group effort to "put the whole thing right" and resolve any remaining conflicts.

Another progression might begin with a scribble drawing for the warm-up activity. The client might be asked to select colors for anger, laughter, and joy to be added to the scribble. Small group discussions of these drawings may suggest the subsequent core activity, or the therapist might proceed with external sound drawings. For these depictions, clients who are not threatened by it are requested to close their eyes, listen carefully and to identify at least five sounds within their immediate perceptual range. They are asked to depict them in color, mass and movement on paper. Another way to approach this exercise might be for the group to listen, eyes closed, while the therapist makes a series of sounds (such as spinning an egg beater or squeaking a screw and nut) and then asks the group to mimic the sounds, one by one. This last exercise facilitates awareness of the qualities of sound such as tempo and pitch. A drawing or mime might be created based upon associations with the sounds or their genesis.

Yet another sound warm-up exercise involves the combination of nonverbal sounds with actions. Long and short sounds, vowel and consonant sounds, emotion and response sounds, question and answer sounds, all can be combined with actions such as thrust and withdrawal, contained and flowing movements, etc. These exercises may then be discussed in terms of individual consistencies and inconsistencies in speech, body language and social relationships. For example, a client's pictures may be monochromatic while his speech is colorful; his pictures dynamic, but his movements constrained.

The core activity might involve mask making and dialogues, such as were mentioned earlier, or the creation of puppets for future dramatizations based upon scripts derived from the warm-up exercises.

Closure might be achieved either through discussion of the preceding activities or through a guided fantasy to a happy and friendly place.

Warm-up Activities

Aside from simple physical warm-up activities, there are a variety of activities designed to facilitate socialization, understanding and physical awareness through dramatic interaction. Emphasis is placed upon clarity of communication, group and partner relationships and the dimensions of sound and silence. Many of these exercises are based on trust, dependency, leadership and cooperation. Contests of balancing and supporting each other's weight; letting another person lift slightly, articulate and lower head and limbs; blind journey in which one person leads the blindfolded partner about, introducing him or her to various obstacles and textures and sounds available; all of these activities can be pleasurable and useful.

Improvisational techniques, such as miming the opening of a package, displaying the contents and passing it about among other members of the group; the mimed passing of ping-pong balls, baseballs, medicine balls and balloons; mimed objects which are passed to another who reshapes and remakes the imaginary object into a new and different one (transformations); enacting a party, complete with refreshments: all encourage a quality of humor and clarity of action.

Art techniques, such as gesture drawings, are a quick way of getting to core issues. Gesture drawings are executed in a matter of seconds, three in a row; there is no attempt to depict or cipher them. After the last drawing is completed, clients are asked to go back to the first one, to title it, and then proceed to the second, and then the third. All three are viewed in sequence and, if a core issue is not present, the linear movements may be enacted physically and discussed in terms of implication.

Core Activities

Family sculpture and tableaux are valuable tools for revealing attitudes towards relationships. Postures and placement of group members are determined by one client who is also asked to include himself in the sculpture. The therapist exchanges positions with each group member in turn, enabling that person to view the entire tableaux. Each group member will state how it feels for him or her to be in that physical position and relationship to others. Then the client is asked to pose the group again, in a different relationship, i.e., idealized or realistic. Each member of the group has a turn at this, providing a complete visualization of attitudes and relationships.

Another approach pertains to dream material. We all dream in images, usually in color and occasionally in sound. It seems only logical to explore this most fertile area of creative ideation while using media the client finds most consistent with the experience. This may begin as a graphic expression which is then discussed and, perhaps, enacted. Dramatization of dream material can often penetrate its silence and give it a multi-dimensional reality, leading to clarification and desensitization.

Guided Fantasies and Closure

Guided fantasies may be used in a number of ways: for warm-up activities, as an introduction to sensory awareness; in core activities, to provide access to the variety of individual responses to the same stimuli; and in closure, to restore clients to a peaceful and constructive emotional state before ending the session.

Closure is an essential part of every session as well as of the therapeutic contract. Most often it is accomplished through discussion; however, it is wise for the therapist to have a variety of closure techniques available, as clients may simply be "talked out." Closure implies the tying up of loose ends, the restoring of the client to no less a position of strength than when he arrived and, if possible, providing him with an awareness of the coping methods developed in the course of the session or therapy.

No one technique for closure is applicable in all circumstances. Although some have been suggested, the best techniques are those which are derived from the core activities, the warm-up, or the course which the therapy has taken.

5   CONCLUSION AND DISCUSSION

In my work with adolescents and young adults, I have identified certain vital areas of conflict which lend themselves particularly well to a multi-arts approach to drama therapy. In addition, this concept is amenable to work with the physically and socially impaired as well as the handicapped.

Adolescents are particularly concerned about their physical changes and appearance. Conflicts of sexual identity; dependence and independence; peer, parent or other adult role models; individual and group identity; as well as idealized and practical political, economic and ecological intervention, occupy most of them much of the time.

Although they are very responsive to dramatic activity, their limited body awareness inhibits much of their movement and mime activity. Many have already accepted codification concerning their creative and nonverbal communications potentials. "I have two left feet, a tin ear and am all thumbs; I can't even draw a straight line," are among the complaints registered. I was recently privileged to work with an adventitiously blinded dyslexic adolescent boy of average or better intelligence, who evidenced most of the conflicts mentioned. This young man had the additional burden, common to the handicapped child, of a sense of guilt and responsibility — whether real or imagined — for the infirmity suffered.

Before his accident, the boy had been reading far behind grade level, which had resulted in a limited self-image of his career potentials. He also suffered from a mixed dominance which interfered with his athletic abilities. He was the fifth child in a family of eight. After his accident, Jay hated himself and identified with his three-year-old brother (an unwanted child).

In trying to ascertain how much Jay knew and could adapt to learning in a sightless environment, I presented him with a series of tactile materials. We were both startled to discover how acute his tactile sense already was, undoubtedly a compensatory measure for his visual dyslexia. I had hopes that, with his innate intelligence, curiosity and this highly developed tactile ability, we would soon have him reading by Braille at or above grade level. Among the difficulties encountered in initiating this plan was the fact that it would be at least a year before total blindness, legal blindness (impaired vision) or partial vision could definitely be identified and a prognosis stated. The State Association for the Blind was forced to defer any Braille instruction until the time when it became absolutely necessary. It never did.

Jay was eager to keep abreast of the academic program being offered to his classmates at school. An English studies project involved the creation of skits and scripts for plays. Taking advantage of the youngster's hunger for and innate sense of humor, we used a basic technique of improvisation involving conflict of interest. We performed a mime routine: an assembly-line task of removing an item from the belt and transferring it to a container while trying to unwrap and eat a candy bar at the same time without losing the timing. The hilarity which followed, as the young man ran through various classroom activities, contrasting them with inner desires inspired by girls and spring fever, was exciting to us both. A script was developed, put on tape and submitted to the teacher. It brought Jay one of the first appropriate grades he had ever received in this subject, with all the associative benefits such academic and peer recognition could bring.

Initially, movement activities were designed to counter the effects of inactivity and medications, and consisted of exercises to increase stamina and coordination. However, it soon became clear that physical contact with a female therapist was embarrassing and inhibiting. A male tutor attended several of our sessions, and exercises in body contact, support, dependence and body awareness were worked out with the tutor's willing assistance. Jay seemed to have a good sense of proportional relationships of body parts (as evidenced by pipe-cleaner figures and other models), but seemed to have no sense of the relationships of these body parts to height, weight or function.

Problems of isolation and socialization were worked through by means of creating a physical environment, complete with assorted textural recesses expressing moods and desires, made out of several huge refrigerator cartons, carpet and fabric samples. Exercises involved both the male tutor and myself being blindfolded and then given or denied access to this environment, according to mood or circumstance. Eventually, as partial vision was restored to one eye, small windows were cut and the doorway enlarged by Jay for easier access and protection.

Family relationships were explored through the use of adjectives or adverbs to describe family members, and then these words were expressed in abstract clay forms. (Using adjectives and adverbs is far less threatening to the uninitiated than asking them to create human figures.) These figures were placed in a diorama depicting the relationships, and several dramatic enactments followed. Sound exercises in which the tutor and I participated by echoing as precisely as possible the way Jay whispered, yelled and cooed his own name, revealed the difficulty we all have in being truly angry with ourselves, and the embarrassment we feel in putting positive feelings about ourselves to voice.

Three years have passed. Jay is a junior in high school now. He has his driver's license, but is not yet dating. He is not involved in physical activities other than farm chores and automotive tinkering (the last has become a passion of his). His teachers and school officials seem disinterested now that Jay is no longer a cause célèbre. I have not worked with him since he returned to school full-time.

Mime has been particularly effective in building towards a positive self-image among adolescents. Allowing the "me" that each of us has locked up inside to find external acknowledgment can transform the whole individual. But the exposure must be done gently, practiced continuously, supported and given sufficient time to come into its own. Opportunities for humor and play make it particularly attractive to adolescents. Students and groups seem to benefit most from a project orientation. Whether the project is an actual performance before a specific or general audience, on tape or live, or merely the development of a completed script, a vignette or a characterization performed by the group itself, it seems to clarify the points of study, crystallize concepts for the individuals and provide unity and motivation for continued work.

"When in great joy, man pronounces words.
The words not sufficing, he elongates them.
The elongated words not sufficing, he modulates them.
The modulated words not sufficing, without even being conscious
    of it —
He finds his hands gesticulating and his feet bouncing."
— Ancient Chinese Proverb[6]

FOOTNOTES

1. Moly Kemp, a music therapist and teacher in Great Britain, defines "internal sound" as that sound which is remembered but not current. "External sound" is defined as that which is heard but not made by the listener. I would define "creative non-verbal sound" as that made by the

individual, consciously or unconsciously, which is not specifically elicited by or abstracted from physiological sources or mimicry.

2. Frank L. Baum, *The Wizard of Oz*, RKO film adaptation of the book.
3. *Random House Dictionary* (New York: Random House, 1967), p. 1043.
4. James Dodding, *Mime One Two Three, Teacher's Handbook* (Dublin: Litho Arts, 1972), p. 2-3.
5. Peter Slade, *Child Drama* (London: University of London Press, 1954), pp. 319-20.
6. Dodding, *Mime One Two Three*, p. 2.

HUGH JAMES LURIE, M.D., Clinical Associate Professor of Psychiatry at the University of Washington, Seattle, also serves as director of mental health media for the Department of Psychiatry and Behavioral Sciences, and is medical director at the Tacoma-Pierce County Child Guidance Clinic, Tacoma.

Chapter 17

THE ACTRESS AS A MENTAL HEALTH TEACHER

Hugh James Lurie

1 INTRODUCTION

This paper describes the role of an actress in a program for the psychiatric education of nonpsychiatrist physicians and nurses.[1] Not only can the actress use her skills in role playing and simulated interviewing situations, but she can also become an active and essential member of the psychiatric teaching team. In the program described here, the actress has come to serve as an individual and group therapist and as a communications facilitator. The situations in which she can effectively serve these functions are delineated, and the general implications for a broader role for an actress in continuing education programs are discussed.

Experiential and participatory teaching and learning have become of increasing interest to educators, especially those mental health educators concerned with the teaching of psychiatric skills.[2] Experiential models using professional actors as a key ingredient in such learning and teaching programs have been described by others,[3] as well as by this author.[4] The following paper describes a program for continuing education of nonpsychiatrist physicians at the University of Washington in which an actress has been utilized as a resource person, as well as an integral and often essential part of the psychiatric *teaching* team.

The paper will attempt to describe: (1) the possible roles of a professional actress within a teaching program in psychiatry; (2)

263

the reactions of physicians and other health professionals to the presence and active intervention of the actress; (3) the roles of the actress as individual and group therapist for the teaching group and as a communication facilitator; (4) guidelines which we have developed for the function of an actress in such a program; and (5) general implications for teaching and learning.

2 THE ACTRESS: QUALIFICATIONS, PREPARATION FOR JOB, SPECIFIC COACHING

S. L. is a professional actress, forty years old, who moved to the West Coast with her husband three years ago when he became a permanent member of the Seattle Repertory Theater Company. She had appeared in various productions on the East Coast sporadically over the past ten years, but had not acted regularly since the birth of her children. Since coming to the West Coast, she has intermittently appeared in children's plays, summer theatre productions sponsored by the Seattle Parks Department, and the Seattle Repertory Theater.

S. L. was first approached about role playing problem patients opposite a Washington family physician in interviews to be video-taped and later discussed by various physician groups. Although initially it was necessary to give her a great deal of background information about the kind of patient she was to simulate (age, occupation, number of children, specific somatic symptoms), together with some material about a possible "life script" for such a patient (ways of relating, crisis points, characterologic features, nonverbal behavior), after several months, during which numerous videotapes were made, the actress learned to improvise the most important ingredients of the many life script situations. Following a few hints on the type of person involved and the characteristic behavior patterns of such a patient, it was only about specific symptoms which might need to be accentuated (such as the character of certain hallucinations, or important features of depressive symptomatology) that the actress needed coaching.[5] At this point, with very little help, she could function autonomously in a variety of teaching and demonstration roles, some of which are described below.

3 CONFERENCE AND WORKSHOP DEMONSTRATIONS

Simulated interviews between actress and psychiatrist have served to demonstrate strategies of interviewing, diagnostic features of specific syndromes, problems inherent in certain patients, or to present dramatically a medical-cultural issue. S. L. has participated in conferences for several hundred people, portraying varied roles: a woman with retarded depression, one with a hysterical character structure who has many vague somatic complaints, an agitated, suicidal housewife, a patient who learns she is dying of cancer, a provocative and hostile woman who demands specific medication, a seductive patient, a woman with problems of sexual unresponsiveness, a patient severely depressed after a hysterectomy, a divorcée with conflicts about masturbating for sexual satisfaction, a woman uncertain about participating in sexual foreplay with her husband, and so forth. These demonstration interviews have been used to illustrate presentations by guest speakers about a particular topic, or to provide a "panel of experts" with material to which they can react.

Audience response to these demonstrations has been very favorable. Many participants in continuing programs have urged inclusion of many more interviews because they so effectively elicit both diagnostic and intervention issues. Since all of the transactions and demonstrations in which the actress participates are "unscripted" and thus have a spontaneous flavor, observers feel encouraged to speculate about what *they* would do as the interviewer, and how *they* might approach such a patient.

Although the actress continues to participate in our large conferences, she increasingly has become more involved in much less formal workshops, offered in small communities for local health professionals (particularly physicians) in order to emphasize the psychological aspects of medical practice. These small workshops focus on encouraging the development of specific diagnostic, in-

terviewing, and intervention skills by the participants, and the roles
the actress is called upon to play are of two types.

The Fixed Role

The workshop as a whole is focused on a particular syndrome or
problem which the actress has studied in advance. Here S. L.
might portray five different types of depressed patients with both
the psychiatrist running the program and some of the participants
in the workshop. Discussion after each short interview allows the
nonpsychiatrist participants and the psychiatrist-teacher to engage
in a dialogue about dynamics, diagnostic signs and symptoms,
strategies of intervention, and specific intervention statements; the
physicians themselves have a chance to try out the suggestions
which emerge in this discussion. The actress's portrayal of the
fixed role at workshops permits the introduction of subjects which
are usually impossible to dramatize with real patients, e.g., taking
a sexual history from a sexually unresponsive woman, interviewing a dying patient, dealing with an extremely abusive and hostile
patient, or interviewing a seductive patient. The fixed role format
works particularly well for new groups, unaccustomed to experiential learning, anxious to see a visible product during the conference, in this case, an interview conducted by a "psychiatric
expert."

The Sudden Improvisation Role

This role has become increasingly prominent in repeat workshops within our program in small communities. On these occasions groups of physicians and other health professionals are asked
about specific problem patients that they encounter in their professional lives. The actress, with a few cues from the professional
involved, then becomes that patient, and the health professional
suggesting the problem becomes the interviewer. These simulations
become problem-solving situations in which the psychiatrist-expert
and the participants can observe a transaction and then present a
critique of it; members of the participating group themselves not
only can propose alternative styles of interviewing, but also have
the opportunity to try them out on the spot. Thus, a physician who

is extremely competent, but who always seems to have trouble with a particular type of patient, can recognize — through this dramatization — that by the way he confronts his patient, he is entering into a struggle with her, and that an alternative way of dealing with the patient would be more successful. Most health professionals involved in these workshops have responded enthusiastically to the teaching of interviewing skills in this problem-solving situation, in which new behaviors and alternative strategies can be tried immediately, while still relevant to particular patients known to the doctors.

Related activities for the actress have included playing the protagonist in family therapy situations or demonstrations emphasizing male-female differences. As will be discussed later, her roles have gradually been modified as many of our workshops, initially aimed exclusively at physicians, became interdisciplinary and began to include nurses, office personnel, social workers, and school counselors. Here the presence of the actress has encouraged the examination of such issues as male and female views of sexuality, areas of conflict between doctors and nurses, and different professional views of helping situations.

4 PARTICIPANT RESPONSE

The response of physicians and other health professionals to the actress has been quite interesting. In the fixed role situations, at both large conferences and small workshops, the reactions have been reasonably predictable. At the start of a demonstration interview, participants tended to view the actress as an "entertainer" and were relatively detached from her performance. As the interview proceeded, however, observers became much more engrossed in the diagnostic and treatment issues being raised and began to see the situation as a real transaction between therapist and patient. If the actress was portraying a hostile or angry patient, the initial reaction of the observing group was often one of apprehension and anxiety: they viewed the actress as threatening the interviewer or as being in a position to "show him up." At times the anxiety was so great that workshop participants refused to try interviewing the "hostile patient" for fear of becoming too angry to be effective, or being humiliated in front of their colleagues. The psychiatrist-teacher conducting the interview could often allay these fears by showing that he is not afraid of the patient and that he viewed the transaction as a problem-solving situation rather than a personal threat.

When the actress has engaged in less structured situations such as sudden improvisations, idiosyncratic responses have emerged, including a projection onto the actress of all those personal characteristics which have been troublesome in the transaction between the physician and a real patient. Thus, interviewers have assumed "bitchiness" on the part of the actress, even when her behavior did not suggest it; the interviewer has become fearful that he was harming the patient by his intervention; and the physician has suffered feelings of intense guilt when the simulated patient began to cry. When such reactions begin to emerge, the actress has to remove herself momentarily from her role to reassure the physician that she is indeed role playing, that she is intact, and that she is able to survive the interventions by the interviewer—even if they are not entirely successful. After simulated interviews, physicians have often asked for feedback from the actress about how their interviews struck her, whether she felt that other women would share her reactions to the interview, whether other mothers saw things the way she did, and so forth. Here the actress assumes a teaching function, different from and complementary to the role of the psychiatrist-teacher.

5   NEW ROLES

The part played by the actress in the "fixed role" and "sudden improvisation role" is not a new one in the history of the search for more interesting and relevant ways of teaching psychiatric skills to nonpsychiatrists.[6] Over the past year, however, the actress has gradually assumed other roles in our program less related to her acting talents. As she has participated in workshops including health workers other than primary physicians, she has been called upon to demonstrate skills not initially anticipated.

In those workshops involving mainly physicians and nurses, the actress has often been a key person in facilitating communication and discussion between both groups. This has come about in several different ways. Sometimes the actress has functioned as co-leader in an interdisciplinary group and, in such a capacity, has been able to draw women, particularly nonphysicians, into a general discussion about the topic at hand. In conjunction with this role, S.L. has demonstrated that she is not afraid of saying what she thinks to doctors (either the physicians within the group or the psychiatrist-teacher of the program), and has thereby indicated a new model of interaction. As a neutral person she mediates between the stereotyped inferior position into which some physicians tend to place nurses (including their own personnel) and the stereotyped godlike position into which many nurses tend to put doctors (including those who employ them). Since the actress does not share these stereotypes and seems equally open in relating to both doctors and nurses, the groups themselves are inspired to begin interacting in a different way.

During the discussion periods of the workshops, the actress and the psychiatrist-teacher may talk about issues which have emerged in the group discussion or the demonstration; here the actress becomes a co-leader also, one whom the groups generally tend to view as "Mother" (with the psychiatrist as "Father"), or as an archetype of "female" (with the psychiatrist as "male"). The actress's group facilitation function is crucial in allowing personnel from different disciplines to consider working as a team with mutual respect, in contrast to the traditional hierarchical relationship.

Lastly, in discussions of adult sexuality or family problems the actress, by her apparent ease in talking about, demonstrating, and dramatizing the issues, allows the group to become more comfortable with these topics.

6 GUIDELINES

(1) If specific issues in a program lend themselves to dramatization, it is definitely desirable to include an actress for that purpose. The presentation is seen as entertaining and often amusing, and the resultant relaxation of tensions allows the participants to become involved.

(2) If the subject matter in some way involves male-female issues

(such as doctor-nurse relationships or male and female sexuality), demonstration interviews with an actress can provide material which otherwise might be overlooked or not emerge at all.

(3)   In keeping with the principle that the amount of structure is indirectly related to the amount of anxiety in the participants,[7] the leader of a workshop can work with an actress in imposing a high degree of structure at particularly tense moments (in fixed role playing), or much less structure (spontaneous role playing with details provided by workshop participants). This flexibility allows participants to get into as much depth in personal feelings and problem-solving as they wish, without involving more self-revelation and personal commitment than seems comfortable at any particular time.

(4)   Whereas a psychiatrist-teacher is often seen as an authority figure within a workshop situation, an actress in the program may be seen as a neutral participant who may legitimately make interventions, comment, and act as a facilitator in a less threatening way.

(5)   The actress's dramatization of characteristic problem situations serves to introduce problems of family or couples therapy and sexual issues without participants having to expose their own personal beliefs.

(6)   Because of her function as "entertainer," the actress often introduces an aspect of humor which facilitates the learning process.

(7)   By actively dramatizing treatment and intervention issues, the actress frees the psychiatrist-teacher to act as a facilitator of group discussion: he is not required to pose all of the problems himself and then in turn be responsible for directing discussion about these issues.

(8)   If a degree of comfort can be demonstrated to exist between the psychiatrist-teacher and the actress, participants in the workshop may be able to view the teacher as an individual and a colleague, rather than as a threatening authority.

7 CONCLUSIONS

This paper has tried to demonstrate how including an actress in a program concerned with teaching psychiatric skills to non-psychiatrist health personnel can increase the degree of learning by facilitating discussion about controversial subjects (such as sexuality), by dramatizing how such controversies can be resolved, and by promoting discussion between doctors and nurses. The actress's role playing of problem patients allows students the opportunity to experiment with new strategies and interventions and to develop specific skills. Finally, the talents of an actress can enable participants in a teaching program, particularly in a small workshop, to realize their difficulties with their own problem patients and confront their attitudes toward them.[8]

FOOTNOTES

1. This investigation was supported by the Public Health Service research grant #MH11984 from the National Institute of Mental Health.
2. M. Knowles, *Informal Adult Education* (New York: Association Press, 1950); idem, "Connative Strategies for Continuing Education: An Overview" (Paper presented at the 11th Annual Training Institute for Psychiatrist-Teachers of Practicing Physicians, WICHF, Boulder, Colorado, 1971).
3. H. Jason, *et al.*, "New Approaches to Teaching Basic Interview Skills to Medical Students," *American Journal of Psychiatry* 127 (1971): 1404–7; D. Naftulin, interview with the author, Albuquerque, New Mexico, March 1971.
4. H. J. Lurie, *Use of Video Tapes, Professional Actors, Structured Games and Role Playing for Psychiatric Education of Rural Physicians.* Film presented to the Fifth World Congress of Psychiatry, Mexico, 1971.
5. It may be pointed out here that in order to reach this degree of acuity and self-sufficiency, S. L. did a good deal of self-rehearsing, trying out in her mind various ways of presenting character types displaying different symptoms. She filed these types, their possible disorders, their biographies, and even scraps of characteristic dialogue—often with labels (e.g., "the lady whose husband drank"). This prevented any confusion of pertinent detail in an interview situation and created a sort of shorthand for communicating with her colleagues prior to an interview.
6. Knowles, *Informal Adult Education;* A. J. Enelow and L. M. Adler,

"Psychiatric Skills and Knowledge for the General Practitioner," *J.A.M.A.* 189 (1964): 91–96; N. Kagan and P. G. Schauble, "Affect Simulation in Interpersonal Process Recall," *Journal of Counselling Psychology* 16 (1969): 309–13.
7. Milton M. Berger, ed., *Video Tape Techniques in Psychiatric Training and Treatment* (New York: Brunner-Mazel, 1970); S. J. Danish and S. L. Brodsky, Training of Policemen in Emotional Control and Awareness," *American Psychologist* 25 (1970): 368–69; N. Kagan, *et al.*, "Methods for the Study of Medical Inquiry" (Unpublished paper, Medical Inquiry Project, College of Human Medicine, Michigan State University, 1970); H. Wilmer, "Television as a Participant Recorder," *American Journal of Psychiatry* 125 (1968): 1157–63.
8. I am indebted to Susan and Clayton Corzatte and to Margit Gerow for their help in the preparation of this paper.

Part 4
DRAMA THERAPY AND THEATRE

The ancient Greek theatre, as Aristotle said, was psychologically healthful for the audience. Prior to that, the theatrical performances of early man were therapeutic for the total community. In the recent past, however, the playhouse provided a form of voyeurism: "naturalistic" theatre was a window through which we examined other people's lives.

Modern theatre forms, however, have consistently pushed back the barriers between actors and audience. Many professional performances today are specifically aimed at participation in order to achieve social and/or psychological health. Interestingly, such professional performances have, as their forerunners, the children's theatre companies of Peter Slade and Brian Way, formed many years ago.

This part has four chapters dealing with drama therapy in theatre in various ways. Al Fann discusses his work with the black community in Harlem in his own inimitable way. His production of *King Heroin* had a remarkable success in the United States, and he particularly describes the effect of his work with two talented people requiring help (Chapter 18).

Jonathan Fox provides a clear picture of his Playback Theater as a community form related to both psychodrama and creative drama (Chapter 19). Actors in the company improvise the stories of members of the audience, and the focus of the form is on the person in society rather than the psychiatric patient.

Ramon Gordon describes his therapeutic work with prisoners in his Cell Block Theatre (Chapter 20). He demonstrates a method that leads from improvisation to performance in ways that are suitable for offenders.

Finally, Louis Miller describes a remarkable social experiment taking place in Israel (Chapter 21). In disintegrated communities, the improvised theatre can provide a form of social cohesion that leads to cultural community action and the rebuilding of psychological health.

AL FANN is a performer for television, radio, films, and theatre. His Broadway credits include roles in *Porgy and Bess* and *The Wiz*, among others. Associated with Cleveland's Karamu House for fifteen years, he is now artistic director of the Al Fann Theatrical Ensemble, which has branches in New York City and Hollywood.

Chapter 18

DRAMA AND THE UNDERPRIVILEGED MIND

Al Fann

1 INTRODUCTION

Although I am convinced that drama is normally self-motivating, it is of paramount importance to stimulate the development of the underprivileged mind. Unlike the majority of young people seeking a career in the creative arts, and specifically acting, the youngsters who come to me are disadvantaged blacks, Puerto Ricans, West Indians, Jamaicans, and so on.

They seek me out, first, because I am black and this fact in itself makes them more comfortable. They anticipate that I will be more sympathetic and sensitive to their cause — better yet, to their effect — their effect of a low self-image, insecurity and inferiority complexes. Second, since I operate in Harlem, they know I will understand that they have no bank account. The third and most important reason is that they have learned that I can help them. They have learned through agencies, unions and word-of-mouth about the achievements of other students, and that Al Fann would not be stopped in his endeavors to help and train them — he would direct their artistic development as well as their personal growth, delve into their lives and help their personal problems. This aspect, I admit, had not been anticipated in my initial endeavor to train youngsters under the anti-poverty program.

In drama, during the process of building a stable foundation, two goals must be placed in juxtaposition: that of a professional

277

actor, and that of a positive, goal-striving individual. One intention will invariably affect the other. The margin between the development of self and the specialized creative art is tissue thin. One cannot hope to succeed in attaining the goal of a solid "person" if the mind has not been nurtured to receive the knowledge that the acting profession demands.

In order to achieve this change (which is basic), there must be reprogramming. This has been my endeavor in dealing with the young people in my drama workshop. The oh-so-delicate minds have walls of defense and insecurity. They have been deprived of a positive self-image which must be reared painstakingly from childhood.

Each person who comes to me with the desire to become an actor also has his own concept of life. The first aim is to establish a relationship. The instructor seeks to find a common ground of communication. He encourages the student to express himself in order to expose a point of interest, which the instructor may use to stimulate further discussion and exploration. That point may be found in a variety of subjects: a hidden desire, a dream of the future, an admiration for a hero, an interest in music, a dislike for certain foods and, in general, a hope for a better way of life.

Because of insecurity, it is common that the student will only mention areas in which he is adept: for example, a sport, his creativity with a musical instrument, or his grades in school. Frequently he will seek a point from which he hopes to gain needed recognition from his instructor. He may studiously avoid conversations concerning weaknesses which may tend to push his self-image even lower. He may purposely refrain from conversations about his parents, home life, relationships with brothers and sisters, school teachers, or other aspects which may have influenced his present state of being. He is usually embarrassed about his lack of success and achievement up to now. Quite often, he has little hope for improvement, although part of his purpose for coming is a desperate search for any sign to believe in himself, as well as hope for the future. He may have yearnings for expression and a somewhat unhealthy ego that seeks constant recognition. The instructor must be careful to select points upon which he can *agree* with the student.

This allows the student to gain some much needed successes, before meeting with the setbacks which are inevitable.

As the instructor democratically guides the student into a series of positive experiences, a form of confidence begins to manifest itself. The student begins to understand the instructor, and his intent to provide techniques designed to help the student understand himself. A bond of trust is established. Repetition of similar techniques causes the relationship between student and teacher to flourish, and an affinity between the minds develops.

This bond is the foundation for motivating the underprivileged mind; it allows for the use of drama as a therapeutic tool. Once this foundation is solid, the student has a basis with which to confront his weaknesses and insecurities. Then the instructor must be willing to risk a loss in the relationship by bringing the student face to face with his wrong decisions and wrong beliefs. The instructor must force him to examine the validity of his negative attitudes. To this end, certain exercises designed as confrontational tools are employed. One of the first of these is "Basic Confronting."

2 BASIC CONFRONTING EXERCISES

Purpose: to train the student to *confront* (with the absence of social tricks, conversation, or compulsive habits); to be interesting; to eradicate insecurity by being honest and himself. This aids him to become stronger and to focus on his intentions.

Training Stress: This exercise is done in two main parts:

(1) The students sit facing each other with eyes *closed.* The idea is for them to sit without undue influence from external stimuli, and to be rid of the fear of the unknown. All irregular breathing, eye blinking, body and facial movements must cease. The students sit, sustaining their posture for some length of time. The exercise must be repeated until their behavior is stable.

(2) The students sit facing each other with eyes open. They must sit and look at each other, say and do nothing for a long time. They must not blink, fidget, giggle or be embarrassed, or in any way try to influence each other verbally or with a body part. The action is to accustom the student to really look at

others, and to counteract any negative or unwanted influences while maintaining control over his own being.

Following the successful achievement of this exercise, the student proceeds to the next confrontation exercise, "Advancement." This is practiced first with an instructor. After an orientation period, the student practices the exercise with another student. In this way, a transition of confidence begins to take place. Previously, the student's only area of confidence has been with his instructor. When he confronts another peer, he begins to transfer confidence into himself. An intensifying of techniques must ensue, designed to build from this spark of confidence to a solid foundation. The student acquires the needed courage to examine himself and, ultimately, understand himself.

When the student is courageous enough to examine himself, the areas of weakness and insecurity (previously avoided) are approached. This is accomplished by encouraging more communication between instructor and student. He is confronted directly by the instructor whom he now trusts, and made aware of certain weaknesses that he has purposely avoided in their talks. The instructor asks for direct reasons "Why?" He then must discipline himself to remain totally silent until he gets an answer. Next he must listen until the student concludes his answer. If he has rationalized to avoid the truth, the instructor must respond with "I *understand,* but I don't believe you've included all the facts, therefore it causes a breakdown in communication." The instructor then proceeds to point out the gaps and inconsistencies involved in the student's response. In this way he induces the student to examine his own courage and honesty and, thereby, learn more about himself. Should the student be truthful in his response, then the instructor simply analyzes the problem, points out the aspects that are important, and advises him accordingly. Through the aid of the instructor, the student is able to see his relation to the problem. He is counselled as to his relationships and responsibilities. He is shown the areas in the problem that have no validity—those which distort the facts and, thereby, cause him to function on false premises and invariably reach the wrong conclusion—and produce frustration.

As the student progresses in self and artistic development, a higher form of communication is required. The improved student is now dealing with scripts, literature, terminology and new techniques at an advanced level. Most of all, he is dealing with people and characters also on advanced levels. He can find he is sometimes painfully inadequate in expressing his thoughts. Consequently, he may be at a standstill in his efforts to communicate. Thus a new exercise is employed, called "Creative Dialogue."

3 CREATIVE DIALOGUE EXERCISE

Purpose: to develop the creation of meaningful dialogue and the art of listening. It is principally intended to increase the student's creative abilities. But it also brings an awareness of the limitations in his vocabulary, induces more confidence in his ability to think, and expands his thinking. The result is added security in communication.

Training Stress: All the students stand, and the coach instructs one student to initiate a story. He may create on any given subject, in the past tense, and avoiding the word "so" which is used as a crutch in most conversations. All students are to listen and follow the story as it unfolds. At a given time, the coach will call on another to pick up the story and continue. The students are not allowed to repeat the cues.

Incorrect Example:
STUDENT 1   I went downtown and saw a lady . . .
STUDENT 2   *I saw a lady* going into a lingerie department . . .

Correct Example:
STUDENT 1   I went downtown and saw a lady . . .
STUDENT 2   . . . going into a lingerie department . . .

The students are flunked for not following the story, repeating the cues, not speaking loud enough to be heard, not speaking at a regulated speed, going into the present tense, and for the usage of "so" — which can be used in terms of quantity only (i.e., so big, so many, etc.).

This exercise helps motivation. The student is questioned about his knowledge of word definition. He is instructed to read various periodicals, trade papers, dailies, magazines (regular and *Newsweek*) in order to gain a working knowledge of writing styles, terminology, techniques, and so on. He must carry a dictionary at all times, and stop immediately to look up a word he is not absolutely sure of before proceeding. He is made aware that there is no way he can understand definition if he does not have a clear picture of even the seemingly smallest word. If he cannot define it in his own words, it simply means that he does not understand and, therefore, there is no use attempting to go further. He is beginning to learn that without definite understanding of old and new words there can be little communication. In addition to defining words, the student must be instructed in the use of these words, incorporating them into his daily vocabulary. He is also presented with a special list of jargon, covering the fields of stage, television, film, modeling, radio and other related professional drama fields. Again, he must get a picture, memorize, understand and use them as part of his dramatic training.

Technical terminology and techniques are examined thoroughly by the instructor and student. A lamp is brought into class and dismantled. Its components are studied until they are understood. Then it is reassembled and its technical usages explained by the students. The same technical analysis is applied to all areas of backstage and onstage activity. A thorough technical knowledge provides the student with a security about the functioning of different aspects of the stage.

His confidence builds and he is presented with opportunities for expression by auditioning for small parts in a workshop production. His first step is to follow the correct procedure for character building, which includes creating a case history up to the character's entrance in the play. He must find the animal counterpart to his character, and then proceed to the zoo to study the live animal—capturing its true behavior, actions, reactions and movements. He must take notes on its origin, reproduction, instincts and purpose. His next step is to develop the animal characterization and present it in class for evaluation by the instructor. After successfully completing his animal counterpart, it is incorporated into his character. This allows the student to dissociate the character from his normal, habitual self. He finds that not only the function but also the mental aspects of the character are completely individual — his thoughts, reactions, sensitivities, fears, confidences, and so on. A comparison between the character traits created for his character and the traits of his character's animal counterpart, quickly make him aware of the accuracy of his choices. The student's attempt to perform an animal characterization also brings him face to face with another of his weaknesses — insecurity.

The disadvantaged mind invariably presents a shy, inhibited and sensitive self that has a thorough lack of confidence. Crawling around on all fours as an animal forces the student to open himself up and begin to lift the protective veil of insecurity. A successful achievement through his performance can be a rewarding experience which gives him an elevated self-image. Before he can venture out to successfully portray another individual, he must gain enough confidence to expose his inner self in the presence of others. Before he can portray an individual at an advanced level, he must first be able to examine the lives of other individuals at his own level. The most difficult task for a student with a low self-image is to open himself up and attempt to play a character on a level lower than his own. Because of his insecurity and embarrassment, he is prone to protect himself from further pain and scrutiny.

4 IMPROVISATION

At this point, various improvisational tools are employed. Students are given simple situations and told who they are. They must call upon past and present experiences, and knowledge of other individuals. Then they must attempt to create realistically, utilizing themselves and their fellow actors; or, if it is a solo improvisation, the realism must be created within themselves. They must discover how they fit into the situation, what their relationships are, and then go on to create the probability of the outcome.

King Heroin was one such group improvisational exercise which resulted in a full-length play by the Ensemble members. The play dealt with the abuses of drug addiction and its aspects.

It traveled around the country, and was performed for the White House staff under President Nixon. It won fourteen awards on national cable television, including first place as the best play of the year.

Students improvised various situations such as pusher-junkie transactions, various forms of obtaining money (including prostitution and boosting—stealing from department stores and reselling the goods), street mugging and automobile vandalism. They were given situations (such as an addict attempting to retrieve her baby from a social agency) and overall conflicts with law enforcement agencies for theft, robbery and the like. Situations of this nature provided the stimuli for creativity, using the students' experience and knowledge. They improvised characters and created dialogue, and from this effort a script was born.

Case History

One history of character portrayal that was successfully adopted was the case of Joseph Johnson, who is now professionally known as Joseph Ray. He was not a typically disadvantaged teenager when he walked into the Ensemble. He was thirty years old and had somehow escaped the chains of the ghetto. He had served in the armed forces and returned to a job as a typewriter repairman with IBM. After his training course, Joe was assigned to travel from office to office, carrying a beeper on his belt for communication with his main office to receive repair calls. At this point in his life, Joe concluded he had established a pretty good position for himself, particularly as he was married and had a couple of youngsters to feed. During his rounds, he met a young secretary who was a student at the Al Fann Theatrical Ensemble, and this young lady invited Joe to accompany her to one of the classes. He readily accepted.

I gave him permission to sit in and he did just that—sat down at the back and remained there quietly observing. During the class, I involved Joe by asking his opinion of a specific point. For a moment he sat stunned, groping for some word or phrase that would articulate his thoughts. He managed to blurt out something which sounded incoherent and confused. However, he did display a spark of gratitude for being acknowledged and given the recognition of being asked for his opinion on a subject of which he had no previous experience.

When the class ended, the secretary introduced him to me. He asked if he could come back and join the workshop. Naturally I agreed, and a glowing student–instructor relationship began.

To begin with, Joe did not have the security to take part in the classroom activities. He sat and watched. One of the characters that evolved from the improvisation was a drug pusher, whom I later named Lucky. Lucky's character was strong, positive, assertive, and he knew exactly what he wanted out of life. He was completely in charge of himself as well as the addicts with whom he dealt. He was definitely "a pusher on the way up." I needed someone to portray this character. I found that Joe was the only available student who had a similar physical image. However, he had none of the innate qualities of Lucky—in fact, his self-image seemed exactly the opposite—except for *desire.* So I asked Joe to do *me* a favor by reading the lines and standing in until I could get someone to play the character. I was well aware that if I had asked Joe to play Lucky at this point, he would have frozen in terror at the thought of being on the stage. By asking him to do me a *favor,* I relieved him of responsibility to perform with any degree of competency. Thus he was able to start developing a characterization without being aware that he was doing so. Since I realized he could not possibly know the motivations behind the functioning of Lucky, I would get on the stage, act out the various qualities involved in the character, and encourage Joe to imitate me. Little by little, Joe began to take on the characteristics of Lucky and, ultimately, found himself permanently installed in the role.

We began playing for small audiences of workshop friends and parents. This allowed Lucky to gain some much needed security in presenting himself on stage. Later we included schools, churches and community centers. Finally we performed in theatres and large auditoria throughout the New York area. The play attracted the attention of cable television, was televised nationally, and secured a full magazine spread and other media publicity. Joe Johnson was steadily growing as Lucky and as a human being. He was gaining much needed recognition as well as self-confidence.

People began to relate to him as a celebrity. After every performance, they crowded round him for his autograph. He found that there were great rewards for playing the character of a villain.

We built portable sets and began to travel by road to other states: Connecticut, Rhode Island, New Jersey, and so on. By this time, *King Heroin* was becoming nationally known. Although Joe's popularity on stage was growing, his life at home was suffering. He was timid and hesitant in his explanations to his wife about his nights away from home. I invited his wife to the Ensemble and had a serious talk with her about Joe's aspirations. I also invited her to accompany the Ensemble on various performance dates and assured her the children would also be welcomed. Not long after this, Mrs. Johnson became a regular outside member of the Ensemble, joining in as a hostess, or working backstage at various performances.

Joe began to miss days from his job as a result of his out-of-town performances. He was called in by his supervisor for a talk concerning his responsibilities. At this point, Joe still suffered from insecurity offstage — although, as the character of Lucky, he had total belief in himself. He did not have the courage to be truthful about his activities with the Ensemble. He gave as an excuse that his children were ill, all the while fearing that his true activities would be exposed. As *King Heroin* grew, so did Joe's fear of losing his job.

In the theatre, meantime, he had so grown in leadership that I appointed him stage manager of the Ensemble. His appointment created new problems. He still felt somewhat threatened in dealing with the problems of others. This necessitated a different form of training. I began to teach him the principles of "what's right" instead of "who's right." I helped him with attitudes, approaches and, most of all, the potential dangers of expressing emotion when dealing with a crisis. (This problem becomes paramount in the mind of the underprivileged. They have so few achievements and are easily threatened by the smallest inference of their inadequacies. A student must be reminded constantly that it is his *choice* and not *he* who is wrong.) For this problem, we use the "Positive and Negative" exercise to strengthen determination.

5   POSITIVE AND NEGATIVE EXERCISE

Purpose: to maintain the student's state of being without becoming distracted, thrown off, or over-reacting to influences. It is designed to discipline the student to focus on his intentions, regardless of outside stimuli. In drama or in life, one must focus in order to successfully achieve a goal because contra-influences may be subtle or obvious, internal or external.

Training Stress: The coach instructs two students to sit directly in front of each other. Each student is assigned a specific state of being, one positive and one negative. They take turns in initiating dialogue. The receiver of the dialogue must maintain his state of being.

Example:

POSITIVE STATE (Initiator)	I just love the way your hair is fixed.
NEGATIVE STATE (Recipient)	It looks horrible this way.
POSITIVE	You look very pretty to me.
NEGATIVE	That's nonsense.

Each must maintain his state of being regardless of influence. When the coach calls "change," the students switch and take turns in initiating and receiving dialogue. The instructor calls "flunk" on the following charges: body reactions, increased breathing, voice inflections, wrong acknowledgments, facial reactions or physical contact with the opponent.

Special Note: This exercise is specifically designed to get at the student's "buttons" (his points of vulnerability) activated by the words or actions of others. These include actions which cause him discomfort, embarrassment, or which can upset him or make him laugh. Each student is to try to get the other to confront his "buttons" without reaction. When inappropriate actions no longer exist for the student, he has become a more secure person.

This exercise allows an instructor or peer to berate the student at length about anything to which he may be vulnerable. The student is watched closely for the effects of his reactions. Some effects are his obvious adjustments: tensing up to withstand the bombardment, eyes flickering or other signs of resentment. The student must realize that what is being said about him holds no other power than the attention he gives to it. His real self remains intact as long as he disciplines himself to remain uninfluenced.

Joseph Ray was given this approach so that he could use it when settling a dispute between two fellow actors. It is a stage manager's responsibility to listen to both sides of the controversy, analyze the situation and determine "what's right." He must not allow himself to become personally involved.

Joe's day to day confrontations with various problems caused him to become more adept in utilizing this new experience. His poise and self-assurance developed steadily. His duties were extended to making travel arrangements for the troupe, which included air and ground transportation. He was also responsible for packaging and transporting sets, props and costumes. These responsibilities brought him in contact with those above and below his personal development level, thereby demanding flexibility in his communication. Often Joe had to exercise force in his negotiations, since performance deadlines had to be met. Offstage, he never shed the positive attributes of the character of Lucky which he had incorporated into his stage management duties. He was directly responsible for the safety of thirty-five adults and children. This added to his burdensome task, but encouraged his steady growth.

By the time the Ensemble had completed its Washington performance for the White House Staff and Congress, Joe had developed into a fully professional and dependable stage manager. It marked a two-year period of Joe's involvement in the Ensemble workshop. About the same time, I became Associate Producer for Warner Brothers, and was involved in a feature film, *Come Back Charleston Blue*. I immediately employed Joe as a production film assistant. Joe's sterling abilities soon caught the attention of the entire cast and crew, including the Executive Producer, Sam Goldwyn, Jr. We all agreed that Joe should be encouraged to continue his efforts in film, and pursue his goal of becoming a full-fledged assistant director. Joe's efforts not only expanded his involvement in the industry, but did much more to broaden his confidence in himself. Following *Charleston Blue,* requests for his services on additional films demanded more time from his job. Then the moment of crisis arrived. Approximately three years from the day that Joe had walked into the Ensemble, he was faced with a decision which could mean disaster. His financial security and seniority with IBM were threatened. He came to me for advice. I reminded him that we had previously discussed this problem and it was now evident that a decision could be avoided no longer. Joe had to decide. To complicate matters, his supervisor gave him an increase in salary and expanded his responsibilities. Joe's intention to continue his film career and possibly abandon his job had been anticipated. It was a big decision, but he made it. He thanked his supervisor for the generous offer, but said: "Well, sir, I've been studying three years and I've learned that my real security must be found within myself. If I am to thoroughly utilize this security, I must burn all the bridges leading back to insecurity and eliminate dependency on anyone other than myself." This statement ended Joe's involvement with IBM. He returned to the Ensemble, and stated: "For the first time in my life, I really feel like a man."

Since then, Joe has continued as a production assistant in films and television. Occasionally, he also uses his talents as an actor. Recently he was finally accepted into the Directors Guild of America. He received his card as a full-fledged assistant director, and is now gainfully employed on the *Kojak* series, starring Telly Savalas. Joseph Johnson, who walked into the Ensemble workshop as an amateur, is now walking out on movie sets as Joe Ray, the professional assistant director.

Not all underprivileged minds develop as smoothly or as quickly as Joe Johnson's. He was an exception rather than the rule. Most students who come to me are usually youngsters in their late teens or early twenties with deep-seated problems. The source of these problems often dates back to their early childhood and is embedded in the unconscious mind. The majority of these youngsters are products of broken homes, with painful needs to be loved, to be recognized and be cared for.

Case History

Chip Fields was a case in point. Her real name was Lavern Fields. I gave her the name of Chip because she chattered all the time, like a chipmunk. She has continued to use the name in her professional career as an actress. Chip came to me at the age of eighteen. She was married and had a daughter, Kim. She had gone to Performing Arts High School and, since that time, had searched around trying to get started in the profession, but with little success. Chip mainly suffered from a serious problem of identity. She requested and was given permission to work with me in whatever way she might be useful. She merely wanted to establish her self-worth. A strong desire for recognition caused her to become a "workaholic." She would work night and day on the smallest project, without pay. She would return the project the moment it was finished and stand there beaming to be recognized, if only for a moment. I would give Chip that moment, and then she would be off again working on an assignment — or creating one if none had been assigned. During this period, she was not too concerned about acting; she was more interested in just being. She progressed so rapidly that I made her my special assistant. This move necessitated her accompanying me to meetings, film assignments, auditions — or just to sit in the car to prevent me from getting traffic tickets while I was inside a building. But she never just sat idly waiting for me to return. She would be armed with various paraphenalia related to projects or studies. She had the opportunity to sit next to me and take notes while I was directing a play, running rehearsals, or conducting a meeting. She occupied a first-row seat in the classroom. She would sit there, eagerly trying to satisfy her insatiable desire to learn. She was an "A" student in her classwork as well as her artistic development.

By this time, Chip had clearly discovered her self-worth and was endeavoring, enthusiastically, to find her identity. But she had problems. Through our private talks, I learned that she had been given to her aunt in South Carolina when she was two years old. Her aunt and uncle had raised her, and provided her with the only family she knew until she was thirteen years old. She knew that her mother and two other sisters were living in New York City, and she was confused as to why she was not a part of the family. She tied together bits of stories and overheard discussions that indicated that her mother had not wanted her. It seemed that her mother thought Chip's birth was responsible for the failure of her marriage.

When Chip was thirteen, her mother came to South Carolina to reclaim her. Chip was not enthusiastic about the move to New York. She had to leave the only mother she really knew for a stranger who had obviously rejected her. This pain ran deep in Chip and, during the five years she lived in New York, it exploded into constant conflicts with her mother and sisters. Chip chose marriage as an escape, and also to release her bottled-up love and affection. But the marriage could not fully develop and fill her needs. The young couple's financial situation forced them to share the apartment with her parents. Chip and her mother were on a constant collision course. Her mother loved the baby, got along well with her husband, but displayed a smouldering resentment for Chip. My first endeavor was to get Chip to look at the reality of her situation. I encouraged her to accept the fact that she was married, had a child, and had a responsibility to her immediate family. I also pointed out that, regardless of her mother's past actions, she was now providing Chip's family with a home. For this Chip had to express gratitude. I made her aware that she could not expect to receive love and happiness until she had first made an effort to give. Chip started to develop a better attitude towards her mother and sisters, and their relationship slowly began to change. I reminded her constantly that it was not easy to change a mind that had habitually been thinking negatively, and that the negative habit of self-pity had to be replaced with positive habits.

Chip also benefitted from my assignment as a producer at Warner Brothers. She was appointed by Sam Goldwyn, Jr. as casting director for *Charleston Blue*. This assignment was the biggest boost to Chip's self-image at that time. She was successful in her task, and also played a small acting role in the film.

By accident, I found that Chip had other underdeveloped talents. She had the ability to write music. She could sit down at the piano and bang out a complete tune in an hour. I encouraged her to write the theme song for the Ensemble, which she approached with great enthusiasm. Then Chip and I collaborated on a musical production, *Strivin'*, which we wrote for the Urban League Guild and performed at their annual ball. We received favorable press notices and other media publicity which did much for her confidence as a musician. Once we had investigated Chip's background, and she had courageously accepted the reality of her situation, together we were able to eradicate most of her negativity and strengthen most of her weaknesses.

Today, Chip Fields is successfully pursuing an acting career. She has performed in film, television and commercials, and on Broadway and radio. She now lives in Los Angeles, California, and commutes periodically to New York in order to continue her studies with the Ensemble. Her most recent visit was a month ago. She flew in to receive help in developing her character for a dramatic role on a television "special." She also needed some assurance from her director that she was a professional and was ready to take her place in the Hollywood environment. Whenever Chip has a problem, the Ensemble is no further away than a telephone call or a plane ride. She makes good use of both. Chip Fields has one unique quality—she has the ability to use the experience and wisdom of others. In other words, she willingly does exactly as I instruct her, with the discipline to resist the influence of her own opinions—a rare quality indeed, and one which has resulted in her most recent achievement. She has been appointed artistic director of "The Al Fann Dramatic Academy," the recently opened West Coast branch of The Al Fann Theatrical Ensemble, in Hollywood, California.

There are many Chip Fields and Joe Johnsons passing daily through the doors of the Al Fann Theatrical Ensemble, all seeking the therapeutic values of drama. They do not realize when they enter what their problems are, or how to solve them. But they all leave with the feeling that this world of conflict and frustration has become a much better place in which to live.

JONATHAN FOX, founder of the Playback Theater, Poughkeepsie, New York, was an actor-teacher for the Young People's Theatre, and has directed community service drama projects. He is a staff member at the Moreno Institute and conducts workshops in psychodrama, action methods, and improvisational drama.

Chapter 19

PLAYBACK THEATER: THE COMMUNITY SEES ITSELF

Jonathan Fox

1 INTRODUCTION

Community theatre is often thought of as the attempt by provincial amateurs to mount Broadway-type productions. Presented in the following pages is a different concept of community theatre: one that is psychodramatic, highly flexible, and has a relation to the community similar to that of the jesters and storytellers in preliterate societies, whose function was to explain the community to itself.

The Playback Theater company, which I formed and direct, currently consists of ten actors and two musicians who perform improvisationally for a variety of audiences: small specialized groups, outdoor festivals, and large conferences. It uses a theatre form where the actors spontaneously enact the personal experience, dreams, feelings and thoughts of members of the audience. The shared scenes emerge from the particular group present and often bear a common theme. The experience has proved to be meaningful, amusing, and often moving—especially for the Tellers who see their own lives portrayed. There are many interesting facets of the approach of The Playback Theater including the specific procedure, underlying concepts, audience workshops, and the different community settings in which it has proven successful.

295

Before detailing our experience, however, I should note that my focus is *the person in society* rather than the psychiatric patient. Virtually every one of us is not as expressive as we would like to be, as open and honest as we need to be, or as fulfilled as we dream we might be. Drama aims at awakening in people a sense of their own creativity—not only for art, but for everyday social life. We are all endowed with creative and expressive capacities: we are all "talented" in this sense. Unfortunately, too many people have had their confidence in their own creativity denied them by parents, teachers, and social pressures towards attributes like earning power and conformity.

2   PERFORMANCE

At a performance of Playback Theater, the actors, after their entrance, sit down facing the audience on stage left. On stage right, downstage, are two chairs, one for the Conductor, who acts as emcee, artistic director, and therapeutic guide for the scenes which are to come, the other chair for the Teller, who will step up from the audience.

There is always a warming-up process. This may take different forms: a song, if the audience is children; some action from the performers or a few words from the Conductor, if the audience is adult. We always include a moment of greeting ("Let us all introduce ourselves") in order to develop trust and confidence in the group. We do not focus on specific subject matter ("Watch this typical scene from family life"); we leave those present as free as possible to reveal their own themes and concerns. Frequently we begin with what we call "fluid sculptures": the Conductor asks an audience member a question, such as what kind of day it has been, or what feelings he had while asleep the night before. The actors then perform a short dance-like response trying to capture, in sound and movement, the essence of the person's experience. In this way, two or three members of the audience can be involved in less than a minute.

The Conductor then asks for a Teller to step forward. Those unfamiliar with the Playback form always ask if there is not a problem getting shy and resistant people to participate in this way.

There are a variety of methods for encouraging the first Teller to step forward, and the Conductor's skill will make a difference. But we have found that people want to tell about themselves. In short, they take advantage of the opportunity.

Once a Teller has come forward, the Conductor asks questions. This interview is designed to elicit basic facts so that the actors have sufficient material to work with, and the Conductor has an opportunity to develop a feeling for the Teller's state of mind. The Conductor encourages the Teller not to tell the whole story, otherwise it loses its impact. It is the actors who will complete the personal account the Teller has begun.

The Teller picks actors to be the characters in the scene — always including the Teller himself, and who or whatever else is significant. While he is describing the setting, the actors set the scene on stage. This procedure serves as a warm-up for the Teller, bringing him back to the moment he has chosen to describe, and getting him in touch with its feeling.

The actors then perform the scene, which may range from thirty seconds to five minutes. Afterwards, the Conductor asks the Teller if he wants to make a correction. It is often at this point that crucial material will emerge ("I didn't mention that there is a man outside on the roof making noise"). The actors then re-improvise the scene.

At this point the Teller may have seen all he considers necessary. Often he will say that the scene was just the way it was in life, but he had not looked at it that way before. The Conductor has the option, however, of asking the Teller how he would like the experience to have been. The Teller can then identify and suggest an alternative way ("I want to fly out the window and run off with the man"). The actors will then act the scene once more with the new ending. Thus a scene unsatisfactory in life will conclude triumphantly in dramatized performance.

One Teller's memory awakens the memory and longings of another. When the warm-up is effective, there are strong connections between scenes. One evening every scene had an animal in it; another evening focused on scenes from early childhood; a third on problems with mates. The tenor of the evening can be sad or horrifying; sometimes it is good memories that people share and the tone is happy and light.

3   SCENES

While the Playback form is simple to describe, it admits of complex possibilities. Here are examples of a few scenes:

- An elderly man, in an outdoor performance, told about watching the town post office being built during the depression.
- A boy, in a school performance, told of being beaten awake by his older brother, then changed it to a peaceful moment.
- A teacher told his favorite moment of the school day — at lunch, when in an empty homeroom he felt love for his students, whose art work surrounded him on the walls.
- A man remembered a traumatic scene from his youth involving the death of a pig and a severe arm injury. In the end, amid tears and laughter, he made the pig his pet.
- A woman told a moment of her youth: both her frustration at not being able to play with the gang and the wholeness of a small child's world emerged.
- A woman, identifying with a painting, imagined herself an Indian chief looking sadly at a wagon train.
- A man, recounting a fantasy, told a horrifying account of infiltrating insurgents with deadly weapons, and did not change it.
- A teacher, picking an incident from history, chose Captain John Smith being captured by Powhatan's braves. "He would submit temporarily," was his instruction for how the scene should end.
- A five year old, before an audience of adults and children, told a nightmare in which his mother had ignored him.

The scenes, as can be seen from the examples, are very diverse. In fact, an unstated tenet of Playback performances is that any moment can be significant and worthy of sharing in this way. Thus we do not restrict ourselves to events of the past. Dreams and fantasies are welcomed. In the "fluid sculptures," we enact

simple feelings about ordinary moments. We have done enactments of evocations and concepts, such as people's associations to
a word like "community" (some of the answers were "folks em-
bracing," "workers in a factory," and "brightly colored chemicals
swimming in a bowl").

It is important to note that while the scenes are in progress, a
subdramatic level exists which can be no less powerful: the experience of the Teller watching the scene. The audience becomes
very involved as they observe a shock of recognition, or laughter,
or tears on the face of the Teller.

4 ELEMENTS

Elements involved in the enactment of scenes include the following:

(1) *Audience warm-up*. A variety of techniques may be used, but
    it is essential that the audience members trust each other
    enough to reveal personal material. When this trust is not forth-
    coming, and occasionally outside circumstances create such a
    situation, then no theatre can take place.

(2) *Interview*. The Conductor's task during the interview is three-
    fold: (1) to elicit the facts in an efficient manner; (2) to help
    the Teller structure his experience so that it is actable; and (3)
    size up the Teller in order to know what kinds of action will be
    appropriate.

      Some Tellers have such weak ego structures that their
    material is more appropriate for a psychiatrist than actors
    and audience in a public gathering. Indications of this are: a
    Teller who cannot choose an actor to play himself; and the
    presentation of explosive material without revealing any per-
    sonal clues as to its meaning for the Teller (the fantasy scene
    listed above, involving the insurgents, was an instance of this
    nature). In such cases, the Conductor is wary of suggesting
    any intensification and must watch the Teller with great care.
    Some Tellers are confused and need assistance in describing
    an event understandably. Some Tellers cannot let go of their
    experience and will elaborate endlessly.

      In all these cases, the Conductor must tactfully direct an

interview which results in a clear presentation of elements and events; otherwise the Teller's attempt at public sharing will be frustrated from the start.

(3) *Scene setting.* Taking time to set the scene accurately ("Where are the windows and doors?" "What was the carpet like?") anchors the experience for Teller, actors and audience, and helps to evoke the emotional reality of the experience.

(4) *Soliloquy.* This technique is an effective way to focus on the meaning of an experience for a Teller. In the example of the teacher in his empty classroom at lunch hour, the actor delivered a soliloquy, intuiting correctly that even though the Teller chose a moment when his students were absent, he really felt great warmth for them. If the Teller had told all this beforehand, the scene would have been much less dramatic. Anyway, he was too shy. If the actor's interpretation had been incorrect, then the Teller would have had a clear basis for correcting the scene.

(5) *Correcting the scene.* As already stated, the first attempt often serves as a warm-up for the second. When vital new information is offered, the re-doing, even though it is in a rough sense repetition, adds to, rather than detracts from, the overall dramatic impact. The first attempt often helps the Teller (who sees actors putting interpretations on his facts) to focus on the meaning of his experience in a new way, which is then incorporated in the correction. This process has taught the actors that a mistaken first interpretation will often help the Teller reveal what is necessary for really capturing the experience; thus they lose their fear, inevitable at first, of doing the scene "wrong."

(6) *Transforming the scene.* The chance to add an ending that did not occur in life enables the Teller to make a creative input into the experience. The Conductor, no matter how grim the scene, never imposes an ending on the Teller. The underlying value here is that individuals are responsible for their own alternatives. An exception is with young children whose sense of self has not yet developed to the extent that this possibility is desirable. In the nightmare revealed by the five year old mentioned above, the Conductor suggested an ending in which the

mother, instead of ignoring her child, gave him attention and comfort, and the actors re-improvised the ending of the scene. A further reason not to impose a transformation on a Teller is that the possibilities are infinite and it is hardly possible to predict that Teller's own choice.

(7) *Music.* Music is a very effective adjunct to the Playback form. It is not considered "background music," but an integral element, like another actor, with the potential to make an active, interpretative contribution to the scene. Actors can mime a scene to musical accompaniment. An example was a nurse's experience of treating three very different patients in the intensive care unit of a hospital. The actor playing the nurse journeyed silently from the bed of one to another while the music identified the emotional states of the individual patients. The scene was a very moving one. Another possibility is to structure the scene so that actors and musicians alternate with each other. A third is to do a scene with nothing but music. One Teller, a war veteran, told of a sign in Viet Nam which announced the mileage to San Francisco. In a short composition the Playback pianist, skilled at improvisation, evoked both the spirit of home and the climate of that war which prevented so many from ever getting back. The Teller wept, and the complex feelings surrounding the Viet Nam war were intensely aroused among everyone else present.

5 PERSONS

The idea that everyone is an actor is one of the basic values of Playback Theater. A person who attends a Playback performance appreciates this in a number of ways.

First are the actors. In a totally visible process, the actors accept the challenge of new performance problems. They trust their spontaneity and creativity to make a real and vital communication. There is always the risk, of course, that the Teller will feel his experience improperly rendered, or that the audience will feel bored. However, audience members are often so enthused by the actors' process that some individuals afterwards express a desire to join the company.

Second are audience-involving experiences — for instance, audience sound effects. Such actions can be more than incidental. A ten year old girl told of almost drowning in the sea. The audience, with great effect, became the waves rolling in to sweep her away. They also did a fine job of reversing their (sound) motion when the child asked that the waves go backward and return her, of their own accord, to the shore.

More significant are audience workshops. These occur when, midway in a performance, the actors take small groups off to private places and, as Conductors, lead audience members in enacting scenes for each other. Such workshops have invariably been successful, with adults as well as children. This emphasizes that we all have a desire to be more expressive and creative than we normally allow ourselves to be. In such scenes, the experience of nonactors performing is often as significant as the moment of the Teller's experience. Nevertheless, the pleasure of seeing one's own scene is so strong that Tellers do not seem to mind considerable confusion and exhilaration on the part of inexperienced audience-actors.

Often audience-actors can be just as sympathetically attuned as the Playback regulars. We consider that each source for dramatic action must be an individual's personal experience, and this eliminates many of the blocks common in acting. The reason for this requires further investigation, but the extent to which actors can intuit and produce accurate and effective interpretations using this principle has at times been remarkable.

When space does not allow for the audience to divide into small groups, a workshop can be conducted with audience members remaining in their seats. We often ask different sections of the audience to find group expressions (a distinctive sound, for example) which are then orchestrated into an impromptu "chorale."

6 SETTINGS

The Playback form has been effective in a number of settings, apart from theatre.

In therapy, it is a useful technique of psychodrama. Moreno made use of a technique similar to Playback,[1] but his emphasis remained staunchly on making the Teller, as "protagonist," the principal actor in his scene. In psychodrama today, Playback has been used as a technique to quickly enact preliminary material prior to the protagonist taking center stage. It has also been helpful at moments when events have become too threatening for the protagonist to be willing to continue. At such times, a temporary use of the Playback format, with the protagonist acting as Teller, will enable the scene to progress until the protagonist is ready to re-enter.

Playback is also effective as a training device for leaders in all action therapies. Although each scene is short, it requires a full complement of skills. Experience as a Conductor is good training in putting verbal accounts into action, diagnosing clients, finding creative ways to help a client find his or her own solutions, and maintaining good contact with the group. Experience as an actor in Playback can provide efficient training in listening, developing a sense of different roles, performing in unrehearsed situations, and communicating effectively. Being a Teller is also valuable for therapists in training because it helps them develop sensitivity to their own experience, and the ability to examine it creatively. The Teller's experience, in fact, has proved to be a very effective aid for those who do not remember their past.

Playback is valid in education and can be an adjunctive method for teaching curriculum material. The scene of Captain John Smith, listed above, is an example. The Teller here was implicitly sharing something about himself, but the focus need not divert the student from the material. Indeed, identifying significant incidents in history or literature may stimulate a student's learning and further research.

During conferences, either between or following speeches, the company enacts scenes relevant to the concerns of the participants. At such functions, Playback Theater has a role very close to the jester in the king's court, with his special license for truth and his ability to provide group cohesion.

In the community-at-large, Playback Theater has special potential because it is a form of public sharing. Family groups provide a good illustration. At a performance, children can share hidden material with parents, and vice versa. For instance, on the pediatrics ward of a hospital with parents and staff present, the children—helped by the actors—could tell about their operations. Another day, during the workshop phase, a father was chosen to play his youngest son; the man did the scene on his knees, experiencing what it was like to be the smallest in the family. Playback can also be an opportunity for sharing between those in different roles in work and community institutional settings.

In short, it can be effective where people will gather in groups, and where the form can be undertaken by a company of actors, or by a single leader capable of using group members as actors.

While the Playback company is interested in pursuing the therapeutic, educational and community potential of this approach, it is also intent on fulfilling its artistic potential as theatre. Art is the embodiment of creativity. It has the power to deliver the hardest truths in a positive way and, as such, is intensely therapeutic.

7 SOCIETY

Writers about theatre, keenly aware of the vital function this art can have in the community, are prone to evoke cultural and anthropological forms. For example, Richard Schechner as a theatre director asks, "How can we get *villagelike* responses from urban Western audiences?"[2] Yet, too often, the attempts of experimental theatre companies to answer that question, and become shamans for their time, produce either artificially forced or grossly provocational pieces. Moreno also approached the matter in terms of society when he wrote:

> . . . we deal with drama at a level where the neat separation of the aesthetic from the therapeutic is meaningless and long before the distinction between individual and universal becomes a foregone conclusion. It is a community of actors without the audience as a special category. Their spontaneity and creativity are our primary concern. Their sincerity and integrity mean more than their artistry. Catharsis moves from the spectator to the actor and from the actor back to the spectator.[3]

Thus the initial task is to create a context of communication between actors and audience, and among audience members themselves. What follows is personal sharing, in itself dramatic because it has empathetic importance for those present.

This approach has been described in terms of education by Paulo Freire. In Brazil, he developed a method for teaching adult literacy amongst groups of peasants which centered on creating "culture circles," and engaging them in dialogue about their own daily concerns. According to him, animals are *of* nature, yet men and women exist not only in nature but *with* it: they have the capacity to *transform* as well as adapt. That power, which follows the development of what Freire has called "critical consciousness," enables individuals to make conscious choices regarding their social institutions, and it gives them the possibility of integration with the real world.[4] Theatre — at least theatre as viewed by Schechner and Moreno — has a similar power.

In Playback Theater, audience members are encouraged to become Tellers, observe their cultural experience, and transform it. It is a step towards social integration.

8 CONCLUSION

A review of some of the concepts underlying Playback Theater shows that:

- Everyone's experience is valid. The actors must be willing to enact whatever people honestly want to share, be it shaving in the morning, fantasizing that one is a bacon sandwich, or looking out of the window as a little child.
- A feeling of connectedness comes from sharing personal material. Thus it leads to cultural cohesion.
- It is up to each person to evaluate and make choices about his or her own experience.
- Everyone is essentially creative in that we all have innate "talents" for expression.

This last point touches on Playback's message for the individual. We are all potential actors: not that kind of performer who speaks other people's scripts under other people's direction, but persons capable of creative human action. The Playback experience encourages us to have a sense of our human creativity and how is can be used in daily life.

FOOTNOTES

1. Jacob L. Moreno, "A Case of Paranoia Treated through Psychodrama," *Monographs*, 13 (New York: Beacon, 1945), p. 6. The methodology of psychodrama was originated and developed by Moreno, and many of his values and concepts helped form Playback Theater, which can be considered a new version of the Spontaneity Theater he organized in the early part of this century.
2. Richard Schechner, *Environmental Theater* (New York: Hawthorn, 1973), p. 73.
3. Jacob L. Moreno, *Theater of Spontaneity* (New York: Beacon, 1973), p. 28.
4. Paulo Freire, *Education for Critical Consciousness* (New York: Seabury, 1973), pp. 3–58.

RAMON GORDON has worked in theatre and films for more than twenty-five years as director, producer, actor, and writer. Among his numerous credits are *Putney Swope, Trail of Tears,* and *The Great Gatsby.* He is the founder and director of Cell Block Theatre, New York City, and for many years has been a leader in prison drama and work with ex-offenders. He is a member of the board of directors of the National Association for Drama Therapy.

Chapter 20

HUMANIZING OFFENDERS THROUGH ACTING THERAPY

Ramon Gordon

In people who spend most of their first twenty-eight years or so in and out of prison, the dehumanization process begins before birth. As legal citizens of a middle-class society whose opportunities, values and rewards escape them, they are forced to live in their own society, created by their forebears, with its own value system and ethical code. Socially excluded, economically hopeless, they become faceless, nameless non-persons groping for the fast money that will make them *somebody*. The concept of future does not exist; the code becomes for many, take what you want now or you will never get it. Prison is the inevitable result — punishment for criminal acts against it by the same society which denied them competence and membership in the first place.

Prison, a microcosm of the society from which they entered, intensifies the dehumanization process. The inmate is classified, numbered and uniformed. He is experimented upon, threatened, punished, ordered about and abstracted. Vocational teachers, social workers, psychiatrists, everyone with a badge of authority becomes, to him, a policeman, with the same goals: to prevent him from being a person in his own right, and from taking what he sees as rightfully his.

How, then, can the offender's attitude be changed so that he may be accepted as a full-fledged member of American society and lead a constructive and fulfilling life? From the time of ancient Greece, theatre, stemming from religious ritual, has been a humanizing force, an educational process and an antidote to hopelessness.

When we speak of a poverty background, we don't mean only the absence of money, but an absence of education. More importantly than academic schooling, education means a higher level of competence in how to get along in the environment and with other human beings. It means knowing the rules of the game and how to play by those rules. Understanding the forces in society, its art and culture, perceptive awareness of surrounding life, makes for better appreciation of, and more fulfilling participation in, that life. Money, of course, *is* the basic survival tool and fast money, in the offender's vision, is the means to acceptance. But, even when there is survival money, poverty still exists in the quality of life. There are no books in the house, no music, no art, no cultural awareness, no conversation which solely stretches the mind. Chances are that friends and relatives are equally poor in these respects and no opportunity exists to acquire friends among higher status-level people.

Art is both educational and therapeutic. Theatre, which makes use of all the arts, best provides this significant education and concomitant therapy.

* * *

Orthodox psychotherapy, stemming from and based upon middle class values and treating middle class people, has irreconcilable differences with the aims and needs of offenders. Since the orthodox method is essentially verbal, insights gained in a session must be tested later in everyday outside settings. In an improvisation, however, the offender tries out his new insight immediately and sees instant results in his own behavior and in his fellow actors' response to him. Through repetition of the improvisation, the insight is reinforced. Acting out in the theatre, or in the literal sense, becomes proof rather than theory. Also, the problem of relieving guilt among middle class people is the opposite among offenders, where the problem is to *instill* a sense of guilt/conscience. It is the lack of guilt/conscience which causes offenders to act without restraint, without consideration of the consequences of their behavior and without responsibility. For example: a middle class man, who, after a time in psychotherapy, discovers a repressed desire to sleep with his sister or mother, experiences guilt and shame. With offenders, the desire was never repressed. Chances are they did sleep with sister or mother, without shame or guilt. The same may be true where mothers earned survival by sleeping with many men and supplied their young daughters to their clients.

In prisons, the psychiatrist is most often used for diagnostic purposes to help authorities classify and place inmates in job and housing situations. When actual therapy is performed, the inmates resist the "shrink" because of language/cultural differences, imposed authority and mistrust. They know that confidentiality most often is missing and that the "shrink's" reports are recorded in the inmates' "jackets" for use by prison authorities in parole hearings, reduction of sentence, etc. For orthodox psychotherapy to be effective among lower status-level people, a new rationale must be created — new language, new orientation among practitioners, new frame of reference. Theatre training, on the other hand, can use the language, the circumstances, the actual life experience of the offender in dealing with his problems.

* * *

Lack of identity, with a resultant lack of self esteem, is the most common character defect among offenders. And professional training of the actor deals with the *total identity* of a person as no other process does. The actor must discover his capabilities and potentialities. He must free and learn to control his emotionality. He must stretch his imagination beyond the familiar and obvious. His sensitivity must be heightened, his memory trained. He must be responsive, articulate and must develop and exercise his body and voice. He learns responsibility to himself and others. Techniques for achieving these results, when taught by skillful, carefully trained specialists, can bring about new identity, new self-confidence and self-esteem among offenders. They will experience a basic change in attitude toward themselves and in turn toward the world in which they live.

* * *

Cell Block Theatre, a program for prison inmates and ex-offenders, uses professional theatre and related methods, tailored to the specific needs and life problems of offenders as a therapeutic process. Conducted in a nonthreatening atmosphere, by people whose authority is *earned* rather than *imposed,* defenses are soon relaxed, tough guy masks are dropped, mutual trust and respect is established and self-revelation comes more easily. In the ambience of the workshop, offenders are able to express freely their hostilities, anger and resentments, to laugh and make mistakes without appearing foolish and without being put down. The process is fun, exciting, interesting and most importantly, the therapy is *indirect.* The offender resists direct, formal therapy in which he is a subjective *patient.* In training as an actor, he is in the role of *student.* Although dealing with *his* person and identity, criticism and evaluation is directed *through* him toward an entity outside himself: the exercise, scene or play. That way it seems less personal; the onus of *patient* is removed.

* * *

Thorough knowledge of the subject, though a prerequisite, is not enough to make a good teacher/specialist. Too often, teachers are hired on paper qualifications or academic achievement. Good teaching can be correlated directly to good acting. Words alone are not enough—they can be read in a play script or book. However, as in good acting, personality, manner, tone, awareness, reaction, compassion and belief are necessary to bring a role alive and convince the audience; so the teacher/specialist with offenders must have all these requirements and more to make himself and the work convincing, and therefore beneficial. Teaching in any situation is a difficult profession, but with offenders the difficulty is compounded. Professional actors already are motivated, essentially toward goals of fame and fortune. In institutions, or with ex-offenders, there is little or no motivation—without which learning cannot take place—and the specialist's goal is therapy, not performance. Therefore the specialist must tailor his approach both to the student and the work.

The specialist is always on trial. From a lifetime of distrust for any person, the offender constantly tests and challenges, to assure himself that the specialist is real—meaning that he can believe him, that he is trustworthy. Only when trust is established can learning take place. The feeling that no one in his life ever cared about or paid attention to him accounts for the offender's lack of caring about himself or his fate. In prison, this feeling is reinforced by virtually everyone, including his peers. The specialist must prove to the offender that he does care and at the same time, must maintain enough detachment to secure the student's respect and acceptance of his authority. It is a *very delicate line* because, if the specialist cares too much, becomes emotionally involved, or conversely, is too detached, his effectiveness is lost.

* * *

Relief of tension through physical relaxation is a technique used by actors. Unless relieved of physical tension, neither the body nor the mind will respond to demands upon them. In a comfortable sitting position, he closes his eyes and puts all his concentration on each specific part of his body in sequence until it is relaxed: starting with the toes, moving to the ankles, the calves, the knees, the thighs, etc., up to the head, eyes and face. When the concentration on the physical self is complete, shutting out all else, the mind, having room for no other considerations, clears in the process. This process is especially important for offenders, who say they have never in their lives had the ability to relax either physically or mentally.

The specialist must be without tension. He cannot bring his own problems into the workshop. Offenders take their cues from the specialist—if he is relaxed, enthusiastic, his attitude positive, it will be reflected in his students. The reverse is equally true. An ill-tempered person cannot teach.

* * *

An important element—taught through improvisation—for the offender to learn is how to deal with the unexpected. I often point out that if everything went as planned, if people reacted always as expected, chances are he would not have gone to jail. Usually, I introduce into each improvisation an unexpected person or event which at first upsets the students, but with which they have to cope. The specialist, also, must be prepared to deal with the unexpected. Keen perception and awareness of what is happening emotionally, psychologically, physically at any given moment may cause the specialist to change his lesson plan and approach. As on the stage, the good actor deals with what is actually happening rather than what is supposed to be happening (the script), the perceptive specialist must be ready to invent, spontaneously, an exercise or improvisation which encompasses the immediate reality. For example, at a Behavior Modification session in a hospital, a volunteer sat and read, without pause, from a prepared script of instructions, to a darkened roomful of alcoholics. She was unaware that the men were soon asleep and not responding to her instructions. When she did look up at her audience, she was unable to deal with the unexpected lack of response and had no other resource but to continue reading the script. The drunks had a nice nap.

The specialist has to perceive individual and group tensions—the natural outgrowth of a long stay in jail—as they change from moment to moment. If, in a session, I see a participant withdrawn and upset, I will stop and ask what's bugging him. He doesn't want to talk about it. But, with some persuasion, the problem comes out and I turn it into an improvisation or exercise. This way, the exercise becomes directly related to that person's problem at that moment. Consequently, he has to respond to that. Example: an inmate has been given a charge that day for cursing an officer. An improvisation is set up simulating the event. The angry inmate plays himself; another plays the officer. Anger and frustration on both sides emerge with the inmate really telling off the officer in the way he would have liked to earlier. He identifies the cause of his anger with the officer at that moment, and acts it out. In the evaluation afterwards, his fellow inmates and the specialist suggest ways he might have avoided the charge. The angry one now feels better for having gotten things off his chest, with no harm done, and participates in the rest of the session with renewed interest. Sometimes the roles may be reversed, with the angry inmate playing the officer, and new insight is gained.

* * *

An indispensable tool for the specialist, often neglected, is humor. I cannot emphasize enough the importance of establishing an atmosphere of humor within the framework of the sessions. Offenders' lives are dreary enough and if the approach is too heavy, too serious for any length of time, they will become bored and turn off. This does not mean joking or making light of the offender's problems, but helping him see the humor as well as the seriousness of his problems, which will make him more receptive to suggestion. A sense of humor makes the specialist more attractive and offenders (as any students) need to be attracted to the specialist or they will resist and become defensive. "Open your discourse with a jest and let your hearers laugh a little; then become serious," says the Talmud.

* * *

The specialist, in effect, is the same as a director of a play and as such cannot *demand* performance. Offenders feel they have been told what to do all their lives by various authority figures and will resist anything that sounds like something they *have to do*. The good director uses the technique of suggestion, asking questions rather than giving answers, so that the result he wants rather than being imposed on the actor seems to come from the actor. Posing the right questions is the first step. The procedure of finding the result is what acting is. If answers are given or found too soon, the actor is forced to play the result mechanically without having arrived at it with understanding. An actor does not like to feel like a puppet, manipulated by someone else.

Neither do offenders, who indeed are manipulated much of their lives. As on the stage, the actor/offender must arrive at revelation himself, and in doing so, better understand it.

* * *

The need for instant gratification, and the lack of concept of future, have consistently led the offender to react purely emotionally, without restraint or forethought in difficult situations. Frustration with the inability to understand or communicate leads to violence as his only means of expression. Violence, too, is his vehicle for demanding attention and recognition. Other antisocial acts — stealing, doping, arson, rape, robbery — are forms of violent reaction to his enemy, the hostile other society. By learning to behave truthfully in prescribed situations (improvisations), he can safely identify and release his anger and learn to control it. In the improvisations, all of which contain conflict, I have established three rules: the solution cannot be through violence, calling the police or walking off stage. Although violence may give momentary satisfaction, it leaves the problem unsolved; calling the police asks others to solve your problem; giving up, obviously, is no solution either. The offender often protests that these are the only possible solutions. Here the specialist must guide the offender beyond the obvious. He may, himself, suggest one or two solutions and ask the audience for suggestions. Even if all the suggested solutions are unacceptable to the offender, he at least learns that his old way of behaving is not the *only* one and that other possibilities do exist. Example: an improvisation wherein the offender reports to his parole officer who threatens to send him back to jail for a violation of parole. The offender feels it is unjust, his anger is real; he identifies the specific cause of his anger and at whom he is angry. He releases this anger in an emotional tirade and threatens violence. Since the situation is "imaginary," he is safe in doing so. If he behaved this way in a real situation, he would surely go back to jail with possibly an added sentence. Evaluation afterward: What are other ways to handle the problem? (1) Be careful your tone and manner remain calm and sincere (think before reacting). (2) Offer proof that violation was unjust. (3) Present valid reasons for behavior which led to violation. (4) Ask for another chance, promising not to let it happen again. (5) Point out your good record until now. (6) Try to change the parole officer's mind by convincing him of your sincerity in trying to abide by rules. (7) Try to enlist his sympathy for your situation. Etc., etc. The specialist may agree that none of these might work, but, and this is important, it may be the offender's *only chance* of avoiding punishment, if only he makes the effort.

* * *

Most offenders have an unrealistic attitude toward society and their own needs and desires. From their limited perspective and need for instant gratification, the long, hard work process between wanting and having, or being, is not within their experience. It is enough for them to *want* to have lots of money, for instance, when the achievement of this is so easily available: steal it! They will want, not to be an actor, but to be a *star*. In other words, they expect the result without the effort. One offender described himself as a painter. When I asked to see his paintings, be indignantly told me he hadn't done any: "I don't have to paint to be a painter!" Others claimed they had written plays or movies. Asked to show the scripts, they said, "Oh, I got the whole thing in my head," and wanted assurances of big money sales before writing a word. One ex-offender had had a small amount of training with a video camera while still in prison and wanted a job in video production. In an improvisation, an interviewer asked what salary he thought he should start with. "Thirty thousand a year," was the reply. The interviewer pointed out that the ex-offender had no experience, didn't even know the simplest nomenclature and if hired would cost the company money to train him. "You know what they get for *one* commercial?" the offender was undaunted, "Six hundred thousand dollars! I must be worth thirty thousand a year."

This indulgence in fantasy is an overcompensating manifestation of offenders' deep lack of self-worth, for to admit their feeling of unworthiness would necessitate a realistic appraisal of their value.

Theatre training begins to remove these unrealistic attitudes

and builds a concept of future. Rehearsal means repetition, practice over and over again. Impatient, at first, with doing the same
exercise more than once, the offender learns, however, that each
time he repeats it, something new is discovered and he becomes a
little better at what he is doing. He sees that the work process
itself is both necessary and rewarding — without it he would never
achieve the result he wanted.

Discipline is an ugly word to the offender. In his experience, it
means only punitive measures imposed on him by authorities. It
means not letting him do what he wants, when he wants, without
regard to the consequences. (Offenders often come late to class or
refuse to participate as a matter of principle.) The demands of
acting and theatre introduce the idea that discipline can be a
positive force which works for their benefit and need not be
distasteful. The offender sees quickly that he cannot develop as
an actor or learn a part without self-discipline. If he does not
discipline himself to do the work, he will appear ridiculous on
stage (an innate fear to begin with) and also ruin the performance
for his peer actors, incurring their disdain.

Rapping, for offenders, comes easily and could go on twenty-
four hours a day if uncontrolled. They like to sit comfortably and
talk; it becomes a substitute for making the effort to do. But, in
the theatre, acting in the literal sense cannot be avoided. Until
the actor gets up, moves, thinks, performs, in short becomes
active, no audience will see anything and little will be learned.
The difference between talking about it and doing it becomes
readily apparent to the offender.

* * *

In a group of twenty-four ex-offenders at Cell Block Theatre,
ages range from eighteen to forty. Although the average level of
academic education among offenders is ninth grade, some will
have achieved a high school diploma or equivalent and a few will
have had a year or two of college. Such disparity in age and
education makes it impossible for each to absorb and respond at
the same rate. However, despite differences in age, sex, and
experience, their emotional and psycho-social ages often remain

at the adolescent level. The specialist must work with each student according to his stage of development both in subject matter and emotionally, because, as with many adolescents, the attention span is short and need for individual attention is great. Therefore, it is essential to involve every participant at all times in what is happening during the session. While two or three students may be doing an improvisation or exercise on stage, the remainder of the students/audience must be instructed in how to observe and evaluate the work, be prepared to answer questions and give criticism when the scene is over. The "audience" must believe it is working as hard as the actors on stage.

There are four stages to each piece of work introduced in the class: (1) explanation of the exercise, (2) a description of the process — how to go about it including, if necessary, a brief demonstration, (3) the purpose of the exercise, (4) evaluation and discussion afterward. For example: a walking exercise. Explanation: to walk naturally, at first, then with certain adjustments, emotional or sensory. Description of process: walk as though you have just won a hundred thousand dollars; as though you are meeting your lover again after five years of absence; as though your best friend has been sent back to jail; as though you are the president of an African nation, etc.; and sensorily, as though you are walking barefoot on very hot pavement; as though walking in water up to the waist, shoulders, completely submerged; as though barefoot in snow; as though very tired and hot; as though on a country road in pitch blackness; as though uphill with a sixty pound pack on your back; as though taking off the pack; as though you weigh three hundred pounds; as though you are seven feet tall and thin, etc. — wherever the imagination of the specialist takes him. Purpose: the way one walks or carries himself reflects his inner feeling about himself. If the adjustments are made real enough so that the student really believes them, his walk will be affected. In life one can give himself adjustments which, with belief, will change his carriage for the better and be reflected in how others see and think of him. On the stage, of course, it helps create character. Evaluation: Did the audience observe change in each adjustment? Did the student make the adjustment real enough for himself? Did you believe him? What differences did you specifically observe? How did it differ from his usual walk? etc. The same questions are asked of the performer, plus which adjustments were easier, or more difficult, and why? This exercise can be done with the whole group participating at once, from which improvisations can develop.

A word of caution for the specialist: use good judgment when explaining the purpose of an exercise. In his need for instant gratification, the offender may ask how this or other exercises, such as sense memory — working with imaginary objects, will help him on the street. Translated, he is asking: Will it make him get fast money, women, big cars and clothes if he is able to do the exercise well, again leaping unrealistically from an exercise in class to the immediate fantasized result. The purpose of an exercise must be explained in such a way that the offender cannot pass judgment on its validity, for he is unqualified to do so. Yet, he must be satisfied enough by the explanation to continue to participate in the work. I point out, for instance, that a boxer skips rope, shadow boxes, punches a bag, runs miles every day for months before a fight — no *one* of which will make him a champion — but when he climbs into the ring, his chances are better than if he had not done the training/exercises.

The most important of the four stages of work is the evaluation afterward. Actors must be encouraged in what they have accomplished, but not to the exclusion of constructive critical analysis. Criticism should not only be in stage terms, but must always relate what happened on stage to real life problems. And *everything* on the stage can be so related — whether exercises, improvisations, scenes or plays. The work on stage is used as a vehicle to stimulate discussion. It is in these discussions where all members of the group participate, and when skillfully handled, that much therapeutic value is gained. Learning is best achieved in company. Without consciously doing so, offenders reveal their own problems, anger, ideas, misconceptions while discussing or criticizing the work of others. The perceptive specialist develops insight into the personalities of the members of the audience as well as the performers while evaluating a theatrical event.

* * *

The humanization process begins the moment an offender is initiated into a Cell Block Theatre group. He is asked to stand on stage before the others, with a spotlight on him, and with all the energy and volume he can muster, to shout his full name, to tell it to the world as though he were proud of it and his life depended on being heard; in fact, to restore his name to himself. It is a brand new experience; never in his life has that much positive attention been focused on him; he has never been "on stage" before. Some take as much as five or ten minutes, amid nervous giggling, fear, delaying tactics, etc., before they can shout loud and clear the simple statement of their own name. One intelligent man gave up after twenty minutes; he could not make his name heard! Many, in this first exercise, unconsciously clutch at their genitals, as if to make sure they are still attached (stemming, possibly, from ancient masculinity rituals among some primitive tribes). This reflex action often continues every time they speak in front of a group. After a time, when confidence is gained, the genital clutching disappears.

The first part of the initiation accomplished, the participant is then asked to sing a song with the same energy as before. Here he generally refuses to comply. Singing alone before a group of his peers is frightening. After much encouragement, part of a song is usually rendered. Asked how he feels afterward, he admits to extreme nervousness, but having done the exercise, feels better, even good about it.

The next step is to sit on stage and in three minutes tell the audience *the story* of his life. Few can fill the three minutes: "There's nothing to tell." Invariably, the narrative (all negative) centers around their crimes and jail sentences. Clearly, these episodes are the most eventful of their lives and uppermost in their consciousness. The audience is asked to comment on the ease, or lack of it, with which the participant handled the story, whether or not he revealed himself, gave information, and what behavioral changes they observed during any part of his presentation. They then question the person on stage perhaps eliciting more information. Asked if there were any *good* moments in his life, he is hard put to remember any, and if so, he considers them insignificant. This exercise is repeated at various stages of progress and differences noted. For the specialist, it serves as a valuable preliminary insight into each new participant.

* * *

With his built-in expectation of failure in trying something new, the offender must be guided and helped to make the effort in order to discover the possibility of his potential. After all, his whole life has been a failure, so he expects to fail. One judge put it, "Jails are ghettos of failure." The specialist must remind him that if he expects failure, chances are he will indeed fail, but the reverse is also true: expectation of success can lead to success.

Cell Block Theatre workshops, where ostensibly it is not a matter of life-and-death survival, offer the opportunity to change the offender's attitude to a success oriented one. In winning approval of his efforts; in discovering capabilities he never knew he had, he soon changes "I can't" to "I did it!" After every CBT performance for outside audiences and peers, the offenders express their exhilaration, their experience of a new "high." In their words, they never dreamed they could do anything like this.

* * *

For so many people of all status-levels, the inability to concentrate fully, to isolate a moment to the exclusion of everything else, robs them of satisfying experience. Among most offenders, who lack real education, the problem is great. Vague, fragmented impressions surround them physically, emotionally and intellectually; impatience and restlessness result.

Ability to concentrate fully is of prime importance to the actor, for without it, he cannot perform truthfully and well. This ability must be trained. Listening and hearing, for example, are elementary for the actor—if one does not listen and hear what another actor says, his own response may be totally illogical. An exercise, developed by CBT is as follows: a member of the group makes a point in a few sentences, which is recorded on tape. The others are asked to repeat *exactly* what they heard. Then the speaker repeats what he thinks he said. When the tape is replayed, it is clear that each may have heard something different, often missing the point altogether. This simple exercise trains concentration, and improvement is measurable. Related to life, it points out a real problem. Not listening, not really hearing, can distort the speaker's meaning and intention, which can lead to undesirable results, even violence; especially in jail where tempers are short and mistrust abounds already. Reasons for not hearing are examined. Aside from lack of concentration, the listener hears from his own frame of reference, trying to fit what the other says to what he is already thinking. Also, as with a bad actor, the listener doesn't hear because he is too intent on what *he* is going to say. Often, a single word, to which the listener may have a negative reaction, becomes magnified out of proportion and context, preventing him from hearing anything beyond that word. A psychiatrist, on first meeting, told a group of offenders that studies showed that most people went to jail because of incompetence rather than evil. Seemingly, the offenders only heard *incompetence* applied to them, and took such offense that the psychiatrist tried for more than an hour to explain what he meant, to no avail — they wouldn't listen.

The opposite side of listening and hearing is articulation in making one's point and intention clear. Here, exercises help the offender to organize his thoughts, be specific and speak clearly. Speech training, of obvious importance for actors, is applied to offenders who learn, in addition, that speech patterns and use of language determine one's status in the view of others. A trained actor knows that he cannot portray anger, love, or any emotion in a generalized way. He must be specific — identify the cause of anger at a particular moment, at whom he is angry, how angry he is, how it differs from other angers, etc., so that he can best express it convincingly within the context of the scene. In learning this need to be specific, the offender helps rid himself of generalized emotions, unthought-out ideas and lessens his frustrations in communicating. He discovers, too, that if he cannot convince another of his point in one way, he must change his approach as many times as necessary.

Complementary to listening, hearing, articulating, is seeing and observing. The offender observes another person for two minutes. Then, without looking at that person, he describes in as much detail as possible what he saw, paying particular attention to things he hadn't noticed before. Or, place an object in the center of the group — a sneaker, a sweater, a can of food, etc. — and have each person in turn verbalize *everything* he observes in the object. For example, different colors, lines, wrinkles, seams, variations of texture, eyelets, labels (in detail), relative size of spaces, etc. They quickly are amazed at how much they do not see. This trains them to observe in depth rather than settle for general impressions. This observation in specific detail of objects, people, trees, buildings, environment, enhances appreciation of the life around oneself.

Another seeing exercise: two people sit facing each other. One describes in systematic detail, the other's features, shape of head, color, hair, etc. When finished, the observer is given, privately, an adjustment — in acting terms, a personalization. He is told to imagine that the other person is someone real to him whom he loves (later change to other emotions), to keep that person in mind and still observing the one opposite him, repeat his description of the other as before. Often using the identical words, the manner, tone, expression of the describer will change to fit the adjustment. This demonstrates that how we see things, or others, is conditioned by our preconceived attitude toward that person or thing and, if our attitude changes toward that object, we will see the very same object differently. The observed one changes his attitude, too, as a result of receiving a different message. Again, relating to life, ask the offender to try this with people he doesn't like — imagined enemies, peers, parole officers, etc. An adjustment in attitude toward oneself creates a similar response. (Previous example of walking exercise.)

As the trained actor knows, he must communicate the subtext (what is *really* happening) more vividly than the words in the script. Thus the offender learns that manner, tone, behavior, feeling, communicate much more than the words we say. This is practiced through improvisations, also, wherein the participants must achieve objectives without the use of words or sounds. A variation on this is to do the improvisation with unrecognizable sounds or gibberish.

The specialist should construct improvisations so as to stretch the imagination, both in situation and in seeking solutions to conflict. Generally, people resort to the familiar in most situations, feeling more comfortable or secure. The offender is no different. His first improvisations, on his own, will deal with criminal activity. Not only does he feel more competent this way, but he also demonstrates whatever expertise he has — a boost to his ego. It is wise to allow him this indulgence in the beginning. But the specialist must guide him surely into other areas which will develop his sensibilities beyond the narrow and familiar, and start him thinking about new ideas, new vision, new purpose, new possibilities of life and behavior. So, too, the selection of plays to be performed by offenders should not perpetuate their criminal/prison orientation, lest the purpose of what they have learned be defeated.

* * *

Theatre training for offenders is a humanizing process. The stage is more real than real life. In real life we present images of ourselves, repress or disguise our feelings and emotions; we are protective, defensive, unrevealing, careful, skeptical. On the stage, however, the actor *must* reveal and *use* all of himself; he is *required* to show passion, to react emotionally, to love, to hate, to be angry, sad, tender, weak, sensitive, to kill, to die, to be foolish, uninhibited, mature, inconsistent, beautiful and ugly. And it is all socially acceptable on the stage — freeing, and safe. But, to act so humanly in real life could result in his institutionalization — hospital, morgue — or prison.

LOUIS MILLER, Israel's Chief National Psychiatrist and a specialist in public health in Jerusalem, has established psychiatric services for Israel's army and air force; directed Jerusalem's public health personal services; and was involved in the promotion of community organization. Chairman of the First World Workshop on Social Action and Community Theatre (Jerusalem, June 1979), he was a visiting professor at Northwestern University and also served as a consultant to the state of Illinois and to other state institutions and countries.

Chapter 21

CREATIVITY AND IDENTITY: SOCIAL DRAMA AND SOCIAL ACTION

Louis Miller

1 INTRODUCTION

In 1973, a number of adolescents from a poor ethnic background in Jerusalem presented an original play about their lives.[1] This powerful play caused bitterness with the traditionalist adults of the neighborhood, and much resentment among the city leaders. At the outbreak of the Yom Kippur War, the protagonists in the play had become socially active in their neighborhood, and remain so to this day. They constitute a new leadership in the community and are now producing their third play. Their dramatic and social action has resulted in a rehabilitatory process for those active in the project, and for the community itself. This community dramatic activity has become a country-wide movement among disadvantaged youth. The social and dramatic techniques described have been the result of a search for more complete and powerful methods of social action.[2]

2 POLITICAL METHODS

Why social action at all? Social action promotes the cohesion, integration and organization of groups for more effective functioning. The functional organization of the social group is an important determinant of the function of the family and the individual. Social action for the promotion of social change is, therefore, a "social mental health" instrument.

It is applied in the forms of community organization to groups in sociocultural change and breakdown. The attention of the mental health worker is drawn to these maladaptive ethnic groups because of the high incidence of personal problems in families and individuals arising out of the failure of acculturation. Sociocultural breakdown is accompanied by the destruction of creative and value-laden group expressions such as folklore, myth and religion. Tradition disappears and, with it, social bonds. The weakening of the social norms and forms is the *anomie* which social action has attempted to combat.

The most effective form of local social action which has been employed in Western democracies to rehabilitate disadvantaged groups, or to prevent social breakdown, has been *community organization*. This method remains the mainstay of social action in the West. It is aided generally by (didactic) formal and social educational methods, and supportive care services, rendered to the target population.

Community organization itself should not, however, be confused with community education, nor with the provision of community services (however urgently such helping services may be sought by the population). Community organization method insists upon the greatest possible participation of the target group itself in order to promote growth, avoid dependency, and to strengthen its social competence and power to act.

Community organization requires that the client defines his legitimate needs himself, and participates actively with those who share in their fulfillment. The group must seek a consensus on the priority rating of these needs, and create or press for resources to meet them. It is a political method that rests on the vote, on broad participation in local decisions, and on the power of the local majority. Community organization is a mental health instrument: it tends to produce individual growth towards autonomy and adaptability through involvement in and the fulfillment of new roles in the group and milieu. This certainly occurs with a limited number of individuals: they develop as leaders with a positive self-image. However, it is rarely shared by the mass of the target group.

There is a curious paradox which community organization is forced to face. One organizes and educates for social and technical efficiency. But on attaining such social functionalism, one falls into the trap of depersonalizing Western industrial society: it may be productive and efficient but it also leads towards a new form of alienation from fellow human beings and from the inspirations of the self. One may lose, therefore, the last bit of human and affectionate relations left to the traditional group in breakdown. They tend to be lost, too, even where the social change occurs relatively smoothly from a rise in the economic standard of living. Cultural breakdown often impairs mental health, but so does social development and reconstruction. The challenge is ultimately, of course, to retain satisfying human relations in the organized society of our day.

3   THE NEED FOR CULTURAL COMMUNITY ACTION

Community organization as a social action method has demonstrated some of its limited positive qualities in Israel as well. Here, it has fostered new role definitions for persons threatened by change, and pushed up some new leadership. But our experience in Israel has indicated to sensitive community workers that community organization is inadequate as a broad mental health instrument. We saw that these deficiencies in the techniques appeared not only because of the gravity of the destruction of the social systems (seen so often in social change), but also because of the impairment of the group culture through the destruction of essential emotional bonds. Community organization had not before perceived this ineluctable association of social *and* cultural failure.

We appeared, therefore, to have hit at last upon a reasonable assumption to explain (at least partially) some of the inadequacies of community organization for social development and mental health. The destruction of emotional bonding in the family and the group produced a poverty of personal and community relations. Community organization as a purely political method was unable to prevent this breakdown. We were then faced with the question of the re-establishment of the emotional bonds, or their conservation, especially among the adults in the community as its leaders and socially active members.

It was, however, a far cry from the perception of the disturbance of emotional bonding to the elaboration of a technique which might foster its re-establishment. The community, for example, could *feel* the shared need for satisfactory housing. But could they feel the need for the regeneration of bonds which had been weakened? And, pragmatically, on what common ground were these bonds to rise again?

This problem had been confronted before; historically, for example, through the agency of religious leaders and their charisma; and more recently in the West, by exhortative and sentimental methods such as "togetherness." The group methods of Alcoholics Anonymous, of the "hippies" and the Growth Centers, were other examples. None of these seemed general or powerful enough in this instance.

Almost by blind chance, we hit upon the idea of shared creative expression: *almost* blind in the sense that we had already perceived that the social destruction of the group was inevitably accompanied by the weakening of its language and its symbols, folklore, legends, ceremonies and religious ritual. (Some awareness of this had prompted earlier movements to attempt to restore the pre-existing cultural contents of the group—often in an artificial and forced fashion.)

The method for fostering cultural contents which we adopted was that of "community drama" or "community theatre." This was to result in a shared community expression, leading to deeper community relations of an emotional quality (re-acculturation) which should result in renewed political community organization.

4   GROUP RELATIONS, IDENTITY AND CREATIVITY

It had been hypothesized earlier that breakdown in group cultural relations induced problems of identity in the individual (a negative feeling about himself and about his own group) which resulted in personal behavioral and developmental dysfunction.[3]

It now began to appear that the breakdown of personal identity (and group feeling) was somehow related to the impairment of personal creativity (and group creative expression). The more focused hypothesis then took shape: *that personal identity and personal creativity are of the same order; that the stifling of creativity leads to a failure of self-esteem and, hence, to impairment of the sense of uniqueness and definition of the self.* This would be true *mutatis mutandis* of the group — the group and the individual being, in effect, a continuity. (We had postulated earlier an aetiological relation between deviance and the failures in individual and group self-esteem and identity.)

In our review of group and individual identity and creativity, we were constrained to re-examine our concepts of creativity. It began to appear to us that creativity, perhaps, was not to be seen essentially as a high derivative of primary (sexual) desires — sublimated finally in art, especially in individuals who were to be considered creative and artistic. It was postulated that *all human beings were born to be creative* (and to have relationships, to develop the self, to participate in the formation of others, to express, to symbolize) *and that the suppression of creativity,* by and of the group, *would lead to anomie in the individual and in the mass.*

These views impelled us to the dramatic-political method: "social action theatre" — a name which indicates both the goals of the restitution of creativity and of group organization for production. We felt that the power demonstrated by the creative group method suggested that community intervention should first be focused on the stimulation of group expression and relations.

5   THE THEATRE OF SOCIAL ACTION

The techniques employed in re-awakening community creativity and expression have extended from group painting to community environmental design. The method which will be discussed here, however, will be "community drama."

Its ultimate goal is community organization, particularly for groups which have suffered social and economic destruction and attenuation. But the paths to community rehabilitation run through the emotional experiences of creative expression. Socially oriented community drama has very important advantages over other creative methods both for creativity as well as organization; this is because the theatre is an embracingly social art, directly concerned with living expression and communication, and given to massive participation. It is comparatively unesoteric. It is explicit in its language and direct in its symbolism.

Our experience in Israel has been with community drama and the personal, cultural, and social changes that flow from it. We have found, too, that community theatre not only has the potential for stimulating these processes in a given target community, but also takes on the quality of a social movement. In its travels away from home, one community theatre group can stimulate a similar development within another community.

6   THE TECHNIQUE OF SOCIAL ACTION THEATRE

The cardinal operational principles which evolved from the underlying hypotheses have been fairly well crystallized. Their applications have been tested in the initial model project. Set out rather loosely in chronological steps, our operational principles are as follows:

(1) An initiating group of the community compiles and writes its own dramatic script. It is stimulated and guided by a drama director and a community organizer (or group worker).

(2) In this creative process, a maximum number of individuals from the community is involved by the initiating group. They may use a tape recorder and/or interviews in order to collect material from their parents, traditional leaders, local political and service people, and so on.

(3) The initiating group (which usually first comprises younger people interested in social, artistic, and self development) produces and acts the drama. As has been found in earlier European experiments in the professional theatres concerned with political propaganda, the theatrical event is likely to be most effective as a variety or musical show. In any event, it

inevitably burns at first with bitterness, angry protests, and the demand for solutions. Movement and other acting exercises are important developmental experiences for the actors. So, too, are the group discussions which evolve during the process of the play's realization.

(4) The initiating group (guided by the drama professional and a community organizer) involves the maximum number of community people in the actual production. Involvement may take the most practical forms such as selling tickets or finding rehearsal space; or more clearly creative activity, such as writing lyrics, performing music or painting a backdrop.

(5) The drama may be first performed before the very community whose life situation, problems and solutions are being portrayed. In our experience, however, the theatre group strives to perform before general audiences both for artistic and political reasons. In such cases, audiences from the original community are present at appearances elsewhere and participate in open rehearsals.

(6) At shows, the dramatic methods are also kept "open." This allows for audience participation. The show usually ends with a free discussion led by a "character" from the play.

The process thus far delineated has been largely a matter of creativity. The creation of the presentation certainly spurs the development of those directly involved towards both a positive self-image and positive relations with the group as it forms. The performance of the community drama before outside audiences, while often shot through with bitterness, usually strengthens these qualities.

Many of the usual problems of working with a dramatic cast may arise, such as: over-identification with a role, "sibling rivalry," intensification of latent problems, and conflicts in the individual or the group. In such cases, unlike the formal theatre, the drama director is usually sufficiently motivated to deal with such problems, and should be aided by a social-work professional. Not infrequently, however, recourse must be made to an individual therapist for the support or treatment of a participant.

(7) The community now moves more firmly towards the goals of continuing impact on the indigenous community, and its organization to solve the social problems which the dramatic representation, and other experiences, have raised in the population group. This may and does take many self-help forms, such as educational and enrichment groups, the opening of clubs for younger brothers and sisters, programs for grandparents, community and folk events at festivals and art exhibitions. But soon the process leads to increasing social and political activity: organizing and pressuring for exposure, or for services and resources which have not been reaching the community.

(8) One community play may run locally and elsewhere for many performances. As it loses its drawing power, it is replaced by another with additional or new performers. Thus the creative and social process may gather momentum.

(9) From in and around the drama groups, leaders will arise who are involved in social, political, and cultural actions.

I cannot here detail the gathering force of this socio-political process with its fears, fragilities and regressions; its imbalances flowing from piled-up frustration and lack of experience of democracy; the conflict between the traditional community and political figures, and the newly awakened leaders searching for changed values, powers, and freedom of expression. But the theatre contributes none-the-less: not only to the awakening of this movement but also to its own consolidation, sophistication, and direction towards legitimacy and achievement. The "actor" of the drama may become the "agent" in his society, and he who holds the dramatic "leading role" may take the leader role in social relationships and organization.

Our experiments have shown that such processes may occur to a degree, even amongst those young people who had been rejected by their own, and by the general, society—and who themselves had rejected the general or local mores (dropouts, culturally retarded, street groups, delinquents). Through working with them on projects, we gained a fair amount of additional experience of the problems of their fantasy life, their incapacity for bodily and verbal expression and communication, and their impaired sense of time and person. In the culturally and economically marginal people, there is also a gross impairment of the self-image/self-value constellation set off by such behavior as brazenness, gang adherence, violence, and hatred of the normative society and its cultural context.

Group and drama experts may re-awaken, with patience and skilled work, the personal and social potential in younger persons. In such cases, community drama directors have used particularly powerful methods for sparking and supporting the process of liberating fantasy through the body: relaxation exercises, particularly those permitting the expression of controlled aggression; physical awareness, body movement and rhythm; and the awareness and sensing of others. From these physical modes, work is generated in the recall of past and shared-present experience, and on to shared decision, activity, and responsibility. Here, too, results vary. They depend on many external and internal factors of the individual, on the group and the professionals.

This is a far cry from the practices of psychodrama with its emphasis on the unconscious. It is a great deal closer to the operation, dynamics and discomforts of the ego in its contextual reality, and is directed towards its socialization. Yet the technique is deeply concerned with the mobilization of fantasy and creativity—bound not so much by hidden conflicts, but mutilated by social frustration and the general lack of stimulation and experience. As mentioned before, such an ego tends basically to undervalue itself, and to be intolerant of frustration and demand. It tends to react rather than work through issues. "Therapy" here means learning and testing new patterns and relations. But until the sense of personal creativity, potential, and value is re-awakened, the learning process may not supervene. This process is nurtured in the group creativity situation. The group, creating and expressing its own drama, develops and supports the individual in what I have called the social elements involved in creativity: self-esteem and identity. The goal of social action drama is ultimately the synthesis of individual and community: individual and group in a creative and satisfying emotional bond; individual and community for social self-action.

7 SOCIAL DRAMA AND THE MIDDLE CLASS

The principles of social action drama have been presented here through material drawn from Israeli neighborhoods and towns threatened by socio-cultural breakdown. The application of socio-dramatic methods for change among the middle classes of the city have not been elaborated, both for lack of experience and of time.

In Israel, especially among students,[3] attempts have been made to bring together individuals from different ethnic or class groups who do not normally communicate. In such cases, socio-drama relies even more heavily upon the open dramatic methods as developed in Europe after the First World War, and in the United States after the Second. Though in such instances, the social action is limited to the actual theatrical experience — both of the actors and the audience — because it lacks the elements of continuity and localization, it will probably remain the method of choice of urban and suburban fully westernized populations. With the middle class, therefore, stress is placed on resensitization and dramatic techniques which include guided compilation or selection of relevant texts, improvisation, self development of the players through guided experience of self and others, deep audience participation in these dramatic preparations and, at presentation, group discussion and the other heritages of "open" and "living" theatres. But these methods are limited. They stop short of community organization and continuing impact and action. The predecessors of these methods go back a long way into the cultural history and folk expressions of Western and Eastern nations. They have been revealed more recently in theatres of the street and basement, experimental and alternate theatre, celebrations, "happenings," the theatre in mental hospitals or in prisons, theatre for addicts, theatre in schools, role playing in education, psychodrama and sensitivity, growth and encounter groups — and in a host of other experiments which explore and communicate with the self and others. They may be seen as reactions against the imposition of stereotypes, and to the interpersonal gaps and suffocation of creativity in modern society. They are also socio-dramatic methods which are more active and effective, perhaps, than the classical dramatic satirists. But they rely, as does the traditional theatre, on a one-time impact on a small group (audience reaction) rather than seeking continuing involvement and the self-action of whole communities as has been described here.

FOOTNOTES

1. L. Miller, "Tiatron V'Khilla: Ohel Joseph," *Bama* 63/64 (1975), Hebrew; idem, "Theatre and Community: The Tent of Joseph," *Mental Health and Society* 3 (1976): 240–47.
2. L. Miller, "Tiatron V'Khilla: (Theatre and Community)," *Bama* 56 (1973), Hebrew.
3. L. Miller, "Identity and Violence," *Israel Annals of Psychiatry* 10, no. 1 (March, 1972).
4. R. J. Miller, "Student Theatre as a Means of Promoting Communication, Self-development and Creativity," *Mental Health and Society* 3, no. 233 (1976).

INDEX OF NAMES AND TITLES

339

GENERAL INDEX